A DANCE

WITH

DECEPTION

CHARLES COLSON

WITH NANCY R. PEARCEY

A DANCE WITH DECEPTION

Revealing the Truth Behind the Headlines

WORD PUBLISHING

Dallas · London · Vancouver · Melbourne

Library of Congress Cataloging-in-Publication Data

Colson, Charles W.
    A dance with deception : revealing the truth behind the
headlines / Charles W. Colson with Nancy R. Pearcey.
      p. cm.
    ISBN 0-8499-1057-9
    1. Sociology, Christian. 2. Church and social problems—
United States. 3. Christian ethics. 4. United States—
Moral conditions. I. Pearcey, Nancy R. II. Title.
BT738.C64 1993
277.3'0829—dc20   93-5322
                                              CIP

3 4 5 6 9 LB 9 8 7 6 5 4 3 2 1

Printed in the United States of America

To Jim Dobson

For years he advised me to limit my
speaking schedule and go on radio.
He was right.

Contents

Preface

The *Atlantic* magazine recently published an article provocatively titled "Dan Quayle Was Right." The good news is that it became the most talked about magazine piece in years, stimulating more letters to the *Atlantic* than any other article in three decades.

The bad news is that most of the letters were negative.

Readers charged the author, Barbara Dafoe Whitehead, with numerous sins against political correctness, ranging from being a raving right-wing Republican to voting for Quayle.

But Whitehead is not and she did not. She's a moderate Democrat who is simply trying to bring some reality to the family values debate.

One of the most poignant images of that reality was captured in a political cartoon that showed a young black mother, thin and exhausted, three small children pulling at her, watching television in a dilapidated apartment. On screen is Murphy Brown's face wearing a huge smile, and emanating from the box are gales of laughter.

The young mother is looking puzzled and saying, "I don't get it."

The problem, it seems to me, is that neither side really gets it. Debates over issues like family structures and sexual conduct have become so politicized that we have nearly lost all shared definitions of such terms as *family* and *values*. A loss that renders us incapable of reasoned moral discourse.

A poignant illustration of that loss was a report entitled "Code Blue," issued a few years ago by several professional organizations. "Code Blue" is a phrase used by hospitals to signal a life-threatening emergency; the emergency in this case was a steep rise in adolescent suicide, school failure, pregnancy, sexually transmitted diseases, and drug and alcohol abuse.

We've all heard these dreary statistics before. But what made "Code Blue" interesting was its analysis of the source of the problem. It pinned the blame directly on changes in family structure. A central factor in the youth crisis, the report said, is changing families and neighborhoods, which has left many children "on their own . . . isolated from adults."

The mobility of American families and the need for second incomes, the report said, "have robbed too many young people of stable families and communities where they are surrounded by caring adults to guide their growth and behavior."

This is great, I thought. Finally we're hearing mainstream institutions admit that many of our social problems stem directly from family decline. I turned the pages eagerly to see what solutions the report would offer. If children flounder when families fail, surely it would recommend strategies to help families succeed. Surely it would recommend ways to bolster the moral virtues that bind families together, like commitment and faithfulness.

Alas, I was wrong. In "Code Blue," all the disorders plaguing youth today, from depression to drug use, were labeled *health* problems. And the solution recommended was guaranteed access to health services, both medical and "psychosocial" services. The report called for the expansion of school clinics, the establishment of adolescent health centers, and even the creation of a Neighborhood Health Corps to "help adolescents and their families actually use health and other services." (Translation: If you decide not to use the clinic, expect pressure from your local Health Corps.)

But think about it: If the problem is that children are being left "on their own," to use the report's own words, is the solution really another health clinic? If the problem is that children have been "robbed . . . of stable families and communities," is the solution really a visit to the doctor?

No, what children need most are strong families, and family cohesion is a direct result of moral choices. What "Code Blue" illustrates is a massive failure among health and education professionals even to conceptualize the moral dimension. We have lost the language of moral discourse.

Americans are finally groping their way toward a correct diagnosis of the problem: namely, that modern society has given adults permission to adopt lifestyles out of tune with the needs of their children. But too many cultural leaders refuse to recognize that this is fundamentally not a health disorder, nor a result of inadequate "services," nor even a lack of government funding; it is a moral disorder.

In *Habits of the Heart,* Robert Bellah argues that American individualism has grown so acute that we no longer even speak the language of transcendent morality. Most Americans no longer think in conceptual categories of overarching standards of right and wrong, good and evil. They think only in terms of what feels right to the individual.

This is the real story behind the "Code Blue" report and the Dan Quayle debate: that Americans have lost the very language of moral discourse. We talk about rights and lifestyles and health needs, but we do not talk about morality and virtue.

Why? Ultimately because a moral law implies a Law-giver to whom we are morally obligated. And that's precisely what so many people are reluctant to acknowledge.

And so the experts hobble along, diagnosing the disease but balking at the cure—because the only effective cure means recognizing the reality of the moral dimension to human life. It's as though a hospital were to issue a code blue alert and the doctors had a perfectly good cure at hand, but they refused to use it because it would obligate them to the pharmacist who offered it.

"BreakPoint" is a daily radio commentary program that aims to revive the language of morality and responsibility without which we cannot resolve our social and cultural dilemmas. *A Dance with Deception* is a collection of commentaries transcribed from "BreakPoint"'s first sixteen months on the air. These are programs designed to equip people with tools to analyze and understand current events and social trends—to talk more effectively with family members, neighbors, and political leaders about what makes the Christian world-view distinctive.

"BreakPoint" takes a close look at people and ideas that shape our world, the books and movies that affect our thinking. The title of this book is a play on words from the movie *Dances with Wolves,* a chilling example of our culture's endemic historical revisionism. The sumptuous costuming and sweeping cinematography nearly obscure the fact that the movie is a neatly packaged attack on Western civilization. Virtually all the Europeans are portrayed as one-dimensional bad guys, all the natives as one-dimensional good guys—as though natives alone in all the human race were untouched by original sin.

But in real life, the Sioux Indians were the most warlike of all the Plains Indian tribes, leading one of the bloodiest uprisings ever. The truth is that both whites and natives are noble—made in the image of God—yet both are fallen into sin. This is part of the biblical grid that Christians ought to build deep into our minds to screen out the distortions purveyed by our culture today in its dance with deception.

I would like to thank the many people who help put BreakPoint Radio on the air: foremost, the program's superbly talented editor and producer, Nancy Pearcey. It was Nancy who created the program from the beginning, and she and I continue to collaborate closely on every stage of commentary preparation, from conception of the ideas to writing and editing the radio scripts. She also has responsibility for working with outside contract writers, editing their work and bringing it to final form for recording. Nancy brings a rich background to the project: a master's degree from Covenant Seminary, graduate work at the Institute for Christian Studies in Toronto, a publishing history in both Christian and secular magazines and journals. This book is in every way a joint effort on our part.

Together we would like to thank the staff at Prison Fellowship who make "BreakPoint" possible: Karen Scantlin, administrative coordinator; Kim Robbins, research coordinator; John Shaw and Larry Frost, media support; the "BreakPoint" volunteer team, especially Jean Epley; Daryl Charles, researcher; and the staff in departments across Prison Fellowship who contribute in a variety of ways: answering telephone calls from listeners, preparing transcripts for distribution, and mailing them out.

Thanks are also due to Ambassador Advertising Agency and to the team of writer-researchers who kept us informed of trends across the country and who drafter material for various commentaries during "BreakPoint"'s first year on the air: E. Calvin Beisner, K. L. Billingsley, John Blattner, Michael Gerson, Mark Horne, Doug Leblanc, Connie Marshner, Jim Manney, Susan Olasky, J. Richard Pearcey, Ed Urban, and Gene Edward Veith.

Finally, we want to thank "BreakPoint"'s five million weekly listeners who keep us going with their enthusiasm and support. The enormous response to this program has convinced us more than ever that Christians are not content to be isolated in spiritual ghettos. They want the tools to expose the secular culture and to challenge its false values—yes, its dance with deception.

And that, with God's grace, is what "BreakPoint" is all about.

Charles W. Colson
Nancy R. Pearcey
July 1993

For more information on "BreakPoint" and for a listing of stations in your area that carry the program, write us at P.O. Box 17500, Washington, D.C. 20041, or call Prison Fellowship at 800-995-8777.

1

The Contemporary Crisis

A Bad Rap
Why Christians Aren't Absolutists

In this past presidential campaign, Evangelicals took a bad rap—and it's time to set the record straight.

I heard it when a friend told me, "I hope the Democrats win. Then you people in the Religious Right will get what's coming to you for trying to impose your values on everyone else!"

We heard the same sneering tone every time the media made bogeymen out of the speakers at the Republican convention. They've captured the Republican party for the Religious Right, we were told. George Bush was just a puppet of Christian Fundamentalists, we were warned.

The media were playing on a well-established fear in America. A Gallup poll found that 50 percent of Americans are worried about Fundamentalism. What worries them is that Fundamentalists actually believe in moral absolutes.

Why does that send a chill down people's backs? Because they have confused belief in absolutes with absolut*ism*—a rigid mentality that is inflexible, irrational, and hostile.

But there's a world of difference between absolutes and absolutism.

This is a critical point for us to grasp. You see, every time you tack "ism" onto a term, you change its meaning. Think of the word *individual*—a good word, suggesting individual dignity and worth. But individual*ism* denotes something altogether different—an egoistic mentality that puts individual interests above everything else.

Think of some other examples: There's a huge difference between material and material*ism*, between human and human*ism*, between feminine and femin*ism*.

So Christians ought to boldly maintain the reality of absolutes. But that doesn't mean we are absolut*ist* in our mentality.

A belief in absolutes simply means we believe that there is a created order. That there are virtues—like courage, fortitude, and patience—which are morally obligatory. That there are normative patterns for marriage, business, and government.

In short, we believe that there are laws for human behavior just as there are laws for the physical world.

Believing these things doesn't make you an absolut*ist* any more than believing in gravity does. And if I try to persuade you of a moral law, I'm not "imposing my views" any more than if I teach you the effects of gravity.

This is what many of our compatriots fail to understand, and that's why Christians are given a bad rap in today's political climate. Every time we raise a moral issue in the public arena, we are slapped down, scolded for being bigots, and accused of imposing our values.

Maybe it's time to take our neighbors one by one and explain what values are in the first place. Values aren't based on private convictions, which we then try to impose on our fellow citizens. Values are based on objective truths about the created order, and we search them out the same way we search out scientific laws.

So the next time someone accuses you of being an absolut*ist*, explain the difference between absolutes and absolut*ism*.

And if you demonstrate a loving and patient attitude while you're talking, you will prove by your own action that believing in absolutes *doesn't* make you an absolut*ist*.

November 6, 1992

Rise of the "New Class"
America's Class Conflict

Christians are becoming politically active. They've entered the fray over abortion, sex education, gay rights, and school textbooks.

They've noticed an interesting pattern: All these issues seem somehow tied together. The same people—whether Christians or not—always seem to be fighting on the same side.

The explanation is that the individual issues all stem from a basic set of assumptions about life—a world-view. America is being torn between two basic world-views, and Christians are being drawn into the battle.

Sociologists call it a class war, but it's a class war of a new kind. Traditional classes were based on economics—the land-owners versus the peasants or the factory-owners versus the proletariat. But the conflict dividing America today is not based on economics. It's a conflict between world-views.

On one side is the middle class, which once supplied most of our nation's leaders and officeholders and shaped America's values. Historically, those values were Christian, with a strong Protestant work ethic emphasizing sacrifice, responsibility, and moral restraint.

On the other side is what sociologists call the "New Class." In the early part of this century America's elites began to develop a distinct world-view. It was secular and liberal; it celebrated America's growing affluence by developing an ethic of individualism, self-gratification, and rebellion against authority.

In the 1960s the elite outlook spread to a large segment of middle-class youth. They broke off from their middle-class roots and formed the New Class.

The New Class is America's intelligentsia. They don't trade in goods and services but in words and ideas. They're sometimes called the Knowledge Class. They're the journalists and anchors on television news networks. They're the educators who write school curricula. They're the lawyers who work for social causes. They're the public-policy analysts who shape government policy. *Newsweek* calls them the nation's "brain workers."

The first empirical studies of the New Class were conducted by Robert and Linda Lichter and Stanley Rothman for their book, *The Media Elite.* They interviewed the people who bring us the nightly news, and their study found that most leading television journalists and news anchors label themselves politically as liberal: 90 percent are pro-choice; 75 percent believe homosexuality is morally acceptable; and only 8 percent attend religious services regularly.

For their next book, *Watching America,* the Lichters and Rothman turned to Hollywood and interviewed the writers and producers of prime-time entertainment. They discovered a remarkable sameness in outlook: 75 percent place themselves on the left politically; 97 percent are pro-choice; 80 percent believe homosexuality is morally acceptable; and only 7 percent attend any sort of religious service regularly. The same values are held by the New Class everywhere, whether they work in the media, the schools, or the government.

Underlying the political conflicts that blare from the headlines is a deeper conflict between the two classes and two world-views: the traditional, middle-class world-view, with its ethic of responsibility and restraint, versus the New Class world-view, exalting individual gratification.

This is not a battle over land or economic power. It's a battle for the heart and soul of America.

November 13, 1993

The Language Gap
Talking to the Other Side

A leader of a Christian organization recently appeared on "Larry King Live" to discuss current issues, especially those volatile values issues. At one point the Christian leader referred to his own group as people who hold "true values."

Instantly, Larry King jumped on him. What do you mean "true values"? What makes you think *you* have the truth? Are you saying everyone else is wrong?

The poor fellow was completely flustered. He hedged and mumbled and was unable to give a coherent response. The worst part is that the man looked sincerely puzzled. He seemed unaware that, in today's secular world, talking about "true values" is like waving a red flag.

You see, in the past, non-Christians rejected the Bible as true, but today many of them reject any notion of truth at all. American society has split into two groups. On one side are those who accept the idea of an objective truth—and, yes, "true values." On the other side are those who believe truth and values are relative and subjective.

The split between these two groups is so severe that some sociologists are calling it a culture war. It is a rift that imperils our very existence as a nation.

Every political order must rest on a moral order, a shared set of beliefs and values. What binds society together is the trust that we will all regulate our conduct according to an agreed-upon moral framework.

But since the 1960s, the very notion of a common moral framework has steadily eroded. Today many people believe that we can set our own standards—that ethics is just a matter of individual feelings and choice.

But when ethics is reduced to feelings, the moral bonds that tie society together quickly dissolve. People have no common standard of conduct they can agree on; they no longer know what to expect of one another.

Mistrust and hostility set in.

You see, in any relationship trust is based not merely on people's good will; we all know *that* can fluctuate. Instead, trust comes from knowing that the other person is committed to a shared standard—a standard binding on both parties.

Think of traffic laws. When we enter an intersection, our confidence is not based on knowing the other drivers feel kindly toward us. It's based on knowing they're going to follow

the same set of traffic laws. If traffic laws were a matter of individual choice, our streets would surrender to chaos.

It's the same with our social life. Trust depends on a shared
set of laws and standards. Until recently, the shared standards
that bound American society together were derived from our
Christian heritage. But no longer.

Today we can no longer assume a shared set of assumptions when we talk to our neighbors—or when we explain our
views on a national talk show. Our listeners may well be on
the other side of the culture war.

And that means we can't just toss around stock phrases—
like "true values." We have to be ready to explain what these
phrases *mean* in language the other side understands.

Otherwise we'll find ourselves, like the man on "Larry King
Live," hedging and mumbling. And wondering why we're always so misunderstood.

October 19, 1992

Biblically Trained Minds
How to Avoid Being Suckered

A Christian business executive, a friend of mine, attended
a three-week course in business ethics at Harvard Business
School. I was eager to hear his reaction. I had said publicly that
Harvard cannot really teach ethics, because it has abandoned
any belief in ethical absolutes.

To my surprise, the executive raved about the course. "I
learned some real practical ethical pointers," he told me. "It's
summed up in what the professor said on the last day of class:
'Never do anything you think might end up in the newspapers.'"

I thought he was joking. He wasn't.

The man appeared to be a mature Christian, the kind of
person who would walk into a Harvard classroom and subject
the contents of the course to a critical biblical analysis. Instead, he himself had been subjected to a crash course in
pragmatism: Good ethics is merely good business; there is no

absolute right or wrong; if it works, do it—just don't get caught.

How had my friend missed it? How had he let a secular view of ethics slip through the filter of his biblically trained mind?

Ah, there's the rub. What does it mean to have a biblically trained mind? Many Christians think of biblical faith in very narrow terms. We think of it as religion—as something expressed in church attendance, prayer, and worship—without much relevance to the larger world outside.

But that's not the biblical view. The biblical view is that faith has to do with all of life. Every decision we make reflects what we believe and what we value.

A vivid example can be seen in the life of Abraham Kuyper, a great Dutch theologian in the early part of this century. Kuyper argued that to stand against a comprehensive secularism, we must articulate a Christian philosophy that is equally comprehensive. We must see Christianity as an all-embracing system of thought that gives us a perspective from which to view every part of life: family, church, work, politics, science, art, and culture.

In short, Christianity must be a world-view: a view of the entire world, an intellectual grid through which we can interpret everything we see or read or do. God created the world, and everything in the world relates in some way to Him.

Kuyper didn't just talk about Christianity as a world-view. He acted on it. He worked vigorously to influence public life in the Netherlands on the basis of Christian truth. He founded a Christian university, published a newspaper, wrote daily editorials, and was even elected prime minister. The social and educational reforms Kuyper instituted continue to benefit Holland today.

One of the great insights of the Protestant Reformation was that it is no higher calling to live in monasteries isolated from the world, performing spiritual exercises. The biblical view is that any honest work in any part of God's creation has dignity and can be done unto Him.

If my friend had understood this, he wouldn't have been suckered in by the ethics course he took at Harvard. When we have a Christian view of all of life, we won't merely absorb a secular outlook on ethics—or on any subject, for that matter.

Instead, we will learn how to challenge the false views of life that are rampant in our culture.

October 29, 1991

Flower Children in the Nineties
The Counterculture Goes to Wall Street

It's become big business to predict the future. Businesses and institutions hire people called "futurists" to tell them what changes to expect in society so they can plan more effectively. One technique futurists use is to survey students. After all, today's pupils are tomorrow's professionals.

In a survey of college business majors, researchers found that, by a ratio of two-to-one, students feel businesses are generally unethical. What's more, fully half the students said that they themselves expect to engage in unethical behavior in their future careers.

What has happened? Why do supposedly idealistic students blandly predict they will do things they know are wrong?

The answer is that modern culture has abandoned more than twenty centuries of Western tradition that adheres to a transcendent standard of right and wrong.

As Christians we believe human laws must be based on divine law, a standard above our own ideas of right and wrong (that's what *transcendent* means), a standard to which we can all appeal, whether princes or paupers, presidents or prisoners.

But this isn't just a Christian idea. The philosophers of ancient Greece were not Christian, yet they too saw the need for a standard above society's own rules. The great philosopher Plato insisted that we cannot be good without a timeless ideal of goodness. Aristotle taught that there is an ethical law based upon universal human nature—what came to be called natural law.

All through the history of Western civilization, there has been near-universal agreement, among Christians and non-Christians alike, that human laws and behavior must rest on a transcendent standard of truth.

But in our own day, this consensus has shattered. Contemporary non-Christians no longer hold either Plato's timeless ideals or Aristotle's natural law—let alone divine law. They see human nature as undefined and changing. It is up to each individual to decide who he is and what is right for him.

Truth is relative.

When the hippies in the 1960s insisted on the freedom to do their own thing, it was part of what I believe was the most profound cultural revolution in American history. When the flower children indulged in cheap drugs and free sex, many of us thought they were simply reveling in old-fashioned immorality. But there was something new here. The hippies were not just violating accepted standards of behavior—they were saying there *are* no accepted standards of behavior.

The idea spread like wildfire.

Today, in the 1990s, the flower children have traded their jeans for pinstripes. But though they have left their beads and braids behind, they brought with them the ideas and values of the sixties—especially the idea that there are no accepted standards.

What are the results? Well, we shouldn't be surprised when business students say they expect to engage in unethical behavior. The students do not feel obligated by any higher sense of right and wrong. They feel accountable only to their own private conscience—which apparently is not a very strong deterrent to unethical behavior.

C. S. Lewis once said that when we mock honor, we should not be surprised to find traitors in our midst. Today it might be said that when we mock transcendent ethics, we should not be surprised to find cheats and frauds in our midst.

October 22, 1991

Love the Sinner, Hate the Sin
How Not to "Impose Morality"

I recently met an old friend I hadn't seen in years. It was a happy reunion as we exchanged news and swapped old memories.

But soon our discussion took a less pleasant turn. "You're really into that Christian political stuff, aren't you?" my friend said, almost with a sneer. "You're into gay bashing and restricting women's rights and cramming your morality down other people's throats."

The anger in his voice was unmistakable.

For the next twenty minutes I tried to calm him down, but I'm not sure I ever really succeeded in getting him to understand my position.

My friend's attitude is not unusual. We Evangelicals have been thoroughly stereotyped: We're pictured as cold, uncaring, judgmental, and bigoted. Just this morning I read an article comparing us to the Nazis.

Where do these extremist stereotypes come from?

For most of this century it has been considered enlightened to believe that there's no such thing as sin—that human nature is basically good. When people do things that are wrong, it is assumed they must be victims of something *outside* themselves—poverty or bad education or maybe even poor toilet training.

With this history it's no wonder people totally misunderstand what Evangelicals mean by the concept of sin. They are stunned when we say that abortion is wrong, that adultery is immoral, that cheating is unethical, or that homosexuality violates God's law.

Our secular neighbors immediately assume that we simply *hate* anyone who does these things, that given the opportunity, we'd march them off to concentration camps.

They just don't get it.

Christians don't hate people. And the reason is that we draw a distinction between the sin and the sinner. We love the sinner, just as God does. We only hate the sin. You know the old adage: Hate the sin but love the sinner.

In fact, it's *because* we love people that we want them to realize that what they're doing is harmful, destructive, and yes, sinful.

This is what we need to get across to our secular neighbors. When we say certain conduct is immoral, we're not setting ourselves up as morally superior. We're not claiming a right to dictate what's good and bad.

It is God who sets standards of right and wrong. We're simply communicating what God has said.

For example, I don't know anyone more outspoken in condemning homosexual conduct than myself. But every time I go into a prison I make a point of asking to see the inmates in the AIDS ward. I don't hesitate to embrace them; I genuinely try to show them God's love.

I'm still trying to explain all this to my skeptical friend. And you might try to help your friends see it as well. Help them understand that when we talk about sin, we're not being bigoted. We're doing it out of genuine concern.

We love people so much that we don't want to see them doing things that ultimately destroy them.

Now, *that's* real love.

October 8, 1992

2

What Are Your Children Learning in School?

PC for the Play-Doh Set
Teaching Tots Political Correctness

Picture books about Babar, the elephant king, are being pulled from the shelves. The stories have been judged to be dangerous for the tender minds of preschoolers.

Just what is Babar's crime? In the words of a prominent educator, Babar is a poor role model for children because he "extols the virtues of a European middle-class lifestyle."

In short, Babar is not politically correct.

We've heard about the attack on the so-called Eurocentric curricula in colleges. Now it's trickling down to the younger grades. It's PC for the Play-Doh set.

The New Republic reports that the hottest things at teachers' conventions today are guidelines for making preschool and elementary classrooms politically correct. A guide entitled "Anti-Bias Curriculum," published by the National Association for the Education of Young Children, is a favorite.

One of the groups defended in "Anti-Bias Curriculum" is witches. Too long, the book says, witches have suffered from disparaging prejudice. Teachers are advised to explain to young children that witches are not evil hags but good women who use herbal remedies to help people.

Story time is a great forum to instill politically correct attitudes. One guide encourages teachers to think of new twists for the old classics. For example, it suggests reading "'Twas the Night Before Christmas" and pretending there is no papa in the story. I guess that's to help children become accustomed to single-parent homes.

There are PC educators who denounce Mother's Day as a regressive symbol of a sexist organization of labor. I wonder what that makes Father's Day.

Then there are schools that celebrate an international Thanksgiving, where each child brings food and flags from his country of origin. In one Brooklyn classroom, a little boy was reduced to tears of confusion because his ancestry was English, Scottish, Irish, German, and Jewish. The teacher finally relented and allowed him to bring an American flag.

Playtime is harder to regulate, but today's PC teachers are up to the challenge. In the dress-up corner, teachers are urged to stock more briefcases than purses to encourage careerism in little girls. They're told to get rid of dump trucks and earthmovers because these reflect the American desire to "conquer nature." Environmentalism is part of PC, too.

If you have children or grandchildren in school, I suggest you find out what they're learning. These stories may sound silly, but they reflect an underlying world-view that is anything but silly. Multiculturalism would be fine if it simply meant teaching children about the culture, history, and geography of other lands. My own ancestry is Swedish and English, and I'm proud of it.

But most of these programs have a more serious agenda. They're out to change our values. They send a subtle message that Western culture is bad and should not be held up as a standard.

In fact, the message is that *nothing* should be held up as a standard, that there is no standard of right or wrong—no transcendent, absolute truth. A report on multicultural education by the New York state board of education actually talks about "multiple truths"—as though each racial and ethnic group has its own truth.

So the issue is not just whether kids should read Babar. It's whether Americans will acknowledge a single, universal truth that transcends all our differences.

May 4, 1992

Why Johnny Can't Learn
Falling SAT Scores

SAT scores dropped again this year. Verbal scores hit a new, all-time low. What's wrong with American public schools?

The decline began in the early part of this century with John Dewey, often called the father of American education. Dewey taught that it's not so important *what* children learn as *how* they learn. Schools shouldn't teach facts, he said, they should teach a process of inquiry.

In a process-oriented history class, Johnny doesn't learn the key events at the founding of our nation. Instead, he grinds corn so he can *experience* how the Indians lived.

In a process-oriented science class, Johnny doesn't learn the basic facts of biology. He writes an essay on what it would *feel* like to be a groundhog.

In social studies, Johnny doesn't learn the facts of geography and culture. Instead, he reads a close-up story about a family living in some Third-World village to get a *feeling* of their way of life.

Process-oriented education is interested not in objective facts and principles but in the student's self-expression. Especially in sex education and drug education, teachers' guides fairly bristle with warnings not to teach that there are right or wrong answers. Instead, Johnny is taught a process of inquiry so he can express his own feelings and choose his own course of action.

Why does modern education stress subjective feelings over objective facts and principles?

The reason is that many educators don't *believe* in objective facts and principles. They don't believe in any overarching, universal truth. And if there is no truth, what is there to teach?

The results of this style of education are devastating, as our falling SAT scores demonstrate. By contrast, scores have gone *up* in Christian schools—not just in the suburbs either, but also in racially mixed, inner-city neighborhoods. This year in Washington, D.C., parochial schools actually registered a twenty-point *increase* in SAT scores.

Why such a remarkable difference?

The answer is that Christian educators believe in objective truth. They teach objective facts and principles—whether in history or math or sex education.

The secular world may mock Christians as anti-intellectual know-nothings. But if current trends hold, Christians may one day be the only ones standing for real education.

It has happened before. In the Middle Ages, after the barbarians destroyed Roman culture, it was the church that kept learning alive.

Today, the new barbarians are those who reject any real truth. And the Christian Church is once again becoming the champion of learning.

March 3, 1992

Educating for Ethics
Choice versus Character

Can adults tell youngsters what to do? The dominant method in education today says no. Adults can only help youngsters explore their feelings and make their own decisions.

For example, one sex education textbook advises teachers to tell children, "Although we adults feel it's in your best interest to delay intimate sexual behaviors, you and only you will decide when you will become sexually involved."

Stanley Hauerwas, a professor of religion at Duke University, explains what's happening in education. Public schools treat ethics as a matter of individual decision making, he says. The goal in moral education is to teach students how to make up their own minds.

The trouble, Hauerwas says, is that, "most students don't have minds worth making up."

Hauerwas does not mean that as an insult. He merely means that most students have not had their minds trained by confrontation with the great principles of truth and justice expounded through centuries of Western culture. Students have been told that all they have to do is look within, judge their own feelings, choose what "feels right" to them.

The result is people who approach ethics as though it were a consumer choice—who insist that they are free to choose their own value systems just as they are free to choose between, say, a Sony or a General Electric radio. In fact, a prominent sex educator says a good program is one that "supports the decision to say 'yes' as well as the decision to say 'no'" to sexual involvement.

"Yes" is a Sony, "no" is a GE. It's all a matter of personal preference.

The implicit message to youngsters is that junior knows best. Making up their own minds implicitly means rejecting the teachings of their homes and churches. In fact, ethical maturity is actually defined in educational theory as the autonomous individual making his own choice. Any external authority is suspect. If you listen to anything outside your own feelings, you are not truly mature, independent, and autonomous.

We see the same theme in psychology. Psychologists say there are various levels of moral development, from blindly following rules to making independent value judgments. But there's an atheistic bias built into the system itself. Consider: If Christians follow an external authority—God's commands, for example—they are by definition at a lower level of ethical maturity.

As a concrete example of this bias, one psychologist conducted a study of the moral beliefs of conservative Christians.

Not surprisingly, he discovered that they appeal to an external authority—to God's will and law. The psychologist triumphantly announced that conservative Christians rank low on the scale of moral maturity.

But, of course, the scale was biased against them from the outset—by its very definition of maturity.

As a result, many moral philosophers and psychologists not only reject a transcendent ethic themselves, they also pronounce those who still hold to one as "psychologically immature."

But moral education based on the psychological theory of autonomy yields disappointing results. Studies show that youngsters who take courses teaching individual decision making as the basis for ethics end up with higher rates of drug use and sexual activity.

The reason should be obvious. Without a timeless, universal set of ethical guidelines that they can rely on—an absolute standard beyond themselves—young people have no means to withstand temptation. They have no defense against the pushers and the dealers.

With this form of moral education, there is little hope that our kids will just say no.

October 24, 1991

The Volleyball Theory of Sex
What Does It Really Teach?

A New York subway ad shows teenagers happily playing volleyball . . . with an inflated condom. "You can play with them," the ad reads. "Don't play around *without* them."

The same lighthearted, isn't-it-fun approach is now being adopted in some schools. The New York City school system has started distributing free condoms. The condoms are handed out to students without giving them counseling, without asking for their parents' consent—or even telling their parents.

This is an approach that gives students no inducement to do any serious thinking about sexual activity and its risks. No, it's all fun, fun, fun. Maybe the next set of advertisements will show teens playing tiddlywinks with birth control pills.

The impact of these ads is to turn sex into something casual and matter-of-fact. Sex educators are worried that teens tend to treat sex as passionate, romantic, meaningful—that they get swept away by their feelings. The theory is that teens are more likely to use birth control and condoms if you strip it of its meaning, treat it clinically, turn it into light entertainment.

Sex without passion, without significance.

But wait, we've heard that before. It's the Playboy philosophy of sex. No commitment, no emotional involvement, simple animal pleasure.

What an incredible irony: In trying to teach young people to be responsible, public schools have adopted an *ir*responsible, Playboy-style philosophy of sex. The only controls on sexual behavior that schools promote are utilitarian: Don't get pregnant; don't get AIDS.

Here, have a condom.

It's preposterous to think this approach to sex education can teach kids responsibility. Consider: Is there any other subject we teach that way? It's like teaching drivers' education by not mentioning any traffic laws and counseling kids to practice "safe driving" by wearing seatbelts. It's like teaching football by ignoring the rules of the game and telling kids to practice "safe sports" by wearing pads. The truth is that educators have abdicated their responsibility for moral training. They've given up. We can't stop kids from having sex, the argument goes; the only thing we can do is help make it safe.

By that logic, *Commonweal* magazine says, schools might just as well offer supervised sex. Provide students with clean, monitored bedrooms, with condoms discreetly placed on nearby nightstands.

Outlandish as it sounds, some parents have actually come to the same conclusion. The *Washington Post* interviewed several parents who allow their children to invite partners home for sex. The kids are going to do it anyway, the parents say; at least they're safer in their own home.

The sad thing is that it doesn't have to be this way. Studies show that teens *do* care what their parents think. They *are* receptive to moral guidance. Sex education programs that teach morality have been well received.

That should come as no surprise. Teens are just like the rest of us: They respond positively to a challenge; they are attracted to adults who expect a lot of them, who believe in them.

No, sex isn't the equivalent of a volleyball game. Teens know it. And they respect adults who know it, too.

November 21, 1991

Heather Has Two Mommies
The Homosexual Agenda for Schools

Gay activists insist they just want equal rights. Opponents say that's just not true—that what they really want is *approval* of same-sex relationships.

Which group has it right?

We get our answer by looking at the literature gay groups are promoting for the public schools.

For example, the New York City school system is embroiled in a controversy over a first-grade curriculum guide entitled *Children of the Rainbow*. The guide says, "children must be taught to acknowledge the positive aspects of each type of household."

What types of households do the authors have in mind? We find out in another passage, where teachers are encouraged to "be aware of varied family structures—including gay or lesbian parents."

If we turn to the list of recommended books, we find the same theme. One book is called *Heather Has Two Mommies;* it's about a lesbian couple who have a child through artificial insemination.

Another book is called *Daddy's Roommate,* about a youngster with two male parents. The child in the story says, "Being gay is just one more kind of love."

These books aren't just teaching kids not to pick on people or make fun of them. They're teaching positive acceptance of homosexuality on a par with traditional marriage and family.

An analogy, says columnist John Leo, would be teaching school children to be tolerant of Catholics by making them read a book called, perhaps, *Heather Finds Peace as a Nun.*

Imagine if we carried this out in an even-handed way. School children would be reading books called *Heather Is Born Again* to promote tolerance of Fundamentalism. *Heather Speaks in Tongues* for charismatics. And if we want to be multicultural about this, how about *Heather Wears a Veil,* showing a happy little Muslim girl? And even *Heather Used to Be a Cow* to promote appreciation of Hinduism?

I'm joking, of course. But the possibilities for cultivating "right attitudes" are endless. The question is where schools would find the time to teach the old standbys like reading, writing, and 'rithmetic.

Schools are going about this tolerance thing backward. If they were really teaching basic skills and attitudes, students would be equipped to respond to *any* group and its beliefs rationally and fairly. Then teachers wouldn't have to single out specific groups for special treatment and endorsement.

And yes, books like *Heather Has Two Mommies* and *Daddy's Roommate* do cross the line from tolerance to outright endorsement. As John Leo puts it, "The traditional civic virtue of tolerance . . . has been replaced with a new ethic requiring approval and endorsement."

Under the old definition of tolerance, schools tried to be value-neutral, asking children to park their values and beliefs at the door. But today's schools have abandoned that goal. They are aggressively teaching a new ethic—and it's one that contradicts the biblical ethic accepted by the majority of our population.

So don't let gay groups or their supporters make you feel as if *you* are the one being intolerant. Their own goal is to impose a new ethic, a new orthodoxy, upon the rest of society.

And they're starting with the people who are most impressionable: our schoolchildren.

September 2, 1992

Condoms for Kids
A New "Sacred" Right

September had arrived, school was opening, and in Washington, D.C., the superintendent was fired up. There will be "a lot of changes" this year, he told a back-to-school rally. We've got to prepare "youngsters to be successful in the twenty-first century."

What was he referring to? Stronger academic programs? Tighter discipline? New computers?

No, what the D.C. superintendent thinks students need is condoms.

The school system had decided to authorize school nurses to hand out condoms to any student who asked. The service was offered "confidentially," which means without informing the student's parents.

When parents heard of the plan, they were outraged. Many requested an opt-out program to exempt their child. Initially the superintendent agreed, but he was overruled by the D.C. public health commissioner.

No one will be allowed to "interfere" with the condom program, the commissioner thundered. *No one* will be allowed to disrupt the "sacred" right of confidentiality between school nurse and student.

And so D.C. has officially decreed that the relationship between school and child is more sacred than the relationship between parent and child.

Parents are of course required to pay with their taxes for this usurpation of their rights. Today D.C. teenagers can saunter into the nurse's office and pick out condoms in a variety of colors and flavors—all paid for by their parents' taxes.

Mint-flavored green condoms are quite popular, district officials confided in a *Washington Post* interview. And for ethnic diversity, schools even offer Afrocentric brands, described by officials as "attractive to the African-American population."

"We try to be attentive to the tastes and choices of our clients," they explained, sounding more like marketers than educators.

Trivialities aside, what we're seeing played out in the office of the school nurse is a philosophical battle over who bears responsibility for children. Biblical teaching gives the primary responsibility to parents, with the support of the church community. Historically, schools were established as an extension of parent and church authority.

But the rise of a public school system challenged all that. From the start, there have been social and political radicals who have seen the public school system as a way of reaching children directly with their political agenda.

As one Princeton scholar puts it, "There is a struggle between the family and the state for the minds of the young." The public school system has become "the chief instrument" for state officials to make "a direct appeal to the children over the heads of their parents."

This is the heart of the condom issue. As D.C. Senator Florence Pendleton warns, the current policy "breaks down the family. It tells the child in a very explicit way that you don't have to do what your parents tell you."

The condom issue is just one front in a larger battle over the role of the public school system. American schools are in the throes of being redefined: Are they going to be an extension of parental authority—or an arm of the state?

There is no middle ground.

November 12, 1992

Virtue and Virginity
Abstinence-Based Sex Education

A comic strip in the *Wall Street Journal* shows a teen-aged couple sitting on a couch, embracing. The bubble over the girl's head says, "C'mon, aren't you a real man?"

The boy answers, "I'm man enough to *respect* you."

So it goes through the rest of the strip, showing teens how they can successfully resist sexual temptation.

Strange stuff for a comic strip, you say. But this wasn't your ordinary newspaper strip. It was taken from a sex education curriculum entitled *Sex Respect,* one of several programs that encourage young people to abstain from sexual relations.

As teen pregnancy rates continue to escalate, abstinence-based programs are starting to be in great demand all around the country. But there are two kinds of abstinence programs—with a world of difference between them.

Programs like *Sex Respect* are openly value-based. They take an unapologetic stand against adolescent sexual involvement. They teach that sexual intercourse is a powerful means of affectional bonding that should be reserved for building strong marriages. Students act out skits to give them practice in learning refusal skills.

These abstinence programs are a radical departure from the nondirective, value-free approach to sex education, where students decide for themselves what is "right for them." Instead, abstinence programs are highly directive about the things that are right for kids—and sex isn't one of them.

There's another kind of abstinence program, however, that looks similar on the surface but is radically different. Like the real thing, these programs do give students reasons to postpone sexual involvement; they do train students in refusal skills.

In fact, some of the exercises look like they were lifted right out of *Sex Respect.*

But here's the catch: These imitation programs put abstinence right back into the context of the old value-free approach. In fact, they're usually written by the same folks who gave us the old materials—organizations like Planned Parenthood or its offshoot, ETR Associates.

In these programs, abstaining from sex may be stressed more heavily than it used to be—but it's still offered as just one "option" among many.

For example, a curriculum entitled *Choosing Abstinence* recommends teaching students that "at this time in their lives it would be a wise choice to say no to sex." But then the text quickly cautions teachers not to give the slightest hint of a "negative reproach" to students who are already sexually active.

In other words, the message to students is that sexual abstinence is a pragmatic choice for certain age groups, but certainly not a matter of right and wrong. One sex education teacher put it bluntly: It's all right to teach kids to say no to sexual activity, she said, but "kids have the right to say yes, too."

This is the underlying premise of wanna-be abstinence programs—that kids have a right to say yes, too. What a sad commentary on how deeply America's educational system has succumbed to relativism.

So check what's being taught in your children's schools. Don't be taken in by imitation programs that teach abstinence as merely a pragmatic option. Find out about programs like *Sex Respect* that bring real values into the classroom.

There's a world of difference between the real thing and the counterfeit.

July 27, 1992

Pumsy, the Magic Dragon
New Age Education

Five-year-old Stephanie sat absolutely still, her hands folded, her eyes closed. For a lively little girl, this was unusual behavior, and her mother was puzzled.

"Stephanie, what are you doing?"

No answer.

"Stephanie, what are you doing?"

"Stephanie!" Finally, the little girl opened her eyes. She explained it was an activity she had learned at school. And she went on to describe what her mother recognized as classic Eastern meditation.

It turned out that Stephanie was in a program called PUMSY: In Pursuit of Excellence. But it would be more accurate to call it In Pursuit of Hindu Philosophy. The techniques taught in Pumsy have all the elements of Hindu-style meditation, dressed up with cute fairy-tale characters.

There's a dragon named Pumsy, along with a guide simply called Friend. Friend teaches Pumsy that her mind is like a pool of water: There's a muddy mind, which tempts her to think negative thoughts, and a Clear Mind, which can solve all her problems through positive thinking.

The funny thing about this Clear Mind is that, the way it's described in the story, it doesn't sound like a mind at all. It sounds more like some separate power or person. Friend tells Pumsy, "Your Clear Mind is the best friend you'll ever have. . . . It is always close to you, and it will never leave you."

This sounds suspiciously like religious language: I will never leave you nor forsake you. And a few pages later in the story, we read, "You have to trust [your Clear Mind] and let it do good things for you."

This "mind" sounds like divine power.

And that's exactly what it is. The Pumsy story is just a fairy-tale way of teaching Hinduism. Hindu doctrine teaches that the human mind or spirit is part of God—a spark in the divine fire, a drop in the divine ocean. The Clear Mind is a euphemism for the divine spark within.

What we're seeing here is New Age pantheism wedging its way into education. It's not sold to teachers that way, of course. It's marketed as a way to teach self-esteem.

The rationale is that teaching kids to look within to solve their problems makes them more self-reliant. Pumsy teaches youngsters to chant slogans like "I can handle it," "I can make it happen," and "I am me; I am enough."

There's that religious language again—like God's name in the Old Testament: I am who I am.

What Pumsy teaches is not self-esteem, it's self-worship.

Educational programs like Pumsy are popping up all across the country. The cover may say it's a program in self-esteem or drug education or whatever. But at the core of so many programs today is a thinly disguised message of New Age pantheism.

Most schools adopt these programs in good faith. Teachers often don't even recognize the underlying philosophy. So it's up to you—as parents and pastors—to find out what your children are learning, to teach them to discern true from false religion, and to equip them with spiritual weapons to fight the spiritual battle.

And yes, that means children even as young as five-year-old Stephanie.

October 2, 1992

Guns at the Door, Please
Violence in School

It was a math class in a Chicago high school. But instead of learning geometry that morning, the students were taught a horrifying lesson about violence.

The teacher was collecting assignments when two students entered the room, pulled out a knife, and attacked a boy. Within moments the boy fell to the floor, fatally stabbed.

It's said that Johnny can't read or write—but he sure can fight.

That's the finding of a new report entitled *National Education Goals*. The study found that one-third of eighth graders can't calculate the cost of a meal from a menu. One-third of eleventh graders can't write a coherent paragraph about themselves—not about history or literature, mind you, but about *themselves*.

Yet, as I said, they do know how to fight. The same study revealed an alarming rate of school violence. Over the past year, one in every five twelfth-graders was injured in school. Many of the incidents involved weapons.

It wasn't so long ago that the weapons of choice among students were rubber bands and spitballs. Today if you check their bags, you're likely to find everything from handguns to knives, razor blades, brass knuckles, and broken beer bottles.

Many schools use metal detectors and security guards to keep their halls safer. Some even issue computerized identity cards, which students slip into a slot before entering the school building every morning. A green light means enter. A red light means stop and be checked by a guard.

What has caused this drastic erosion of school discipline? The answer is a changing view of rights and authority. The traditional view is that schools are an extension of parental authority over their children. But beginning in the 1960s, the Supreme Court issued a series of decisions granting students many of the same rights as adults.

For example, in 1967 the Supreme Court ruled that any school disciplining a student has to provide notice of the charges, right to legal counsel, right to confront and cross-examine witnesses, privilege against self-incrimination, and right to appellate review.

Remember, we're talking about high school kids here.

Rulings like this may have prevented abuses of authority in a few cases. But the greater effect by far has been to undermine school discipline. Litigation soared. Teachers' hands were tied. They hesitated to impose discipline for fear of being drawn into costly legal battles. Students openly defied teachers, saying, "You can't suspend me."

But there really is a better way.

I began by telling you about a fatal stabbing in a Chicago school. Not far away is another school, where discipline is strict, students are well behaved, and academic scores are high. One educator describes it as a "pocket of excellence" in the heart of a violent, drug-ridden neighborhood.

What makes the difference? This is a parochial school. The teachers here are not frightened off by charges that they're violating student rights if they maintain strict standards of conduct.

As Christians, these teachers know that courtesy, respect, and hard work are part of the image of God in all people. They also know that teachers who demand such things of their students are only asking them to live up to their best potential.

What our school system needs today is more of these little "pockets of excellence."

March 9, 1992

Unhappily Ever After
Lopsided Literature

Manny was an orphan, living on the streets of Mexico. Daily he faced hunger and beatings. One day he was caught trying to heist the wallet of a depressed Vietnam veteran, and the American befriended him. But shortly afterward the man was attacked by a street gang. Dying in a dirty alley, he gave his wallet to Manny and urged him to flee to America.

It's a dreary story without any redemptive message. Not the sort of thing you'd expect to find in a book for teenagers. But that's exactly what it is. The title is *The Crossing,* and it's on the American Library Association's list of Best Books for Young Adults for 1987.

Death, divorce, poverty, crime—it's all in contemporary teen literature. I'm not talking about cheap paperbacks, either. I'm talking about the books most widely recommended by library and education groups.

Literature used to be taught as an art form; its goal was to express beauty and truth. Today, literature is taught as a therapeutic tool for coping with personal problems.

Anyone who objects to such bitter fare for teens is attacked as a censor: "Don't you want kids to learn how to face the real world?"

Of course we do, but these books raise problems without offering solutions.

In her book *What Are Your Kids Reading?* Jill Carlson reviews the most frequently recommended books for teens. A full quarter of the books, Carlson says, revolve around death as a major theme. Yet none offers a biblical perspective on death or suffering.

Another common theme is teen sex. But it's never portrayed as morally wrong, Carlson notes. It's never even followed by

negative consequences, like teen pregnancy or sexually transmitted diseases.

And the portrayal of adults is sharply skewed. In most
books for teens fathers take a real beating, Carlson reports:
They're overwhelmingly portrayed as cruel and abusive.
When you can find them, that is. Most have died, divorced, or
deserted their families.

Mothers have been dressed up by Women's Liberation and
usually appear as career women.

And clergy are almost always bad guys—lecherous and
lewd.

This new teen literature is described as "contemporary realism." But realistic is just what it's not. America has its problems, I'll admit, but to portray *most* American fathers as
abusive, *most* mothers as careerists, *most* preachers as hypocrites, and teen sex as fun without consequences is statistically
and morally inaccurate.

What are your teens reading these days? If you're a parent,
I suggest you find out. When teens read, they enter into a dialogue with the author. As Carlson puts it, "From cover to
cover, your child is alone with a skilled author whose beliefs
may not be yours."

Make a habit of reading with your teens. Dig up the clas-
sics—books by Charles Dickens, Jane Austen, Thomas Hardy.
Acquaint your family with Christian fiction, too—from
Pilgrim's Progress to J. R. R. Tolkien, C. S. Lewis, and George
MacDonald. Contemporary Christian novels are exploding
onto the market these days, too, and many are excellent.

What educators say is true: Kids *do* need to be prepared for
the real world. But that means being armed with the truth.

November 25, 1992

Garbage In, Garbage Out
Out of the Mouths of Babes

What do kids think about these days? A group of teachers
found out recently.

And the answer shocked them.

According to the *Education Reporter,* it started when a California school district participated in a creative writing project. The assignment for all the children was to write a story beginning with the same opening line: They were to imagine coming to school on a "misty, foggy morning" to find a strange car on the field, with the teacher's voice coming from the car.

The tone of the opening line suggests mystery, but the stories the children came up with had a lot more than mystery. They had savagery, violence, and sexual innuendo.

One child's story was about his teacher holding the class hostage with a machine gun. The police lure the teacher out and blow her up. In the end, the child wrote, "Ever body was happy."

Well, that gives a new definition to happy endings.

Several other stories were just as gruesome. One was about a teacher kidnapping a student and stuffing him into the trunk of the car; another was about a teacher planning to assassinate the principal; another was about a teacher teaming up with aliens to capture her students.

The teacher wasn't always a perpetrator of violence, though. Sometimes she was a victim. One student wrote a story about taping his teacher's mouth shut and pointing a gun at her head.

Other children laced their stories with sex. One little girl wrote about seeing her teacher in the car with a man, passionately kissing him. Another child wrote about his teacher being brutally raped. Another wrote about finding his *father* in the car with his teacher.

How old would you suppose these kids were?

Incredibly, they were only third-, fourth-, and fifth-graders. What a stark testimony to the early age at which children are being exposed to the sordid, ugly side of life.

Just thirty years ago parents could pretty much control their children's access to unwholesome material. Society cooperated by protecting kids from explicit sex and violence.

But today society no longer cooperates. Just the opposite: Everywhere, from movies to television to so-called problem literature, kids are fed a steady diet of murder, suicide, abortion, incest—you name it.

And with the rapid increase in divorce and two-career families, there's been a sharp drop in the amount of time parents spend supervising their children's activities.

The result is that children are no longer protected from the corrupt and dangerous side of life. In fact, some scholars say we are losing the very concept of childhood as a special and protected place in the life cycle. In recent years several books on the subject have appeared, with titles like *The Disappearance of Childhood* and *Children Without Childhood*.

In this presidential campaign we're hearing a lot about family values. Well, here's a concrete example of the decline of family values. And it's something you and I can work to change.

It may mean rethinking our priorities so we spend more time with our children; it may mean putting up with screams and hollers as we wean them off the lurid stuff they've become used to. But it's worth it.

It's time we gave our children back their childhood.

September 28, 1992

Textbook Tales
Don't Bother Me with Facts

Quick: When did America drop the atomic bomb?

If you said, "at the end of World War II," you're quicker than some of the people who write our children's history books.

That's right. One history textbook places the bomb at the end of the *Korean* War. And that's just one of more than two hundred errors contained in this year's new history textbooks.

The errors came to light when the Texas Board of Education met to approve a textbook list. The books had already been reviewed by a panel of experts.

But it took an independent monitoring group to catch the mistakes: a group run by Mel and Norma Gabler, a Christian couple who periodically review textbooks.

Among the errors they found was a textbook describing Sputnik as a nuclear missile. Another book cited the wrong number of Americans killed in World War I. And several books gave wrong dates for the invention of the telegraph, the bombing of Pearl Harbor, the assassination of John Kennedy, and the first moon walk.

Well, the Texas board was chagrined, as well it should have been, and ordered the publishers to correct the mistakes. But the incident raises a larger question. How did such obvious errors creep into the books in the first place?

This carelessness about factual accuracy didn't come out of nowhere. It came from a shift in educational theory—away from objective truth and toward social engineering.

It began with John Dewey, who said schools should not be in the business of teaching facts; they should be teaching kids how to change in a changing world.

Dewey's followers took that a step further. They said schools should become *agents* of change.

The result: Educators began to downplay facts and focused instead on changing students' values to solve social problems. Schools aimed to raise a new generation free from racism, sexism, and discrimination.

Contemporary history textbooks reflect that goal. In a review of some of the most widely used history textbooks, Paul Gagnon of the University of Massachusetts discovered that profiles are reserved for certified minorities: for women like Anne Hutchinson; for blacks like Benjamin Banneker; for Native Americans like Tecumseh; and for a Chinese pioneer named Fatt Hing.

But, Gagnon writes, we search in vain for a serious discussion of American leaders: George Washington, Thomas Jefferson, James Madison—the people who shaped America's political thought and institutions. Apparently these men committed the social crime of being privileged, upper-class, white males; hence their treatment in several modern history text-books is scant.

What a lopsided view students are getting of American history. Textbook authors are too concerned with their social agenda to worry about such trifling matters as historical accuracy.

But Christians ought to take history seriously. Biblical religion is a historical religion; it rests on events that occurred at a particular place and time. We don't want to see history debased, as though it were just a tool for reshaping society.

So perhaps it's fitting that the people who caught the two hundred errors in the history textbooks are Christians. They ought to be an inspiration for us all.

Read your children's textbooks. Find out what picture of America *they're* getting.

January 15, 1992

Why Sail the Seven Seas?
Christopher Columbus—Man of God

In 1992 we marked the five hundredth anniversary of the arrival of Christopher Columbus on American shores.

And what a firestorm it has ignited.

On one side are Columbus's supporters, who paint him as enlightened and progressive. Their account is not much different from the simplistic stories we learned about famous people when we were in grade school.

On the other side are the protesters, who set themselves up as debunkers of cultural myths. In recent years they've made a new interpretation popular: Columbus set sail for America merely to gain wealth and extend Spanish dominion. They mutter angrily about exploitation and greed.

But the new story told by the debunkers is just as simplistic as the old myth. If we really want to know who Columbus was, we need to read balanced literature on the subject, like George Grant's *The Last Crusader* and Robert Royal's new book *1492 and All That*.

The story these books tell casts new light on the controversy. The historical records show that what motivated Columbus above all else in his ventures on the high seas was his Christian faith.

Yes, Columbus was a committed Christian. Like Joan of Arc and Saint Francis of Assisi, he was convinced that God had personally called him. "With a hand that could be felt," Columbus once wrote, "the Lord opened my mind to the fact that it would be possible to sail from here to the Indies, and He opened my will to desire to accomplish this project."

That's genuine religious conviction.

Columbus's desire to travel was first inspired by the Franciscan monks, who taught that the end of the world would come as soon as the gospel had spread to the ends of the earth. Columbus believed he had been called by God to accomplish this task, to become an instrument of universal evangelization. Whenever he encountered native peoples, he sought to bring them the Word of God.

This is the real Christopher Columbus—a man set on fire by missionary zeal.

Modern historians often make the mistake of reading contemporary concepts back into history. Take the idea that Columbus sailed for Spain and its imperial ambitions. Impossible. In late medieval times, Spain wasn't even a nation.

Most of Europe at the time consisted of loose collections of kingdoms, each with its own separate administration, laws, and customs. What tied medieval Europe together was a common faith and a common civilization known as Christendom.

Columbus saw himself not as a representative of Spain but of Christendom itself.

How many of you learned about this side of Columbus in your elementary school classrooms? I certainly didn't. And the current controversy over Columbus isn't helping to set the balance either.

Both sides are trying to impose modern categories on a historical figure. One side makes him out to be a progressive explorer, the other side denounces him as a racist and imperialist.

Both sides are overlooking the real story. It's the Christian story—of Christopher Columbus as a sincere Christian, doing his best to follow God's call on his life.

Now there's a story worth passing on to our children.

October 12, 1992

Who Needs Literacy?
Education for Ignorance

Here we were, decrying the decay of America's schools, the decline in test scores—and now it turns out we had it all wrong. A *Washington Post* column by Leonard Steinhorn tells us we shouldn't be worrying about kids who can't read or write.

Today's kids have a *new* kind of literacy, he says, and it's better than the old verbal kind: They have visual literacy, from watching so much television and playing video games.

You see, when youngsters play Super Mario Brothers, they're not just having fun, Steinhorn says. They're "processing information."

So who needs Aristotle or Shakespeare? Why worry about geography or history? In the modern world, Steinhorn tells us, it's much more important for kids to be able to "dissect a Madonna video or a Nike ad."

But there's the problem. Are they really learning how to "dissect" a Madonna video—or anything else?

Just picture a group of teenagers analyzing each frame of Madonna's latest video, engaging in serious intellectual debate over why the technical director chose a particular camera angle, or what artistic considerations lay behind the choice of black fishnet stockings.

Teens *don't* talk like this, of course, and the reason is that sheer exposure to visual images doesn't teach people how to understand or analyze them. The facts show that even with television blaring seven hours a day in the average American household, people aren't processing very much of what they take in.

The American Association of Advertising Agencies ran a study in which subjects were shown thirty-second video-tapes from news clips, commercials, and prime-time programs. They were then asked simple true-or-false questions about what they had just seen. Many could not answer the questions. On average, the study found, Americans fail to understand a quarter to a third of what they watch on television.

So while American society is becoming more *visual,* that doesn't mean we're becoming visually *literate*—in the sense of comprehending what we watch.

The truth is that the electronic age still requires old-fashioned verbal literacy. Words heard on television or read off a computer screen are comprehended exactly the same way as words in a book. We still need the ability to understand sentences and follow a line of argument.

People like Steinhorn mean well, but they're merely providing the education establishment an excuse for incompetence. Sure, we've failed to teach literacy, they say. But don't worry—people don't need it anyway. They get all they need from watching television and playing Nintendo.

That mentality is a sure ticket back to the dark ages. In medieval times, when only the priests could read, people were intellectually enslaved to the church. They had no way of searching out the truth on their own.

A major work of the Reformation was to translate the Bible into the language of the people. For the first time, people were free to search the Scripture for themselves and come to God through His Word.

If we fail to teach our children how to read and write, we condemn them to return to intellectual and spiritual slavery under some form of elite group in society, which will tell them what they should know.

Literacy is much more than just a practical skill. It's a door-way to freedom.

May 18, 1992

Who Teaches the Teachers?
Ed School Follies

Picture a classroom with groups of people sitting around tables working on a math problem. It's a simple task, but the groups are having trouble and keep asking for help. Finally a teacher breaks up the class, singing out, "If you're happy and you know it clap your hands . . ."

Sounds like a typical grade-school class, doesn't it? But it's not. The students are adults attending a teachers college. The idea is that the students are learning how to *teach* children by *acting* like children.

But the story also illustrates how teacher education courses are being "dumbed down."

For all the controversy over the sorry state of American education, no one has taken a look at the teachers themselves or at the training they receive. No one, that is, until recently. Journalist Rita Kramer spent a year visiting education schools across the country, sitting in on classes and talking to students and teachers. Her findings were published in a book called *Ed School Follies: The Miseducation of America's Teachers*.

And it is anything but reassuring.

Education departments are not known for attracting the brightest university students. And Kramer met many who were woefully unprepared to go out and teach. Their language was often sprinkled with adolescent slang; some couldn't get through a sentence without using the word "like." One professor even told Kramer, "We can't assume our students know anything. They've never even learned the states and their capitals."

Unfortunately, the courses offered by education departments do little to remedy these shortcomings. Would-be teachers learn that the goal of education is not excellence but equity. Grades are disdained as elitist. Any standards of behavior are frowned upon.

In one class, a student teacher suggested handing out motivational stamps to kids who come to class on time. No good, said her classmates—that would make the children who *don't* get them feel bad about themselves.

Today it seems that the major goal of education is to make kids feel good about themselves. Popular psychology seems to assume kids' self-esteem is so fragile that a single low mark could turn them into dropouts and drug addicts.

But without any external standards, the only standard of reference left is the "self." So today's curriculum doesn't stress objective knowledge but *self*-knowledge. Social studies doesn't develop awareness of the world but *self*-awareness. Art is supposed to encourage not expression but *self*-expression.

There was a time when education was about teaching basic skills and transmitting a common culture. But today's upcoming teachers see schools as agents for solving social problems, not by equipping kids to think, but by boosting their self-esteem.

When child-centered education was first developed by scholars such as John Dewey it was a helpful counterbalance, stressing experiential learning in a system that had become arid and abstract. But today child-centered education has gone to the opposite extreme: It elevates personal experience to the end-all of education and has lost all sense of transmitting objective truth.

We often hear American schools accused of failing to meet their goals. But as Rita Kramer makes painfully clear in her book, they *are* meeting their goals—because their goals are no longer academic but social. Upcoming teachers see themselves as agents of social change.

And *that* they are doing . . . all too well.

September 30, 1992

Feminquisition
The New "Gender Feminism"

Probably no piece of classical music is better known than Beethoven's Ninth Symphony, that paean to freedom and joy. One section has even been turned into a hymn: "Joyful, Joyful We Adore Thee."

So it's startling to hear what some feminist critics are saying today about this symphony.

Feminist music critics insist that all music is shaped by sexual themes—themes of male domination and control. Feminist professor Susan McCleary writes that in Beethoven's Ninth, what she hears is not an ode to freedom but frustrated sexual energy—energy that builds up until it "finally explodes in the . . . murderous rage of a rapist."

Well. Welcome to the strange world of feminist scholarship.

It used to be that feminists just wanted to open opportunity for women in all fields—a worthy goal. But today there's a new movement of so-called *gender feminists*. They want more than equal opportunity. They want to change the very content of what is taught in every field—to create a feminist music, a feminist art, a feminist science.

For example: In architecture, gender feminists say the development of square-cornered buildings has nothing to do with economy or space. It represents simply "the male takeover of power in architectural shapes." If females were architects, they say, we'd be living in oval mounds and other rounded shapes.

In advertising, gender feminists read fashion photos as symbols of suppressed male violence. A model wearing a high collar is said to represent strangulation. Bracelets denote slavery.

Even science is interpreted as an expression of male dominance. In biology, DNA is sometimes called the master molecule because it directs the cell's activities. But for gender feminists, any concept of mastery is masculine. They reject the master molecule theory, saying it pictures the DNA as "a male controller in a female body."

But criticism goes beyond individual scientific theories. Gender feminists say the scientific method itself is an outgrowth of male bias. They like to quote Francis Bacon, a sixteenth-century scientist, who quaintly described science as a "marriage" between the human mind and nature. He said the mind "penetrates" nature and turns her into his "slave."

Gender feminists pounce on this kind of imagery and insist that *all* science is based on the metaphor of sexual subjugation—of dominance and control. One feminist even suggests that Newton's mechanics be renamed Newton's rape manual.

Those examples are so outrageous they're almost silly. But the underlying theme is far from silly. Gender feminists deny any objective truth. Every theory, they say, is distorted by gender.

This ought to be disturbing for people like you and me who believe there *is* an objective truth and that the heart of that truth is in the Scriptures.

There's no denying that women's perspectives and experiences have been excluded from the public arena. Christians should be the first to recognize that both men and women are created in the image of God and both have something important to contribute.

But we should also stand against the attempt to deny the existence of objective truth, to reduce everything to sexual themes.

There's much more to art and science than the battle of the sexes.

June 4, 1992

The New Apartheid
Segregation on Campus

Some say the university campus sets the trends for the wider society. If that's true, then we may be headed for a jarring crackup of American culture.

Student groups today seem to be splitting into ever-smaller subgroups. *New Republic* magazine reports that at Oberlin College, for example, the Asian-American Alliance has splintered into East Asians and South Asians. Similar splits have broken up the Korean, the Jewish, and the Muslim student groups.

Not to be outdone, a group of homosexual students has split four ways: one subgroup for black males, another for black females, another for white males, and finally one for white females.

Today's students seem determined to congregate only with clones of themselves. Many campuses have special theme houses where students can live with people of their own race: an Asian house, a Jewish house, a Latino house, and an African-Heritage house.

The same separatism has even invaded the academic program. The curriculum has splintered into East Asian Studies, Judaic Studies, Latin American Studies, Women's Studies, Black Studies. Many colleges have dropped required courses that treat Western culture as a whole.

This is nothing less than intellectual balkanization. Black students want to read only books by black authors; women want to read only books by female authors. The assumption seems to be that race and gender determine how people think.

Some may try to justify this in the name of ethnic pride, but it's much more than that. It's a blow at the very principles upon which America was built.

America is a nation of immigrants. What gives us cultural cohesiveness is not a common ethnic background but a common belief—belief in such principles as the rule of law, the value of the individual, and the freedoms outlined in the Bill of Rights.

Indeed, America depends for its very existence upon the conviction that we can *transcend* our native cultures and commit ourselves to a unified national vision. This is expressed in our national motto: *e pluribus unum,* "out of many, we are one."

That motto, of course, is a secularized version of a biblical vision of unity. In the first century, Jesus' apostles scattered across the globe with the message that the biblical God is the God of the entire universe. The gospel is for Jews and Gentiles, Greeks and barbarians, men and women, rich and poor.

But today's university students are being taught that there is no single set of principles that can command allegiance from all people. As a result, we are in danger of splintering into a thousand squabbling nationalities, each hiding out in its own cultural and intellectual ghetto.

What's at stake here is not only the future of American culture but the very notion of truth itself. When black students, women students, or Latino students refuse to even read the works of other people, what they are saying is that each group has its own truths—that there is no single, overarching, universal truth.

But Christianity makes the bold claim that it *is* an overarching, universal truth—the truth about ultimate reality. So the breakup of the universities is not just a disaster for American culture. It's a disaster for anyone trying to communicate the Christian truth.

It will be impossible to preach that Christianity is true . . . when truth itself is splintered into a thousand ethnic fragments.

July 30, 1992

3

Law and Liberty

A Tale of Two Ads
Selective Freedom

America, land of the free!

At least that's what we've been taught. But today freedom is sometimes selective. Freedom of speech is granted to some groups . . . but not to others.

Consider the opposite treatment given to two advertisements in recent weeks. The first was in Georgia, where a pro-life candidate for Congress, David Becker, aired several political ads showing an abortion in progress.

Pro-choicers were outraged and appealed to the Federal Communications Commission to declare the ads indecent. The ads were admittedly pretty gruesome—but then abortion is a gruesome business.

The FCC upheld Becker's right to show the ads, but then the Georgia Supreme Court stepped in and ruled the ads indecent. By law, indecent programming can run only between midnight and 6:00 A.M. So while prime time is free to show murders in living color, abortion is relegated to the dead of night—along with smutty programs that really *are* indecent.

So much for Becker's freedom of speech.

The second story is set in Washington, D.C., where a country music radio station was approached by a gay-rights group to run an ad promoting the organization and its agenda. The station manager politely turned down the ad, citing a long-standing station policy of refusing to air any "issue advertising."

Immediately the gay group swung into action. The next business day, the station manager received a call from none other than the mayor of Washington, D.C. He was told in no uncertain terms that if the station refused to carry the ad, he would be prosecuted. The charge? Denying a minority group access to the "cultural life" of the city.

Unfortunately, the radio station caved in—a response that will only encourage gay groups to continue to use coercive tactics.

Liberal groups often present themselves as open and tolerant, as people who just want a pluralistic society. But I'm not so sure. The gay activists in Washington certainly weren't being very tolerant when they enlisted the city government to overrule the radio station's policy. They were just as absolutist—just as willing to force their will on others—as Fundamentalists are often accused of being.

And the Georgia Supreme Court certainly wasn't being very pluralistic when it banned those pro-life ads. The judges were just as exclusivist in promoting a single point of view as Christians are often accused of being.

Appeals to tolerance and pluralism may sound good, but they are not always sincere. Often they are merely a tactic to undermine *one* set of values in order to make way for a *new* set. And the new values are just as absolute, just as dogmatic, as the old ones.

So when you hear a group say, *We just want everyone to be free to make up his own mind,* don't necessarily take that at face value. Pro-choicers are not for real choice when they use the courts to suppress the opposition. Pro-gay groups are not for real tolerance when they use the arm of the law to force their views on others.

Yes, America *is* the land of the free, but not when the government uses its coercive power selectively—to promote one point of view over another.

November 11, 1992

The Reindeer Rule
Banning Christmas Carols

Christmas is coming, and for towns and municipalities across the nation 'tis the season to be worried—worried about lawsuits, that is.

Local officials in Vienna, Virginia, a suburb of Washington, D.C., were so worried that they banned religious carols at their annual Christmas celebration. "Frosty the Snowman" and "Jingle Bells" were permissible, but not "The First Noel" or "Joy to the World."

What made officials so skittish is that last year Vienna was the target of a lawsuit by the American Civil Liberties Union (ACLU) for allowing a local group to set up a Nativity scene in front of a community center.

The town had been careful to add secular displays alongside the Nativity scene: plastic reindeers, Santas, and snowmen. This was in accord with a 1985 Supreme Court ruling known as the "reindeer rule," which requires any religious display on public property to be balanced by secular displays in order to avoid any hint that the state is endorsing religion.

But in Vienna the careful balancing act was all for naught. The ACLU charged that, in spite of the Santas and reindeer, the crèche was still the primary focus of the display and hence violated the separation of church and state. Now the Supreme Court hadn't said anything about primary focuses, but no matter. A federal judge sided with the ACLU, and the crèche was taken down.

This year the controversy was about Christmas carols. At the advice of nervous lawyers, Vienna officials banned all religious songs at the annual town celebration.

In protest, the Vienna Choral Society withdrew from the program. And on the day of the festivities, two hundred people massed in the parking lot across the street to hold a counter-celebration. They erected a crèche and lifted their voices in song: "Away in a Manger," "Silent Night," and all the well-loved carols.

A few protesters brought banners. One banner read: "A baby in a manger or a fat guy in a red suit? The choice is yours."

Another banner took aim at the ACLU. "The ACLU is jealous of manger scenes," it read, "because it doesn't *have* three wise men or a virgin in its organization."

It was a well-aimed jab. But all humor aside, I will never forget the pathos of the image on the news that evening. The protesters were huddled behind barricades—carefully keeping their feet off public property—praying and singing their carols.

Instead of Christmas joy, the atmosphere was one of confrontation and protest.

I was grieved. Have we really come to this? Here in the shadow of the nation's capitol, the beacon of religious freedom for the whole world, Christians are having to fight for the right to sing traditional religious carols. The image recalled scenes from Eastern Europe before the fall of communism.

It ought to be a sober lesson for all Christians. If we don't speak out against the secularization of society—if we stand by quietly while the ACLU takes away our rights one by one— then America will lose what our forefathers called the first liberty: the freedom of religion.

And then the message on the banners in Virginia will no longer apply—because we *won't* have a choice anymore.

Instead of being able to choose the baby in a manger, we will be left with only a fat man in a red suit.

December 15, 1992

Battle of the Crosses
Do Americans Care about Religious Freedom?

When the communist tyrants held power in Poland, they ordered all crosses removed from classroom walls, factories, hospitals—all public institutions. But the Polish people rose up in a great wave of protest, and all across the land government officials backed down.

Yet in one small town the officials were determined to prevail. They insisted on taking down the crosses hanging in school classrooms. Students responded by staging a sit-in. Heavily armed riot police chased them out.

Then the students—nearly three thousand of them—carried the crosses to a nearby church to pray. The police surrounded the church. Violence was averted only when photographs of the confrontation were flashed around the globe and sparked a widespread protest.

With grit like that, it was no wonder Poland was the first country in Eastern Europe to throw off communism.

Compare that story to events in our own country. In 1963, the Supreme Court banned prayer from public schools. Many people took the decision as a signal that religion was no longer welcome in public places. And ever since, the courts have been busy ordering Christmas crèches removed from public parks and the Ten Commandments taken down from courthouse walls.

One small town was enmeshed in lawsuits for years. Zion, Illinois, was founded at the turn of the century as a religious community. Streets still bear names like Ezekiel, Gideon, and Galilee. The city seal still bears a cross, along with other Christian symbols.

I should say, it *used* to bear a cross. The seal came under the scrutiny of a group called American Atheists. Their Illinois director noticed it on one of his many trips, which seem to take him to and fro throughout the state looking for Christian symbols to remove.

The man took the city of Zion to court, demanding that the seal be purged of its cross. After years of court battles, in the summer of this year, the American Atheists finally won. The crosses are now being removed from city stationery and police cruisers.

But what is this resounding silence I hear?

Where is the outcry that greeted Polish authorities when they tried to remove crosses throughout *their* country?

The residents of Zion are disgruntled, to be sure. They rather liked the religious imagery in a cultural sense—as a reminder of Zion's unusual history. And the police department grumbles that it will cost a lot of money to replace the city seals on all those cruisers.

Hardly a ringing protest.

The courts say the state must maintain strict neutrality toward religion. But removing religious symbols from public places is not neutrality. On the contrary, it sends a highly negative message—that religion is something shameful, embarrassing, or at best strictly private.

We've come a long way from the day of the American founders, who regarded religious freedom as the first liberty. What they meant was that without the liberty to express our most fundamental beliefs, all other liberties inevitably crumble.

Alas, today the people of Poland and all of Eastern Europe seem to understand that better than we do here in America.

September 15, 1992

Making America Safe for Atheism
The Supreme Court Prayer Decision

The Supreme Court has struck another blow for liberty— liberty for the secularist and the atheist, that is.

The Court recently prohibited the use of nonsectarian prayers in graduation ceremonies in public junior and senior high schools. The justices ruled that prayers create "peer pressure" on kids to participate, or at least to stand and listen respectfully.

Now, I earned my doctoral honors in constitutional law, but I confess, this is a new one. I don't read any requirement in the Constitution to avoid peer pressure. And I always thought listening respectfully was exactly the kind of thing we *wanted* to teach kids in the name of tolerance.

Mind you, we're not talking here about prayer in the classroom, led by the child's teacher. We're talking about a public ceremony—a community event with parents, civic officials, and community leaders.

At a typical graduation you might hear a mayor exhort students about civic responsibility. A local businessman might inspire them vocationally. And a local religious leader . . . well, what would you *expect* a religious leader to do? He might pronounce a benediction over the students or recite a prayer on their behalf.

People don't have to *agree* with what the priest or minister says, any more than they might agree with the mayor's politics or the businessman's financial policy. But then, the First Amendment was not designed to protect us from ever listening respectfully to a person we disagree with.

What it *was* designed to do was to protect the free exercise of religious beliefs and to prohibit the establishment of a national church.

You see, many of the American colonists came from England, where every citizen was required to financially support the state church. Church tithes were collected by government officials just like taxes—under threat of legal penalty. And the English government appointed the church's bishops.

This is what the American founders were adamantly opposed to. The First Amendment was meant to protect religious people from legal coercion. It was *not* meant to protect atheists from psychological discomfort or "peer pressure."

Why have the courts moved so far from the original meaning of the First Amendment? The answer is not so much legal as cultural: a shift across American culture from an objective view of truth to a subjective view. Americans have come to see truth claims as individualistic and privatized—*especially* religious ones.

They resent any suggestion that Christianity is a universal truth.

The Supreme Court justices are not immune to these cultural attitudes. Like everyone else, they read the papers, listen to the news, and belong to professional associations. Eventually they may absorb the prevailing cultural mood—where it's more important to protect a junior high girl from feeling excluded than to protect America's historical religious heritage.

If the cause of this shift is cultural, the solution must likewise be cultural. Beginning in our churches, families, and neighborhoods, we must win over people's hearts and minds. We must show them that the political system we cherish—the religious liberties we enjoy—are rooted in a biblical worldview.

The lesson of the recent Supreme Court decision is that is we lose on the cultural front, we will also lose in the courts—even with judges we thought would be friendly to religious rights.

We cannot place our hope in the courts. Legal battles will be won only when Christians truly act as salt and light in our culture.

June 29, 1992

Facing Up to the Law
Are the Ten Commandments Legal?

When you pay a traffic fine in Cobb County, Georgia, you have to face up to the law of the land—*and* to the law of God. To be precise, the Ten Commandments, which are displayed on a wall plaque beside the ticket window.

The plaque has coexisted peacefully with the courthouse wall for thirty years, and no one ever objected to it. But in recent months it has threatened to become a national issue.

A sharp-eyed law clerk spotted the Ten Commandments—right there on government property!—and called in the American Civil Liberties Union. The ACLU demanded that the plaque be removed, claiming a violation of separation of church and state.

The state court judges refused unanimously. They argued that it is perfectly constitutional for a courthouse to decorate its walls with historical examples of codified law.

The judges are right, of course. Otherwise even the U.S. Supreme Court building would be unconstitutional. Right above the head of the chief justice, carved in marble, is a tablet representing the Ten Commandments.

You see, the Constitution doesn't even use the words "separation of church and state." The First Amendment simply says, "Congress shall make no law respecting an establishment of religion or prohibiting the free exercise thereof."

The purpose of the amendment was to prevent the federal government from setting up an official national church—like the Anglican Church in England or the Lutheran Church in Sweden. It was *not* intended to prevent the government from treating religion favorably.

The historical record on this is clear. On the very day Congress passed the First Amendment, it also passed a measure setting aside a national day of prayer and thanksgiving. Government officials back then saw no contradiction between the two acts.

They saw no contradiction either between the First Amendment and the appointment of a congressional chaplain, even though his salary came out of federal funds.

It was Thomas Jefferson who coined the phrase, a "wall of separation" between church and state. But even Jefferson, when he was president, signed a law making churches tax-exempt. He also used federal funds to build churches and establish missions to bring the gospel to the Indians. He never saw these measures as violating the separation between church and state.

When we talk about what is or is not constitutional, we need to consider what the writers of the Constitution themselves had in mind. From history it is obvious they did not intend anything like the completely secular state envisioned by the ACLU.

Under the ACLU's interpretation, even the Declaration of Independence would be unconstitutional, because it refers to the Creator as the source of our rights.

Down in Georgia, ACLU lawyers are threatening to take the Ten Commandment case to federal court. And one wag has suggested a way to outsmart them. Just decorate the plaque in some obscene way, he suggests, and call it "art." Instantly the ACLU will defend your right to free expression.

You might even get funding from the National Endowment for the Arts.

The idea was meant as a joke, of course, but what a bitter truth it expresses. In our day, you can *mock* religion in public and even get funds for doing it.

But you can't show *respect* for religion in public—or you risk being hauled into court.

July 16, 1992

Don't Blame Me
My Hormones Made Me Do It

Rose Cipollone smoked a pack and a half of cigarettes daily for forty years. And then she developed lung cancer.

Did Rose blame herself for ignoring the warning labels on cigarette packs? Did she kick herself for turning a blind eye to the reports on the health hazards of smoking? Did she resign herself to the fact that she had gambled with her health—and lost?

None of the above. Instead she insisted that her illness wasn't her fault at all. I'm just a victim, she said—and launched a lawsuit against three tobacco companies.

Several years ago, a young man named Dan White sneaked into San Francisco's City Hall and savagely gunned down the mayor and the city supervisor, Harvey Milk. Hauled into court, Dan pleaded temporary insanity. He insisted that a steady diet of junk food had raised his blood sugar and addled his brain.

It became known as the infamous "Twinkie Defense."

These are only two examples of what has become a growth industry in America—the cult of victimization. Here's how it works.

Western civilization traditionally understood that human beings are moral agents who can distinguish right from wrong, and who can therefore be held accountable for their actions. Law codes and social morality were based on the notion of individual responsibility.

But in the cult of victimization, individuals are not seen as moral agents. They are victims—of racism, sexism, capitalist exploitation, or an unhappy childhood.

Victims of tobacco companies and Twinkies.

There are advantages to claiming victim status. For one thing, it confers a sense of innocence that allows one to get away with outrageous behavior. After all, it wasn't really I who did it; I was driven by outside forces.

Victim claims can also be used to cover up one's shortcomings. A woman was stopped recently by a Virginia police officer for erratic driving. She cursed, kicked, and scored above the legal limit on a Breathalyzer test. Yet she successfully argued in court that she was not drunk, she was merely suffering from premenstrual syndrome, or PMS.

Her hormones made her do it.

Of course, there are *real* victims. As our culture moves further away from the biblical norms of behavior, more people break their marriage vows, more children are abandoned, more criminals stalk our streets. In short, more people suffer. The vocabulary of victimhood stems partly from a humanitarian concern for the suffering that may lie behind people's actions.

But it is not humanitarian to deprive people of their status as moral agents. It may be appealing to be a victim, since it frees one from having to admit wrong or guilt. But there is actually greater dignity in admitting guilt—for it affirms the moral dimension to human nature.

As C. S. Lewis once said, to be punished because one is truly guilty is to be treated as a human being made in God's image, capable of making moral choices—even if the choice is wrong.

As Christians we weep with those who weep. But we do not use their sorrows as an excuse for their shortcomings. That would be to treat them as pawns moved about by outside forces.

People made in God's image deserve better than a Twinkie defense.

September 27, 1991

Crybabies and Whiners
Should Life Be Perfect?

Judith Haime says she has psychic powers. At least, she used to say that. Several years ago, during a CAT scan, Judith was injected with a dye, which she claims caused her to lose her psychic abilities. Judith sued the doctor and the hospital, and a jury awarded her nearly $1 million in damages.

Americans are playing the blame game and taking their neighbors to court in record numbers.

A man in California was upset by the noise from his neighbor's private basketball court. He sued; the neighbor countersued. Both sought more than $100,000 in punitive damages.

Today there's even something called "hedonic" damages—from the same root as "hedonism," which means living for pleasure. The assumption is that everyone is entitled to a life of perpetual pleasure. After an accident, lawyers bring in an economist to calculate a dollar amount for every moment of lost fun the victim has suffered.

Well, the victim may win a jackpot, but the rest of us foot the bill. We all pay when companies are forced to charge higher prices to cover their liability insurance; when cities close playgrounds and swimming pools for fear of lawsuits; when industries abandon research in high-risk fields; when doctors stop practicing because of malpractice suits.

Often these costs are unnecessary. A Harvard study of malpractice suits found that only one in eight involved genuine wrongdoing by the doctor.

People just want someone to blame when things don't turn out right.

The assumption seems to be that things *ought to* turn out right, that life ought to be perfect. It's an assumption so widely shared that *Time* magazine calls it an "American faith"—with lawyers as its priesthood.

The American faith in a perfect life has its source in modern science and medicine. The astonishing success of science has persuaded many people that one day it will solve all human problems. It will conquer suffering and create social harmony.

Who needs heaven? Science will create a perfect society right here on earth.

But, ironically, faith in perfection, which started out as a proud boast, has turned into a whine. America has become what *Time* magazine calls a nation of crybabies. We expect things to be perfect, and when they aren't, we resort to a grown-up version of a temper tantrum: We stomp off to court.

It used to be that when people hurt, they opened the Bible to find comfort and meaning. Now they open the yellow pages to find a lawyer.

Taming the litigation monster will take more than blaming lawyers. We also have to persuade ordinary people to give up the idea that they are entitled to a life of fun and ease.

Christians, of all people, should know better. The Fall is real. Sin and suffering are here to stay until God creates a new heaven and a new earth.

Christians ought to be in a position to give a crybaby society a bracing dose of realism.

January 9, 1992

"Rights Talk"
The Right to Have Rights

A huge tangle of rights has overgrown America's legal landscape in the past few decades. Today we have criminal rights, minority rights, women's rights, children's rights, gay rights, animal rights.

The Supreme Court has even defined citizenship as "the right to have rights."

Without a doubt, this wild growth of new rights is a major cause of America's litigation explosion. The classic conception of rights was simply the freedom to act by your conscience without interference. Take the Bill of Rights. Freedom of religion means Americans can worship without state interference.

Freedom of speech means we can express our convictions without fear of a knock on the door.

But in the 1960s, a new concept of rights arose: a right to receive benefits from the government—like a job, medical treatment, a certain standard of living.

I was working in government at the time, and I saw it in the very language we used. Where once we had spoken of government "aid" programs, we began speaking of "entitlement" programs. Suddenly, it wasn't just an act of compassion to help the poor, the sick, or the elderly. It was a *right* to which they were entitled.

Rights came to mean basic needs, which in turn gave way to wishes. In *Rights Talk,* Harvard law professor Mary Ann Glendon says that people today use the language of rights to give moral force to what are merely personal desires.

So how does this fuel the fires of litigation?

Well, every right I claim imposes an obligation on someone else. If patients have a right to medical treatment, then doctors have an obligation to administer it. If criminals have a right to a lawyer, then the state has an obligation to supply one. If people have a right to financial security, then the government has an obligation to dole out welfare benefits.

For each new right that is created, a whole network of laws and regulations is written to enforce the corresponding obligations.

No wonder our courts are logjammed with lawsuits.

Notice the irony here. The old concept of rights was designed to *limit* state power—to define areas free from government interference. But the new concept of rights *expands* state power. It asks government to regulate all sorts of areas that were once private.

And if that doesn't work, people can resort to another form of government power—the courts. Private contracts, private conversations, the most intimate details are fair game for scrutiny by the courts.

The result: A larger and larger portion of our lives is vulnerable to government control—exactly what the old kind of rights were designed to prevent. The entitlement mentality is threatening the fundamental freedoms that were once the whole point of human rights.

What a sad irony: As Americans demand more and more rights, we enjoy fewer and fewer freedoms.

Christians should be calling their neighbors away from a selfish preoccupation with rights—reminding them that they also have responsibilities.

It's the only way to save the fundamental freedoms that have made America a light to the world.

January 10, 1992

In the Lawyers' Den
Using Law to Soak the Rich

When Vice-President Dan Quayle delivered a speech to the American Bar Association, his remarks reverberated through courtrooms and law schools for months afterward.

His message: America has too many lawyers.

Needless to say, some of the lawyers present were not very happy to hear it. The president of the ABA even stood up and scolded the vice-president on the spot.

Reporters called the story "Dan in the Lawyers' Den."

But the question the vice-president posed was a good one. Why does American need 70 percent of the world's lawyers, he asked, when it has only 5 percent of the world's population? No wonder America is suffering from a litigation explosion. Lawsuits are even driving some businesses out of the country.

What's behind this staggering increase in lawyers and lawsuits?

At its root is a change in the concept of law itself. The classical view is that law is based on unchanging principles of justice. The duty of a judge is to apply the law objectively, without being biased by personal feelings or preferences.

But in the 1920s and 1930s a new theory of law appeared: legal realism—so called because it claims to be more realistic than the classical view.

The new theory says judges are just ordinary people. They can't help being influenced by their own concerns. They can't be completely objective.

So let's stop asking them to try, legal realism says. Let's stop talking about objective principles of justice and just admit that judges make decisions according to their own personal or political agendas.

In legal realism, law was redefined as social engineering by judges.

The new theory really took hold in the 1960s, when the judiciary turned to the left. Judges came to believe that the rich were rich because they oppressed the poor. They came to treat lawsuits as a means of punishing the rich and redistributing the wealth to the little guy.

It's this new theory that we see at work in many of today's far-fetched lawsuits. Take the case some years ago when angry unionists set fire to a large hotel in Puerto Rico.

Lawyers for the victims of the fire didn't sue the individual arsonists. After all, they were union members; they represented the little guy.

No, the lawyers went after the corporations that made the carpets, the wallpaper, the bar stools. They argued that the companies should have made their products fire-resistant. They even sued the company that made the dice used in the hotel casino.

It was a classic case of using lawsuits to soak the rich.

If you read the Old Testament law, you won't find this bias against the rich. In Exodus 23:6, Scripture demands justice for the poor. But in the very same context, it warns us not to be *partial* to the poor either.

This is the classical view of law—impartial justice for rich and poor alike.

If lawyers today were to revert to that view, our nation would not be overrun by lawyers whose hidden agenda is to change the social and economic structures of society.

And Dan Quayle would walk unscathed out of the lawyers' den.

January 8, 1992

It's a Natural
The Real Basis of Civil Rights

Most Americans like to fall comfortably in the middle of the road on most political issues. As a result, politicians typically present their own views as the mainstream, while painting their opponents as extremists—on the fringe.

Call it the weirdo factor.

If you can't undercut someone by rational argument, just make him look weird, out of the mainstream.

We saw that tactic at work in the debate over the nomination of Clarence Thomas to the Supreme Court. Judge Thomas believes in natural law—a belief that human laws must be measured against an objective standard of morality and justice.

A higher law.

Opponents were quick to label Thomas's ideas as weird. Harvard Professor Lawrence Tribe said that no Supreme Court nominee had held a natural law philosophy in fifty years.

But that's a wild exaggeration. In fact, *most* people hold some belief in natural law. How about you? Do you believe the government can pass a law that is unjust? If so, you believe in natural law. You believe a law has to measure up to some outside standard of justice—otherwise it is unjust.

Natural law has been the dominant legal philosophy throughout Western civilization. Its roots reach back to the ancient Greeks and Romans—to Plato and Aristotle, Cicero and Seneca.

It was the dominant philosophy of law in the Middle Ages. The great theologian Thomas Aquinas related the secular concept of natural law to the biblical concept of divine law. Both refer to an objective standard against which human laws are measured.

The Reformers talked about natural law, too. John Calvin wrote that God's law is "engraved upon the minds of men" through conscience and natural law.

Our modern nations are based on the writings of men such as John Locke and Montesquieu, who offered their own theories of natural law.

Need we belabor the point any further?

Clearly the idea of natural law has a long and venerable heritage in Western thought. It is hardly novel or unusual. And certainly not weird.

In fact, it is the only basis for human rights. Judge Thomas argued that minority rights depend upon the idea of natural law found in the Declaration of Independence. The Declaration talks about certain rights as inalienable—which means a just government can't take them away.

But rights are not inalienable unless they are based on something beyond the government.

As the late Francis Schaeffer so eloquently put it, Where do inalienable rights come from? From the state? Then they are *not* inalienable. Because what the state gives the state can also take away.

That's why the Declaration of Independence says inalienable rights are endowed "by the Creator." The state doesn't *create* these rights; it merely *recognizes* them as preexisting by divine creation.

A Jewish rabbi named Joshua Haberman, writing in *Policy Review,* argued that without a higher law—a law above the state—there is no standard of justice to which we can hold the state accountable. And then there is nothing to prevent it from falling into tyranny and totalitarianism.

Rabbi Haberman knows what he's talking about: He had to flee Germany for his life when the Nazis came to power.

For Jews, for blacks, for all of us, the only sure basis of civil rights is natural law. And there's nothing weird about that— whatever Clarence Thomas's detractors may say.

September 9, 1991

When Lewd Is Illegal
Can Law Be Based on Personal Taste?

A man puts his arm around a female co-worker and gives her a quick hug. He's done it many times before . . . but now he stops himself. Is it OK? he wonders. Did I offend her? Did I do anything illegal?

Welcome to the American workplace after the Clarence Thomas hearings, where the rules of conduct have suddenly become very murky.

As Christians we have no quarrel with condemnations of sexual harassment. We have always trained our children to be pure in thought and action. But there's the crucial difference: What *we* have done by moral training, modern America is trying to do by law.

And that just won't work.

It used to be that parents, church, and school all spoke with a single voice, exhorting the young to follow accepted moral precepts. Social civility was woven into the very warp and woof of people's character.

But today many reject those moral precepts. They've bought into the Enlightenment philosophy that says each individual is autonomous and makes up his own rules of conduct.

Unfortunately, give people free reign like that, and sin quickly takes over. People do whatever they want. Civility decays, gutter language increases, women are harassed.

What should America do about it? Restore the old moral code? That seems to be the obvious answer. But don't even hope. Modern political activists shudder at the thought.

After all, these are the same enlightened progressives who have always pushed for a free and easy social attitude toward sex, who fight legal restrictions on pornography, who plead a First-Amendment right to produce smut for movies and television, who support government funding for obscene art.

No, it would be totally contrary to the progressive agenda to suggest that lewd language in the workplace is morally wrong.

Yet, at the same time, they do want to put a lid on offensive behavior. As a result, they're trying to solve the problem by making the behavior illegal.

Not wrong, just illegal.

The distinction is clear in the literature on sexual harassment. Prohibitions are carefully worded to avoid suggesting that the behavior in question is morally wrong—only that certain people don't like it.

For instance, the Capitol Hill Women's Political Caucus distributes a document listing several examples of sexual harassment. One example is—note carefully—"unwelcome propositions." The idea is that propositioning a woman is OK; it only becomes illegal when it's *unwelcome.*

Another example of harassment is—get this—"ill-received dirty jokes." So dirty jokes are OK; it's only *ill-received* ones that become illegal.

Language like this gives no one any clear guidelines. A man cannot know ahead of time whether his actions are going to be "unwelcome" or "ill-received." What one woman may enjoy another may find offensive.

To avoid committing a crime, a man has to be a mind reader.

This is ludicrous. The old moral law was wonderfully egalitarian. It applied equally to everyone; everyone played by the same rules; right and wrong depended on objective principles everyone could know. But modern sexual harassment laws hold people hostage to the fluctuating feelings of whoever happens to be present at the moment.

As Christians, we should be telling our feminist friends the *real* reason sexual harassment should be illegal. Not because it offends this woman or that woman, but because it offends a holy God—whose very character demands purity in speech and in action.

November 7, 1991

Whatever Happened to the ABA?
Loss of Legal Objectivity

The American Bar Association used to be a crowd of gray men wearing gray suits. But today they've become noisy and radical. According to one news report, the 1992 ABA convention was marked by whoops and cheers never before heard at Bar conventions.

And the whooping and cheering was all in support of radical causes.

First, the ABA officially endorsed an unrestricted right to abortion. More whoops and hollers sounded when the ABA presented an award to Anita Hill, the feminist hero who charged Judge Clarence Thomas with sexual harassment.

The excitement reached fever pitch when Hillary Clinton was invited to speak. Mrs. Clinton is well known in legal circles for her activism in support of radical causes, like children's rights.

Clearly this convention marked the demise of the ABA as a purely professional association and its rebirth as a cheerleader for radical politics.

Why has the legal profession become so radicalized?

The answer must be found in a change in philosophy of law. The Western tradition with its Judeo-Christian roots holds that law has an objective basis: Human laws should reflect principles of divine justice. But in the early part of this century a new philosophy emerged called "legal realism." It argued that law has no objective basis; it's just a tool of government to enforce social policies.

Judges don't have to wrestle with principles and precedents, says legal realism; they're free to make their decisions based on what they see as socially desirable outcomes.

One incident in the recent convention tells it all. It was not as showy or well publicized as the appearance of Anita Hill and Hillary Clinton, but it was even more revealing. The ABA presented two awards to retired Supreme Court Justice Thurgood Marshall. During the presentation, a former law clerk told a story about a time he heard Justice Marshall asked to describe his judicial philosophy.

The justice summed up his philosophy in a single sentence: "You do what you think is right, and let the law catch up with you."

That, my friends, is legal realism. Judges are not bound by an objective law; they simply do whatever they think is right and hope the law will eventually be changed to match.

Here is the explanation for what's happened to the ABA. Legal realism as a philosophy has taken over the law faculties. A young law student recently said to me, "You know, Mr. Colson, there isn't a single professor on the law faculty at my university who believes in an objective basis for law." And when these students join the legal profession, the predictable result is an ABA committed to abortion rights and radical feminism.

The lesson is that ideas have consequences. What young people learn will eventually transform institutions and even change the basis of the law.

The greatest challenge for Christians is educating the next generation. As early as elementary school, they should be learning that the real basis for law is a transcendent standard.

Human law must be rooted in divine law.

August 25, 1992

4

Who's Minding the Media?

Calvin and the Comics
Cartoons That Preach

Comic-strip superheroes have always had their secret identities. But the concept of secret identity has just taken on a new meaning. Northstar, a superhero for Marvel Comics, recently announced that he's gay.

I guess superheroes don't just come out of phone booths these days. They come out of closets.

Well, the comics aren't just entertainment anymore. But maybe they never were. You see, people everywhere hold to some set of beliefs, some world-view—whether they're university professors or comic-strip writers.

And their world-view is bound to come out in their work.

The writers at Marvel Comics obviously hold a humanistic world-view that worships at the altar of tolerance. The president of Marvel said the purpose in making Northstar gay is to "preach tolerance" of homosexuality.

Isn't it interesting to learn that a cartoon is supposed to preach anything at all?

But, thankfully, humanism isn't the only world-view preached through comics. Think of the classic comic strip "Peanuts," created by Charles Schulz. Schulz is an active member in an evangelical church and sees the world through

Christian eyes. His humor is never cynical or vicious but filled with sympathetic insight into human nature.

Insights from "Peanuts" have even been published in books with titles like *The Gospel According to Peanuts* and *Short Meditations on the Bible and Peanuts.*

Another Christian cartoonist is Doug Marlette, creator of "Kudzu." Its characters are from the Deep South, including the pastor, Will B. Dunn. The strip pokes gentle fun at the foibles of imperfect Christians living in an imperfect world.

The cartoonist Ray Billingsley is also a Christian. His strip "Curtis" depicts the stark life of the inner city, but his characters model strong family values that have grown out of the black church.

One of the most popular cartoons today is "Calvin and Hobbes," which features a little boy and his stuffed tiger, who comes to life in the boy's imagination. The cartoonist is a bit of a recluse. I'm not sure about his religious faith, but the title plays off the names of John Calvin, the great Reformation leader, and Thomas Hobbes, an English philosopher.

What these two historical figures held in common was the belief that human nature is depraved. The little boy in the strip portrays on a childish level all the sin and weakness that flesh is heir to.

What we're seeing are Christians working to shape popular culture.

So often Christians fall into the habit of merely complaining about the bad aspects of our culture—suggestive lyrics in music, sex and violence on television. Our major goal seems to be to criticize popular culture and keep our kids away from the worst of it.

But we should also make it our goal to produce good, wholesome products to take its place. We need to create an alternative culture.

If we're artists and musicians, we can create wholesome art and music—and not just for Christian audiences but for the mainstream culture as well. If we're businessmen, we can help support these efforts financially and market them.

The point is, there's no such thing as "mere" entertainment. Whether it's movies or music or comic strips, everything has a message; everything preaches a world-view.

Our calling as Christians is to make sure the biblical world-view is heard—in church, in business, in politics, and, yes, even in the funny pages.

August 3, 1992

Television Teens
Not-So-Subliminal Messages

Doogie Howser, television's teen-aged doctor, lost his virginity in the series' premier this season. He's one of several teen-aged characters scheduled to have their first sexual encounter during television's fall season.

Why is teen sex suddenly the big trend on television?

The bottom line, of course, is that sex boosts ratings. But no one ever admits his motives are that crass. The executive producer of "Doogie Howser, M.D.," says that the show is just trying to be honest.

"Doogie's been in love with this girl for two years," the executive producer told a newspaper reporter. "It seemed it would be dishonest, it would make him kind of weird, if nothing happened."

(Don't miss the implication here: The teen who *doesn't* have sex is weird.)

Television's attitude toward teen sex highlights an interesting phenomenon. I'll call it selective civic responsibility.

Remember the detective show "Cagney and Lacey"? Every time one of the detectives climbed into the squad car, she buckled her seatbelt. It was part of an organized campaign to boost seatbelt use. The idea is that if people see television characters buckling up, that will have a subliminal effect on them.

Likewise, population control groups are trying to get television to depict people using contraceptives. They hope that hearing references to birth control on television will make people begin using it themselves.

Behind the campaign for seatbelts and birth control lies the belief that television has the power—and the moral responsibility—to make a difference in people's attitudes.

But when it comes to sex, that sense of moral responsibility evaporates. If anything, the subliminal message seems to be that sex is OK any time, any place, any context.

The impact on young people can be tragic. Television teen characters function as coming-of-age role models to many American teen-agers. They imitate the hair styles and clothing they see on screen.

Can anyone pretend teens *don't* imitate the sexual attitudes they see as well?

Just last May the script of *Beverly Hills 90210* called for teen character Brenda to lose her virginity. Shannen Doherty, the actress who plays Brenda, protested, saying Brenda provides a role model to many young girls. But Shannen lost the battle with her producers. And Brenda was portrayed having sex with her boyfriend on prom night.

We will never know what *other* battles were lost that night in the hearts of minds of American teens.

Anyone who reads the news knows that sex is not healthy for teens. It has produced an epidemic of abortions, sexually transmitted diseases, school dropouts, and babies born into poverty. So why don't television moguls use their power to persuade teens *not* to have sex outside of marriage?

The answer must be sought deep within the human heart—in what we can only call religious motives. Hollywood worships at the altar of sexual freedom. Many actors themselves drop easily in and out of relationships. They conceive children out of wedlock, have abortions, and engage in homosexuality.

In his comments about "Doogie Howser," the executive producer was just reflecting the world he lives in. In Hollywood, abstaining from sex *is* weird.

So when your children watch television, watch it with them. Help them to identify the subliminal messages conveyed by so many programs.

Because if you don't, Hollywood might teach *your* kids to just say yes.

September 30, 1991

Pretty Sappy
World-Views on Screen

Last year, Hollywood gave us *Pretty Woman,* a sappy—but highly successful—movie about a charming young prostitute who ends up marrying a business tycoon.

The story is completely unrealistic, of course. It portrays hookers as cute, independent-minded young women for whom prostitution is just another occupational choice.

So this year, Hollywood gave us a movie called *Whore.* The name itself says it all: This movie is blunt, coarse, ugly. The prostitute in this film is a frumpy, hard-jawed, bleached blonde. The producer, Ken Russell, says his intention is to give a harsh corrective to *Pretty Woman.*

He wants to administer a bracing dose of realism.

But is this heavy-handed approach actually more realistic? That depends on what you think is real. Which is to say, it depends on your world-view.

Judging by the movie, Ken Russell thinks the only reality is physical reality. Russell's specialty is lurid detail. Graphic scenes are filmed with close-up, clinical precision. Through the cold camera eye, we see the dreariness of sex for hire, the horror of violence.

This is reality all right—but it's only *part* of reality. All we see here are bodies moved by animal passions, recorded through the impersonal lens of the camera. The film conveys no sense that the characters were created for anything higher.

This is called naturalism in art. People are portrayed as just a part of nature, without any spiritual purpose or meaning.

Both of these movies fall short of the full-orbed biblical view of reality. *Pretty Woman* dresses up sin with cute shots of a pretty prostitute falling in love and denies the evil, ugly side of human nature.

The Bible will have none of that fluff. It doesn't flinch at calling sin by its proper name. It points to a fatal flaw jagging through the center of the human heart.

Whore, on the other hand, is presented as a corrective to the silly romanticism of *Pretty Woman.* But it's equally unrealistic. Sure, it shows the ugly side of life; it even hits us in the face with it. But in its own way, it's just as incomplete as *Pretty Woman.*

It shows life as if there were nothing beyond sheer physical existence. It doesn't show the transcendent side of human nature, the side that yearns for meaning, that reaches out to know God.

Yet these things are just as real as our physical nature.

The Bible presents both sides of human nature. It teaches that we are not just organisms, reacting by biological impulses. Every person—even a prostitute—is someone made in the image of God, someone Jesus died to save.

So if you thought movies were just entertainment, think again. Every movie producer has a world-view, a personal philosophy, that he expresses through the film.

Colossians tells us not to be taken in by vain philosophies. That word doesn't just mean abstract intellectual systems. Philosophies are everywhere. People express their philosophy— their outlook on life—in everything they do.

So as Christians, we need to think biblically wherever we are. Even in the movie theater and video store.

January 30, 1992

Hollywood Helpful
How Celebrities Treat the Family

Ever since Dan Quayle uttered his famous line about Murphy Brown, Hollywood has been waxing indignant. Attack family values? Wage a culture war? Not us. We're just here to entertain.

But the fact is that even entertainment expresses a point of view, a set of beliefs.

And Hollywood's beliefs about the family are pretty obvious. Just look at all the entertainers who have borne children without bothering to marry: Goldie Hawn and Kurt Russell, Jessica Lange and Mikhail Baryshnikov, Farrah Fawcett and Ryan O'Neal, to name just a few.

Choosing not to marry is a statement of genuine conviction for these folks. Film critic Michael Medved found that out the hard way. He once mentioned in public that a particular Hollywood couple was married. They were film producers who had been together more than fifteen years and had raised two children.

Later Medved received an angry letter from a friend of the couple saying they certainly were *not* married—and that they would be offended to hear themselves described that way.

Offended?—Hollywood may be the only place in the world where the assumption that a long-term couple is married would be taken as an insult.

Where does such an attitude come from?

It began with the Enlightenment, with its cavalier rejection of religion and tradition. John Stuart Mill wrote that each generation ought to free itself from tradition and find its own answers to life.

Mill even encouraged the deliberate flouting of social rules. In his own words, "the mere refusal to bend the knee to custom, is itself a service."

Now *there's* a positive spin on immorality. If you deliberately reject moral and social rules, Mill is saying, you're actually performing a service. You're helping free people from the grip of oppressive moral traditions.

This is exactly how the Hollywood crowd thinks. That's why they actually take pride in turning their back on marriage.

Nothing highlights better the deep moral rift in America today. What to some of us is base immorality, to others qualifies as a service to society. Americans no longer share even the most fundamental moral assumptions.

As a result, the public debate over things like family values just grows louder and angrier—without any hope of resolution.

You see, a debate is like a game. If you and I are both playing chess, we can resolve any argument simply by appealing to the rule book.

But if you play chess while I play Monopoly, how can we settle our disputes? There are no common rules that apply to both of us.

That's exactly what's happening in our nation's moral life. We have no common set of moral principles—no rule book—that all of us can appeal to. And so our debates have degenerated into shouting matches with no hope of real resolution.

If we're going to speak effectively to our culture, we must understand how people think. Many people share the same outlook of the Hollywood stars. They are not merely immoral—they have rejected any concept of morality at all.

They're playing by a whole different rule book.

We will never end the culture war until we can persuade both sides that they need to start playing the same game.

October 21, 1992

PC Comes to the Theater
Robin Hood, the Revised Version

Consider this for a movie plot.

A former POW comes home from an unpopular war. He discovers that his country has been taken over by corrupt politicians. He joins a group of environmentalists in the woods. With the help of a feminist girlfriend and a minority activist, he works with the homeless and organizes the poor people of the community.

Sounds like a nineties sort of movie, doesn't it? It has the Vietnam syndrome, multiculturalism, and all the politically correct poses.

But surprise! It isn't a movie about the nineties; it's about the Middle Ages. It's Hollywood's latest version of Robin Hood, recently released in video.

In the original tale, Robin is branded an outlaw because he accidentally kills one of the king's deer. In the new version, he is an escaped prisoner-of-war from the Crusades, a thinly veiled parallel to the Vietnam War.

The original Maid Marian was a damsel in distress. The new version is a feminist—tough and assertive. She'd probably prefer to be called Ms. Marian.

In the old tales, Friar Tuck was an important religious symbol, representing down-to-earth Christian faith. The new Friar Tuck is a drunk and a lush. His faith is depicted as superstitious ignorance.

Not content with changing the old characters, Hollywood has added a new one: a Muslim named Azeem. Azeem helps Robin escape from the POW compound and becomes his sidekick.

In fact, Azeem becomes the real hero of the movie. Repeatedly, he demonstrates the superiority of Muslim culture to backward, medieval Christianity. In a scene where a woman is suffering a difficult childbirth, Friar Tuck solemnly says she must die because it is God's will. But Azeem rolls up his sleeves and delivers the baby by C-section.

There are other historical revisions. In the movie, Azeem brings gunpowder to England. But this is two hundred years before gunpowder was even invented. Then Azeem makes noble speeches about tolerance and democracy, as though these were Muslim inventions.

Tell that to Saddam Hussein.

There's no Muslim in the original Robin Hood. So what's he doing in Sherwood Forest? The answer is that white males are not allowed to be heroes today. Multiculturalism dictates that the true heroes be from non-Western cultures.

So the new Robin Hood is not the original, idealistic swashbuckler, he's a guilt-stricken liberal. And it's not the Christian characters in the film, it's the Muslim who exhibits the highest moral stature, who exemplifies the energetic ideals that transform society.

Some might argue that the new Robin Hood merely updates the old one. But it does so by falsifying the story's basic themes. It is part of a bigger pattern in which the cultural elites are trying to change our culture by rewriting historic literature—and slamming Christianity in the process.

It's legitimate to disagree with the past, with things people did or said. But it's *not* legitimate to *rewrite* the past. Today, people are revising history books, literature anthologies, and time-honored folk tales to make them conform to modern attitudes.

The result: History is lost. Our traditions and heritage are erased. We drift without the perspective or the wisdom of the past and at the mercy of those with the cultural power to define the present.

February 5, 1992

Modern Mythmaker
Oliver Stone's JFK

The movie was blasted by the critics. The *Washington Post* called it "riddled with errors." *Time* magazine said that it distorted history. The *New York Times* dismissed it as paranoid.

Yet the movie grossed some $7 million in its first two weeks at the box office.

What *was* this movie that the columnists hated and the people loved?

It was Oliver Stone's *JFK*, which portrays the assassination of President Kennedy. What had the critics steaming was Stone's cavalier approach to history.

Stone's thesis is that Kennedy was not really anti-communist, and that he was secretly planning to pull U.S. troops out of Vietnam. To forestall his plans, Kennedy was knocked off by a mega-conspiracy involving the CIA, the FBI, the Mob, the Dallas police force, and the entire "military-industrial complex."

The only way Stone makes this implausible thesis seem plausible is by a slick blending of cinematic techniques. He moves from real footage to black-and-white reenactments so smoothly that it's hard even for alert viewers to tell the difference.

And to young people raised in the celluloid age, Stone's scenario looks like real history.

But what really ought to concern us as Christians is the rationale Stone offered for his skewing of history. When critics challenged him on his reckless disregard for historical truth, he appealed to a higher truth. He admitted that *JFK* is "not a true story per se." But after all, he told *Newsweek,* what filmmakers care about is not historical truth but cultural myth.

In other words, who cares if the portrayal of Kennedy is inaccurate in the mundane, factual sense? It can still be true in what Stone calls "a mythic sense"; it can still convey "a larger issue."

And for him, the larger issues have to do with politics—with exposing the big, bad government. Stone is an aging 1960s radical, and he still seems to see everything through the ideological grid of the sixties, where the world is divided between young idealists and the establishment.

Any story that conveys this basic world-view seems to fit Stone's definition of "mythic" truth—even if it fudges on the historical facts.

This is a strange, divided notion of truth. But it's nothing new; it's the same idea that's been laying waste our schools and universities.

There it goes by the arcane name of "deconstructionism," and it means there is no objective interpretation of history. History means whatever the individual takes it to mean. Deconstructionism has been fiercely debated in the ivory towers of college campuses for years, but in *JFK* it has invaded popular culture. Stone openly admits he's not interested in historical accuracy; he's interested only in what Kennedy's death symbolized for him.

In short, Stone has deconstructed the Kennedy assassination. He has used the medium of film to convey what the events meant in his private, subjective world.

So the critics are right to be concerned about the film's historical inaccuracy. They are right to worry that young viewers who didn't live in the 1960s are going to absorb a false picture of what happened.

But there's something much more dangerous here.

The film's deeper message is that there is no objective truth, historical or otherwise—no objective reality. And if the movie succeeds in passing on *that* message, it will mean a lot more than the death of a president.

It will mean the death of a culture.

January 17, 1992

Music from Hell
What Happened to "I Wanna Hold Your Hand"?

One radio station calls it "Heavy Metal from Hell." It's a new style of music that glorifies death, blood, and Satanism.

Some people call it "death metal."

The bands sport names like Megadeth, Slayer, Carcass. They decorate the stage with upside-down crosses and Satanic pentagrams. The audience greets them with index finger and pinky raised: the devil's horn salute.

The music features fast guitar runs and pounding rhythms, but no melody. Instead, the vocals are a low, growling sound. And no wonder, given what they're singing about. Listen to these titles: "Under the Rotted Flesh," "Covered with Sores," "Raining Blood." A band called Cannibal Corpse sings about babies being torn apart.

It's frightening how fast our culture is deteriorating. Only three decades ago, the Beatles were all the rage singing, "I wanna hold your hand." Death metal bands would be more likely to sing, "I wanna chop off your hand."

Fortunately, most commercial radio stations are refusing to carry death metal music. And retailers objected when an album came out entitled "Butchered at Birth," with graphic pictures of mutilated babies.

Still, death metal albums are selling by the hundreds of thousands. Concert halls are packed.

Why do some teenagers *like* this music?

Defenders of death metal say that it helps kids let off steam. Megadeth says their music gives kids "an outlet to vent their frustrations, their anxieties, and their hostilities." A record producer says, "Kids are angry. They want to go out and kill people. This way, they can get it out in a civilized manner."

This is known as catharsis theory—the idea that art gives people a harmless way to get hostility out of their system. Unfortunately, it doesn't work that way. Recently a television talk show ran a program about children who had committed murder. Every one of them said they listened to death metal.

It sure didn't get rid of *their* hostility.

And several court cases have been brought by parents who say that their children committed suicide after listening to lyrics that exalted death.

No, art is not catharsis. Just the opposite: Art is rehearsal. Watching or listening to other people do something is a way of mentally rehearsing it—which makes it easier for *us* to do the same thing.

After all, that's why businesses spend untold millions of dollars on advertising every year. They know that if we see an actor using product *X*, we're more likely to use it ourselves.

Well, product *X* may be harmless enough, but what death metal is selling is gore and destruction. When those words and images take hold in the mind of a young person, the impact is not so harmless.

So when it comes to psychology, the Bible is right. It tells us that sin gets a foothold in our minds through the things we see, hear, and talk about.

As Job says, we need to make a covenant with our eyes—and with our ears—not to indulge in things that could cause us to sin. And surely that includes music glorifying blood and violence and Satanism.

Music that even non-Christians call "music from hell."

August 26, 1992

Rappers and Rioters
Is There a Connection?

The warning came a full ten years ago.

"Don't push me," sang the rapper, "'cause I'm close to the edge / I'm trying not to lose my head."

Soon there were other warnings. A rap group that sang about shooting police officers, with lines like: "Taking out a police[man] will make my day."

Another rap group sang, "Get rid of the devil, real simple / Put a bullet in his temple." One group even rapped about killing Korean grocers.

Yes, the warnings were there. And then came the explosion: the eruption of violence in South Central Los Angeles.

There's no shortage of explanations for the riots: racism, poverty, family breakdown, welfare dependency, and, of course, the Rodney King verdict itself.

No doubt all these factors must be taken into account if we are to come to terms with the riots. But even taken all together, they do not explain the blood and ugliness that fractured South Central Los Angeles.

If we probe deeper, we discover one answer in the lyrics of rap music. Leonard Pitts, Jr., a black music critic for the *Miami Herald*, says, "The music these rappers make grows out of a paralyzing despair, deeper than any we've seen in over twenty years."

I believe Pitts is right. Nothing but paralyzing despair could inspire the attitudes expressed by some rappers. Some of them openly took credit for helping to inspire the Los Angeles riots. A few publicly criticized the rioters—but what they criticized them *for* was that they didn't go far enough!

One rapper said on television that he was "honored to be living at a time when people are looting and robbing and stealing"—and then went on to criticize the rioters for waiting so long instead of rising up when the King videotape was first shown.

Another rapper lamented that the riots weren't better organized. In an organized revolution, he said, people wouldn't have burned their own neighborhoods, they'd have headed over to Hollywood and Beverly Hills and burned them down instead.

These are words that could only be spoken by someone on the hard edge of despair—who sees nothing left to build, nothing to care about. Who sees life, in the words of philosopher Thomas Hobbes, as "solitary, poor, nasty, brutish, and short."

Pitts suggests there is only one solution to this kind of despair: We must become truly "one nation under God." He's right. The disorder in Los Angeles is fundamentally a disorder of the soul—the souls of men and women, the soul of our nation itself. For years our cultural and intellectual leaders have been telling people there is no God, that life is nothing but a Darwinian struggle for survival, that the earth is just a speck of rock hurtling through space in a silent, impersonal cosmos.

That's the secular world-view that reigns from the universities down to the streets of the ghetto. It tears into a person's very soul and says, "You're only an animal; your life means nothing."

But the rappers who counsel despair have got it all wrong. We're *not* just animals locked in a Darwinian struggle of one group against another. We have the high dignity of being created in the very image of a holy and loving God.

Only if we believe that can we hope to truly become "one nation under God."

June 11, 1992

Filthy Lucre
Making Money Off Desperation

If it hadn't been for the riots in Los Angeles, most middle-class Americans might never have known much about rap music. But rap groups were quick to step forward and take credit for predicting the riots, maybe even for inciting them with their lyrics about shooting and killing.

But after the initial rush of public attention, these same rap groups are discovering that the limelight can be pretty hot. With the public eye upon her, Sister Souljah is squirming for her infamous line urging black thugs to stop killing other blacks and to start killing whites instead. And rapper Ice-T is on the hot seat for his song about pulling on his black gloves and ski mask to stalk and shoot police officers.

No wonder this stuff has been dubbed "gangster rap."

It's good to see decent Americans calling the rappers to account. They should not be allowed to fill the minds of young fans with language suggestive of murder and mayhem.

But there's someone else who should be called to account as well. I'm talking about the companies who make money *producing* the albums that suggest murder and mayhem.

After all, Sister Souljah and Ice-T could sit in their rooms all day and spill their violent lyrics onto paper with absolutely no effect—if it weren't for corporate businessmen willing to make a fast buck by marketing their verbal garbage.

These businessmen ought to be called on the carpet alongside the rap artists they're supporting.

Perhaps they warrant even harsher judgment. Many young black artists grew up on the streets. They've watched friends get shot in drug wars; they've seen family members go to prison.

At Prison Fellowship, we work with prisoners and we know their stories firsthand. There's no question the rappers go too far with their rough lyrics, but their songs are often rooted in the desperation of personal experience.

What is utterly reprehensible is the business world's willingness to make money off that desperation. Well-heeled white businessmen in their paneled boardrooms are quite happy to let young people rant about murder and revenge—as long as it makes money.

It wasn't so long ago, in a gutsier America, that corporate executives would have taken one look at lyrics filled with such hatred and thrown the album in the trash. They might even have taken these young artists by the shoulder, looked deep into their eyes, and said, "You were made for something better than this."

But our business community has imbibed the ethic of secularism: Anything goes as long as it sells. Large companies no longer even raise an eyebrow over songs that say, "Let's go shotgun the cops."

Well, several police organizations and civic groups *are* raising their eyebrows—and their voices, too. They're organizing a boycott against Time Warner, the multibillion-dollar conglomerate that markets Ice-T's vicious song "Cop Killer." Sixty members of Congress have signed a letter expressing outrage against Time Warner for refusing to withdraw the album from sale.

These are practical strategies Christians can support. It's time to let corporate executives know they can't hide behind the rappers whose products they market.

They've got to come forward and take the rap themselves.

July 7, 1992

[Update: Early in 1993, Time Warner, citing "creative differences," announced that, by mutual agreement, Ice-T was no longer under contract with them for future recording.]

Selling Sex
Ethics in Advertising

The boys have been hunting and fishing all day. Now they kick back with a bottle of Stroh beer and sigh, "It can't get any better than this."

The slogan is one that Stroh has used for years.

But several months ago, the format changed. Things *can* get better than this, it turns out, when the Swedish Bikini Team—a group of scantily clad blondes—parachutes out of the sky to serve the beer.

The new ad raised a furor among feminist groups, who say it presents a demeaning stereotype of women. There's even a court case in the works.

Stroh argues that the exaggerated ads were meant as a parody of the typical beer commercial; beer companies are notorious for using sex to sell their products.

But, of course, that's precisely the point.

Advertisers have come to feel that in our sex-saturated culture, the only way to catch the audience's attention is to give them sex, sex, and more sex.

I don't know if anyone remembers, but the functional purpose of advertising is to convey information about a product. Today's ads don't do much of that. They're geared to arousing emotions—especially sexual ones.

Just combine a theme song with some hot footage. A jingle with a jiggle—that's what makes the sale.

And in today's equal-opportunity environment, it's not just women who are used in the body-parts approach to advertising. Men can be turned into sex objects, too. In spots this summer for Coors Light, young women in bikinis were flanked by well-built young men in tight, wet swim trunks.

A recent issue of *Vanity Fair* featured a Calvin Klein ad with a close-up photo of a naked male model, from shoulders to knees, covered only by a tiny scrap of denim.

The photo was part of an advertising booklet by Calvin Klein—116 pages of suggestive poses: men caressing women, men caressing men, women caressing women.

Advertising turned into soft porn.

Supposedly, all this R-rated photography had something to do with selling clothes. But sometimes the ads don't even bother to connect the sexual images with the product. A Toyota ad for television flips rapidly back and forth, MTV-style, from a car to a young couple dancing nearby. The dancing grows ever more suggestive—and never relates in any way to the car.

Its only purpose is to excite the glands.

The real tragedy here is that business has historically acted as a conservative force in society. Even recently, a state supreme court justice from West Virginia remarked that, compared to other elite groups in America (like journalists and politicians), businessmen hold the most conservative moral convictions.

Well, you'd never know it by the tenor of these ads.

It's time for folks in business to realize that they are responsible not just for *what* they sell but also *how* they sell it. In the process of selling cars and clothing, they are selling a lifestyle that is not only morally wrong but dangerous.

Just ask Magic Johnson.

The rest of us have a simple way of letting businesses know how we think: We can stop buying products from companies that use sex in their ads.

If enough of us do that, well, then the Swedish Bikini Team will just have to pack their bikinis and go home.

February 6, 1992

Press Voyeurs
What's a Good Story Worth?

On a balmy day last summer in wealthy Montgomery County, Maryland, a group of teenagers blew their minds out on the hallucinogenic drug LSD.

They were all nice kids, the kind who get good grades and lead the student council. No one suspected they were indulging in a dangerous drug that night—not their parents, not their teachers, not the police.

No one, that is, except a reporter.

A *Washington Post* reporter stayed on hand all night to observe the party. She calmly watched as minor children broke the law by popping four, five, and six hits of acid. She listened as kids described their hallucinations: faces appearing in the woodwork, paper bursting into flames, images in the mirror turning into devils.

The reporter observed and took notes. She made no effort to stop the teens. She offered no moral comment. And when she wrote up the story for the *Post,* she concealed the kids' identities.

Even now, many parents probably don't know whether their own children were involved.

Public reaction to the story was swift—and outraged. Was it right for a reporter to stand by passively as teens took an illegal and dangerous drug? Should she have notified their parents? Called the police?

What *was* her ethical obligation as a reporter in a situation like this?

The *Washington Post* gave its ombudsman, Richard Harwood, the task of answering the onslaught of letters. And remarkably, Harwood wrote a piece *defending* the reporter. He advanced the utterly crass argument that journalism has no ethics anyway, so what was everyone so upset about?

This is so astounding, I want to give you his exact words. Harwood said that journalists are "in a business with no fixed moral or ethical formula." Their ethics just "get invented as [they] go along."

For example, should a reporter publish state secrets? Harwood said, "It depends." If a reporter finds an injured man in the street, should he help the man or grab a camera and film his death throes? Harwood said, "It depends." And what should a reporter do if he stumbles upon a crime in progress? Harwood again, "It depends."

In other words, journalism is ruled by situation ethics. Right and wrong depend on how the reporter reads the situation.

To tell the truth, Harwood confides, for journalists "ethics is not even [a] concern." Getting a good story is. *How* you get the story doesn't matter.

This is sheer pragmatism, and Harwood freely admits it. All that counts, he says, is the result. The end justifies the means.

The entire article is an amazing admission by a prominent member of the press, revealing just how much journalists have rejected any transcendent, God-given standards to guide their conduct. They have become mini-gods, making up their own rules as they go along.

Of course, journalists aren't the only ones. Most of our major institutions and bureaucracies operate on pragmatism and situation ethics. Our corporate life is carried on in a gaping ethical vacuum.

The Book of Judges describes a time when the people of Israel lived in ethical anarchy, when "everyone did what was right in his own eyes."

What a fitting description of life in America today.

January 21, 1992

What's the Big Joke?
The Vice-President Nails Television

Well, Dan Quayle has done it again—this time by criticizing television character Murphy Brown and her now-infamous foray into single parenthood. It was a bonanza for cartoonists and comedians. Johnny Carson ended his thirty years on television quipping that he was thankful to Dan Quayle for giving him some of his best comic material.

Doesn't the vice-president have better things to do than worry about a sitcom? people asked.

Well, now that everyone's had his laugh, let's see what's so funny about what Quayle said. The comment that grabbed the headlines was just a passing line in a speech blaming the Los Angeles riots on family breakdown. Quayle then criticized the example set by television character Murphy Brown, making single motherhood the latest in celebrity chic.

The point the vice-president was making was actually quite serious. With the poverty rate for fatherless families running at about 34 percent, compared to only 6 percent for two-parent families, the last thing we need is more bad role models.

What's so funny about that?

The problems of single-parent families are not only financial. Even with economic conditions factored out, a huge disproportion of fatherless children drop out of school, succumb to drug addiction, and commit crimes. A recent study found a catastrophic correlation between crime and fatherless households.

Nothing funny about that either.

The vice-president noted that the young hoodlums who shocked the nation by rampaging through the streets of Los Angeles were mostly from fractured families. All four of the young men who savagely beat truck driver Reginald Denny had known fatherless homes.

It's hard to laugh off those kinds of facts.

The real irony is that only two weeks after these events took place, the folks in Hollywood—just a few miles away—put on a program that praised single motherhood as courageous. Yes, I'm talking about "Murphy Brown." Producers from competing networks went so far as to loan big-name anchorwomen and interviewers from their real-life news shows to celebrate Murphy Brown's decision in a fictional baby shower.

All the network news departments seemed to agree that Murphy Brown was making a major social statement.

That's why Quayle's criticism hit so hard. As film critic Richard Grenier put it, Hollywood was caught with its hand in the cookie jar. Right in the wake of the Los Angeles riots, they were supporting the very behavior that contributes to that kind of anarchy.

Quayle was raising a serious issue about the responsibility that a powerful medium such as television has in influencing the morals and behavior of the public.

The network's response was to go on the defensive. They turned the whole thing into a joke. It's an old technique, and the media are master at it. Ignore the issue and attack the man. Reason is no match for ridicule.

The scary thing is that so many people accepted the strategy and laughed along with them.

The Los Angeles riots were horrific. But if there's anything more horrific, it's that people in the media have lost the moral sensitivity to recognize that its major cause is family breakdown.

And that they mock and ridicule anyone who tries to warn them.

May 29, 1992

Golden Age of Film
Morality in Movies

Four years ago Robert McFarlane, President Ronald Reagan's former national security adviser, was indicted for his role in the Iran-Contra affair. McFarlane was crushed. His career was ruined. In desperation, he tried to commit suicide.

Then a stranger mailed him a video of the old classic *It's a Wonderful Life*.

The movie portrays a young man named George Bailey who suddenly faces the prospect of bankruptcy and arrest and decides to kill himself. But he is stopped by an angel, who persuades him that the simple things in life—like loving his children and helping a friend—are more important than business success.

It's a Wonderful Life is a touching movie, and reruns appear every Christmas season. But Robert McFarlane had never seen it. In an interview, McFarlane said that the movie gave him the inspiration to go on.

What a tribute to Frank Capra, who created the movie back in the 1940s. When Capra died recently, critics took the occasion to reflect about the way movies have changed over the past fifty years.

In Frank Capra's day, films conveyed a moral message. Like *Mr. Smith Goes to Washington,* another Capra favorite. It's about a young senator who stands up for moral principles in the face of practical politicking.

We don't hear that kind of message from Hollywood anymore. Today's filmmakers insist art should be free of moral overtones. But look what they give us instead: tired formulas—endless rehashing of chase scenes, slashers, nudity, and gore.

Sure, today's special effects are spectacular. But when the film itself has no substance, that's like frosting with no cake.

Glitz and glitter that leave the viewer feeling empty afterward.

Many modern filmmakers feel that morality gets in the way of serious art. But Frank Capra proved them wrong. He successfully portrayed characters who stood for traditional moral values—honesty, courage, sacrifice, loyalty.

Characters who turn to prayer as easily as breathing. In *It's a Wonderful Life,* when George runs into financial trouble, his wife asks the children and her neighbors to pray. And they do, right there on screen.

Frank Capra described his goal in these words: "I deal with the little man's doubts, . . . his loss of faith in himself, in his neighbor, in his God." And then, "I show the overcoming of doubts, the courageous renewal of faith."

This is the stuff of real life. Homey, yet heroic.

Capra's creative period, the 1930s and 1940s, is considered the golden age of film. Even feminists say the old studios cast women as strong, interesting characters. By contrast, today's films portray women one-dimensionally, either as sex objects or female Rambos.

The truth is that a moral framework doesn't *limit* art, it makes *better* art.

Characters who demonstrate moral integrity are complex and interesting. But characters who live for pleasure and self-gratification are shallow and childish.

The American public is so used to shallow characters and formula films, we've almost forgotten what a good movie can be. Try educating yourself. Do what Patty and I have been doing lately: Rent some of the older classics and see the contrast.

If Christians start demanding real quality in films, we just might spark a cultural revolution—where movies once again portray the moral drama in the souls of ordinary men and women.

December 16, 1991

5

Politics and Policy

Understanding the Underclass
The Real Cause of Poverty

Welfare has been a failure.

That fact seems to be nearly universally recognized today. Government aid has created an underclass of people who are chronically poor and an army of politicians and bureaucrats who draw fat salaries by keeping the welfare machine running.

Which group do *you* think really benefits from the system? I'll give you a hint: It isn't the poor.

Government does have a duty to help the poor, of course. It ought to erect a safety net to catch people when hard times hit. But the question is, What *kind* of help should government give? How can it help the needy without making them dependent?

If we look back at nineteenth-century America, we see a very different way to help the poor. Back then there *were* no government welfare programs. It was all up to the church.

As historian Marvin Olasky tells it, the church at that time recognized two categories of people among the poor. The first were called the "worthy poor." People who were willing to work—even at odd jobs—in return for help; who studied hard to get an education; who were faithful to their spouse and children; who stayed off drugs and alcohol. These folks rarely stayed poor for long.

The second group were referred to as the "unworthy poor." These were people who wanted a handout with no strings attached—no demands that they work or give up alcohol. Simply giving these people money only reinforces their irresponsible behavior. What they need most is to be held responsible.

In *Help Is Just Around the Corner,* Virgil Gulker gives a modern example. Harry was an alcoholic who managed to survive on odd jobs and handouts. Eventually, it became clear that the handouts were just allowing Harry to continue his unstable lifestyle.

A Christian charity worker told him, "Harry, it's time for you to take responsibility for your life. We can find you a job and a place to live. But if you aren't willing to work, we won't give you any more money."

Harry left the office in a huff. But after several weeks of scrounging, he thought better of it. He accepted a job, joined a church, and began putting his life together.

Calling people to responsibility—that's the approach the church used in the nineteenth century, and it works just as well in the twentieth. It's the only approach consistent with the biblical view of human nature and our dignity as individuals created in the image of God.

In modern America chronic poverty doesn't stem from low wages or lack of opportunity. It stems from dysfunctional behavior—kids dropping out of school, unmarried teens having children, fathers deserting their families, and drug and alcohol abuse.

Helping people trapped in dysfunctional lifestyles takes a lot more than a bigger welfare check. What has to change is the behavior—which in turn requires a change in values.

And changing values is a task for the church. What would happen if the church took back its historic role to reach out to people in need? Unlike the government, the church can distinguish between types of poor people—between those who have been dealt a tough blow in life and just need help getting back on their feet and those whose poverty stems from dysfunctional behavior.

The church can reach out to each type with the *right kind* of help: to the one, emphasizing God's love, and to the other, emphasizing God's law.

September 6, 1991

The Great Emasculator
How Welfare Undermines Families

Homelessness.

A few years ago the word didn't exist. Even now it's not in the dictionary. But everyone knows what it means, and everyone knows it's become a major problem in urban America.

Who are the homeless? The word conjures up images of bag ladies and destitute families. But statistics reveal that the overwhelming majority of the homeless are single men.

So if we want to understand the problem of homelessness, we have to ask ourselves: What is happening to America's men?

Yesterday's homeless consisted mainly of older white men living on skid row. Today's homeless are mainly poor minority men in their early to mid-thirties, typically the age for marriage and childrearing.

What could be inducing young men to give up the normal satisfactions of family life?

The answer has much to do with welfare policy. Our welfare system has been designed primarily to help women and children. Aid to Families with Dependent Children, food stamps, subsidized housing, free medical and legal services—all are targeted to the poor mother.

But what effect do they have on the poor *father?*

The answer is, they undercut the most powerful force in men to pull themselves up out of poverty: namely, their desire to provide for their families.

The welfare package often equals what a father is able to earn working at a low-skill job. So a woman is sometimes forced to choose between being married and receiving government aid. As one journalist writes, the result is that low-income men become ghost husbands and ghost fathers, always one step ahead of welfare workers ready to disqualify families for having a man around.

Eventually, the men become drifters, living off one welfare woman after another. Or they give up entirely and live in abandoned cars and vacant buildings.

Homeless.

Before we judge these men as failures and bums, we need to understand how their social role has been undermined by federal policies. Consider the man who works hard at a low-paying job, struggling to be a good husband and father. How does he feel when he sees his friends—unmarried and unemployed—living off various welfare women?

His efforts to do right are mocked. He's made to feel the sucker.

It doesn't have to be this way. Back in the Depression, when the welfare system was established, it was paralleled by programs providing work for men; for example, the Civilian Conservation Corps and the Works Progress Administration. The idea was welfare for women, work for men.

Well, we still have welfare for women, but where is the work for men? Where are the programs that reinforce men's role as provider?

The standard solution for homelessness is to build more shelters. And that may well be necessary in the short term. But the long-term solution is to reform the welfare system.

You and I need to confront our politicians. Tell them that we want programs that reinforce responsibility, not irresponsibility, in fathers.

When we do that, we'll be doing something much more basic than building shelters.

We'll be helping men feel like men again.

August 20, 1992

Who Are the Poor?
America's Real Poverty

The United States Census Bureau reports that more than 30 million Americans live in poverty. That's more than 10 percent of our population. Statistics like that paint a picture of millions of hungry children crowded on the doorsteps of crumbling tenement houses.

But the reality is much different.

The official poverty threshold for a family of four is a cash income of about $13,000 a year. That sounds pretty poor to most of us. But government surveys reveal some strange facts.

Did you know that 38 percent of all households classified as poor own their own homes? More than 60 percent own cars. A poor American is 40 percent more likely to own a car than the average Japanese—and fifty times more likely than the average Mexican.

They do pretty well compared with their own parents, too. Poor households today are more likely to own consumer items such as televisions and refrigerators than the *average* American family did in the 1950s. Nearly a third own a microwave oven. Half have air conditioning. Seventeen percent have automatic dishwashers.

What about those visions of hungry children? There's no doubt they exist but they're only a small percentage of the officially poor. Studies by the Department of Agriculture show that households labeled poor consume roughly the same amount of food as average American households.

Obviously, most of the people labeled poor are not living in destitution. So why does the government continue to include them in the statistics? The reason, says a Heritage Foundation report, is that the Census Bureau counts only one form of income—cash income—and ignores other kinds of wealth.

For example, it ignores the family's existing assets. If you own a car, a home, or other valuables, those are not counted in determining whether you are poor or not.

The Census Bureau also ignores most welfare benefits—like cash welfare payments, food stamps, Medicaid, and public housing subsidies. Taken together, welfare benefits add an average of $11,000 a year to poor households in America.

The Census Bureau numbers also fail to take into account the money poor people earn but fail to report. A recent study of welfare mothers in one city found that 90 percent had jobs they concealed from government authorities.

The result is a highly distorted view of poverty in America. In fact, another Census Bureau survey found that for every dollar of income *reported,* low-income households actually *spent* $1.94. That means nearly half their income fails to find its way into the statistics.

The truth is that the more widespread problem in America today is not material poverty; it's spiritual poverty.

Vast welfare spending has generated an underclass whose lives are distorted by social pathologies—broken families, drug abuse, violence. This is a poverty not of things but of spiritual resources.

And it is much more destructive. A person who has strong character but little money can work hard and climb out of poverty. But a person who grows up in a subculture that doesn't nurture basic values or teach basic skills lacks the tools to work his way out of poverty.

Here is a task for the church. We might not know the latest theories on poverty and wealth. But we do know how to minister to those who are spiritually poor—and lead them to the riches of God's grace.

And from there to the skills and self-assurance they need to make if off the dole.

May 27, 1992

Middle-Class Welfare
It's Not Just for the Poor Anymore

In the last presidential election we heard a lot of moaning over the federal deficit. But there's one aspect of the problem we *didn't* hear about. It's what one economist calls the government's "biggest little secret."

The secret is that the real budget buster has little to do with welfare mothers or stealth bombers. It has to do with government subsidies of the middle class.

That's right: the middle class.

Whenever a politician talks about cutting government programs, there's a hue and cry about abandoning the poor. But did you know that only 2 percent of federal spending goes to the poor?

Two percent! The rest goes to programs for the middle and upper classes.

Hard to believe? Well, think for a moment. Who benefits most from farm subsidies, Amtrak, and student loans? The middle class. Who benefits most from art subsidies and public broadcasting? The middle class. (After all, who do you think visits art museums and watches "Masterpiece Theater"?) Who benefits most from Social Security, Medicare, and civil service pensions?

Right. The middle class.

A few government programs have income ceilings to ensure that they go only to the needy—programs such as food stamps and aid to families with dependent children. But attempts to put ceilings on other programs have been beaten back.

Just this year Congress stymied efforts by the administration to limit farm subsidies and Medicare payments to people earning more than $125,000 a year.

Come on. Do people earning $125,000 a year really need government assistance?

Back when entitlement programs were started, their goal was to provide a safety net for the needy. But in the 1960s, the Great Society fostered a new philosophy, treating government benefits as a universal right.

As a result, today 80 percent of entitlement programs go *not* to the poor but to the middle and upper classes.

The irony is that no one is actually helped by all this. It's all a game of smoke and mirrors. Think about it: When entitlements go to the middle class, who foots the bill? There aren't remotely enough *rich* people to subsidize the middle class. So the bill for the middle class is paid by . . . the middle class.

It's all a grand illusion. The government picks one man's pocket and offers it to the next man—while picking *his* pocket for the next man. And we all enjoy the illusion that the government is giving us something for free.

The ethical label for this is covetousness, pure and simple. We're being encouraged to think it's okay to plunder our neighbors for government benefits.

This whole arrangement is not only wrong but inefficient—because government *doesn't* just hand the money on to the next guy. First it takes out a good chunk to pay for its own huge bureaucracy.

That means we would save a lot of money if we paid *directly* for the programs we want, instead of channeling that money through the government.

Politicians are afraid to cut middle-class benefits because, of course, middle-class people vote. That means it's up to us to change our tax policy. You and I have to decide this is an unethical and inefficient way to run a government.

You and I have to stop demanding something for nothing.

October 7, 1992

Glitz versus Gumption
The Real Solution to Health-Care Costs

"I don't mean to glitz up the issue," says Ron Silver, "but, well, I do mean to glitz up the issue."

Silver is one of a growing breed of movie stars who use their celebrity status for political causes. His latest cause: getting Congress to adopt national health care.

But glitz is just what we *don't* need to reduce health-care costs. What we need is gumption: hard work and responsibility.

Let's look at some of the reasons for skyrocketing health costs. In every case, the solution comes down to personal responsibility.

Reason number one: the way we finance our health-care system. The government gives a tax break to companies, not to families, for buying insurance. That means consumers have no incentive to shop and compare medical insurance, the way they do for everything else they buy.

The solution? Give tax breaks to individual families, not to companies, so they can choose their own insurance—and the competition will drive costs down.

Reason number two: medical costs are shifted to a third party, namely, an insurance company. Which means neither the patient nor the doctor has an incentive to hold costs down, to ask if this procedure is really necessary?

The solution? Create an incentive by giving individuals more responsibility in paying for medical care. A tax credit or deduction would be a good step because it gives families more choice over benefits and forces them to ask which ones are truly necessary.

Reason number three: many states require coverage for certain procedures. Marriage counseling is mandated in California, hairpieces in Minnesota, sperm-bank deposits in Massachusetts. Even if you never buy a hairpiece or use a sperm bank, if you live in that state, you pay higher costs for the mandatory coverage.

The solution, obviously, is to get rid of government mandates. Families should pay only for the coverage they really need.

Reason number four: a change in the purpose of insurance. Insurance used to provide protection only against major illnesses and accidents—heart failure, broken bones, that kind of thing. But now insurance often covers every office visit, every test, every prescription, no matter how minor the illness—which vastly inflates the costs of health care.

The solution? Families should pay out of pocket for minor ailments. It's actually cheaper in the long run. Financial guru Charles Givens advises families to raise the deductible on their insurance to $1,000 and pay all lesser expenses themselves. That would cut insurance premiums up to 45 percent—*and* make you think twice about running to the doctor for every sniffle.

It's striking that in each case the solution to rising health costs is greater personal responsibility: to compare insurance companies, to choose only the benefits you need, to pay for minor ailments yourself.

Personal responsibility—that's a concept that should resonate deeply within the heart of every Christian. It may not be a glitzy answer—the kind politicians and movie actors like.

But it's a profoundly biblical answer to our health-care crisis.

February 12, 1992

Clean Livin'
Protecting Ourselves from Ourselves

Health care. It's one of the hottest items in today's political debate. Every group is offering its own proposal for reforming America's health-care system.

But we don't have to wait for some expensive, sweeping health-care policy. The most common health problems are best solved on the personal level.

That's right. It turns out that the United States, more than any other developed country, is paying staggering medical bills that stem from individual behavior.

Take drug abuse, for example. It causes horrendous health problems—not just for those who indulge in it but also for tens of thousands of babies born to addicted mothers.

And crime. Americans pay steeply for our high rate of violence. A better crime program would do more to clear out emergency rooms than any new health-care program.

And if you choose to sleep around, you'd better expect some big medical bills—for syphilis, gonorrhea, herpes. And now there's AIDS, which is costing billions.

Addictive habits cost a lot, too. Like smoking. Last year the cost of health care provided to smokers totaled $52 billion. And still some four hundred thousand people died before their time from smoking-related illnesses.

Alcoholism is a killer, too. It is involved in a staggering proportion of homicides, suicides, and injuries. Not to mention nearly half the motor-vehicle deaths every year.

If you think none of this applies to you, here's one that probably will. Dr. Louis Sullivan, secretary of Health and Human Services under the Bush administration, has warned that eating unhealthy food—too much sugar, salt, and fat—is related to five leading causes of death in the United States: heart disease, cancer, stroke, infant mortality, and diabetes.

To put it bluntly, many of America's health problems are caused by our own bad choices and bad habits. Sullivan estimates that 40 to 70 percent of the disability and premature death in America is linked to behavior people could control.

In our most common afflictions, we are not so much victims of disease as victims of our own behavior.

So if we're looking for a solution to our health-care problems, here's a major part of it. As the old saying goes, what we need is "clean living"—don't smoke, don't drink, don't sleep around, don't eat junk food.

As Secretary Sullivan put it, health depends on personal character, on "personal values . . . such as self-discipline, integrity, honor, taking responsibility."

Too many Americans view the health-care system as an all-purpose "fix-it" shop. We choose behavior and lifestyles that are harmful to our health and then we expect the health-care system to compensate for our bad habits, to protect us from the consequences of our own behavior.

No wonder the health-care system is overburdened.

So don't get caught up in the hype over multimillion-dollar health-care programs. The solution lies with us. From crime to bad habits, America's health depends on the millions of choices made every day by people like you and me.

Good health is not a commodity we buy from experts. It's not something Congress can purchase by spending more money. Basic good health depends on our own values and choices.

It's a matter of character.

February 14, 1992

Madness in the Streets
What Happens to the Mentally Ill?

Sheila seemed to have it all. She was young, beautiful, a graduate of Vassar, with a coveted job at the *New Yorker* magazine.

But then something went wrong. Sheila started muttering that her apartment was bugged and that there was poison in the water. Within months she had completely lost touch with reality.

What happened next is a tragic example of what often happens to the mentally ill in modern America.

Sheila moved home with her family. But soon she was more than her family could handle. Her parents tried repeatedly to commit her to a mental hospital so she could get round-the-clock help.

But Sheila refused to stay. And, under current laws, the mentally ill can't be held involuntarily, even when they are clearly psychotic.

So Sheila took to wandering the streets.

A few months later, they found her body in an alley in Washington, D.C. In her disoriented state, Sheila had been an easy prey for criminals. Her body was mutilated beyond recognition.

The story is told in a book by Rael Jean Isaac and Virginia Armat called *Madness in the Streets,* which explains why the mentally ill have been pushed out of hospitals and onto the streets. The reason was not primarily economic, as many people think, but ideological.

The trend began in the 1960s, when mental illness became a civil liberties issue. It became fashionable to deny the very existence of mental illness.

You see, young radicals at the time were experimenting with psychedelic drugs, like LSD—and discovering that they could reproduce many of the symptoms of schizophrenia: hallucinations and intense color perceptions.

They decided schizophrenia wasn't an illness; it was merely a different way of perceiving reality.

Soon the mentally ill were portrayed as just another oppressed group—like blacks, gays, and women. Psychiatrist Thomas Szasz wrote his influential book *The Myth of Mental Illness.* Civil libertarians began to champion the absolute right of everyone, sane or insane, to live by his own perceptions of reality. The American Civil Liberties Union pressed the point home with several lawsuits.

In response, hospitals began a process of deinstitutionalization. They discharged patients by the tens of thousands.

But many of these former patients couldn't cook a meal or wash their own clothes. Many were too disoriented even to live with their families. Like Sheila, they ended up on the streets. Today, 30 to 40 percent of America's homeless are mentally incapacitated.

Let's be clear about what happened here. This vast increase in the homeless population had nothing to do with a decrease in available housing. It had nothing to do with Americans being heartless to the plight of the poor.

What it stemmed from was a radically anti-Christian world-view—a relativism that insisted that all perceptions of reality are equally valid. That the hallucinations of the mentally disturbed are not intrinsically different from normal thought.

As Christians we should be the first to offer programs to help the homeless—shelters and soup kitchens. But we should also take this as an opportunity to show people the practical outworking of the relativistic world-view dominating American life today.

We ought to be arguing the principle that ideas have consequences.

Nowhere is this more obvious than in the field of mental health—where a false view of truth has doomed thousands of people to a life on the streets.

August 21, 1992

Pork Chops
Waste in Government

Not long ago Congress passed a transportation bill that's just the ticket for solving some of our nation's most pressing needs.

Just consider the $30 million earmarked in the bill for the city of Altoona, Pennsylvania. The money will go toward the construction of a high-tech, moving sidewalk.

I don't know about you, but this warms my heart. Just think of all the poor people of Altoona who until now have been forced to get around on old-fashioned, stationary sidewalks.

It's pure coincidence, of course, that Altoona is located in the district of Representative Bud Shuster, the ranking Republican on the Surface Transportation Subcommittee.

Critics might charge that the moving sidewalk project is pure pork barrel. But I'm sure there's *something* in it of great national significance.

Pressing on to other worthy plans in the transportation bill, Representative John Paul Hammerschmidt had the foresight to insert a provision to erect signs along a national highway in Arkansas. The signs will identify that part of the highway as the John Paul Hammerschmidt Highway.

Now, isn't that resourceful? Here I was, wondering how our government could possibly improve the transportation system—it certainly needs it—and along comes one of our hardworking representatives in Congress, always ready to serve the greater good, who tells me that my tax money can be used to plaster his name all over Arkansas.

I never would have thought of it myself.

And there's more. The transportation bill allots nearly $150 million to West Virginia for a demonstration project on how to eliminate traffic congestion.

Now, if you've driven through West Virginia, as I have, you're probably wondering where all the traffic congestion is in that low-population state. But not to worry. The traffic solutions we figure out there can be applied to other places.

Like Montana. Or Alaska.

I hope no one is cynical enough to think this bill has anything to do with the fact that the chairman of the Senate Appropriations Committee is from West Virginia.

Critics like to point out that the national debt is already more than $4 trillion. And it's jumping $1 billion a day. Right now, paying off that debt would require $15,000 from every man, woman, and child in America.

But just look at all the wonderful things Congress is doing with that money. It's creating jobs. That's what President George Bush said when he signed the transportation bill. "Jobs, jobs, jobs," he said.

You see, says journalist Dave Barry, when the *government* spends money, it's creating jobs. But if you leave the money in the hands of *taxpayers,* well, there's no telling what they'll do with it. Dig a hole and hide it maybe. *Anything* to avoid creating jobs.

So when members of Congress appropriate several million dollars to build a shrine for Lawrence Welk in North Dakota or when they earmark millions for an Abraham Lincoln Center in Illinois, we really should trust their judgment.

They know what's best for the nation. *They* know what to do with our money. After all, that's why we elected them.

And if we didn't agree with them, why, we'd just kick them out of office. Right?

April 15, 1992

Paying *for* Taxes
The Real Cost of Government

The Internal Revenue Service is costing the country a lot of money. And I don't mean just tax money.

You see, what most of us don't know is that for every dollar you and I send in, there's an additional sixty-five cents in hidden costs: the cost of collecting those taxes.

The government agency that does the work of collecting taxes is, of course, the IRS. On the surface, it appears to do a very efficient job. The agency reports that its own operating costs use up only about 1 percent of what it raises in taxes.

But that figure hides the real costs—because most of those are borne by other people.

What kinds of costs are we talking about? According to an article in *Policy Review*, it begins with the record keeping and paperwork we do to comply with tax laws. That includes the time it takes to keep receipts, learn about tax requirements, make calculations, and fill out tax forms.

The more complex the tax code grows, the more time these things take. Many businesses have to hire expensive professionals to maintain their tax records. And remember that businesses also keep tax records and collect taxes for their employees.

All told, it takes American taxpayers more than five billion hours—the equivalent of three million people working full time—just to comply with tax laws.

Another cost is the economic disincentive created by the tax system. You see, a tax acts as a penalty. If you are required to pay out money every time you do a certain activity, the effect is to discourage that activity.

For example, income taxes penalize us every time we engage in productive labor. The effect is to undermine the incentive to work. And taxes on corporations undermine *their* incentive to invest in production.

One study calculated that the amount of production lost due to tax disincentives comes to a staggering $300 billion every year.

There are other costs as well. As the tax burden becomes greater, more people look for loopholes and tax shelters. The IRS spends more of its time plugging loopholes. Audits are made. Tax attorneys are called in. The whole process becomes more and more time consuming.

All together, the real economic costs of the tax system are much more than the 1 percent of tax revenue reported by the IRS. In fact, every dollar paid in taxes actually costs the economy an *additional* sixty-five cents.

So every time you hear politicians downplay how much a government program costs, remember that the real price tag is much higher than the figure cited. Every dollar the government spends actually costs the economy $1.65.

So if a housing program costs $20 billion in tax money, its total cost is $33 billion. When representatives of Congress raise their salary to $125,000, they're actually asking the country for $206,000.

You see, since the costs for tax collection are borne by citizens and corporations, the government calculates its budget as though tax collection costs virtually nothing. But that's like thinking you can buy a car by paying only for the parts and not the labor.

The policy exemplifies a growing trend on the part of government to push its costs over onto the private sector and then pretend the program doesn't cost anything.

The Bible urges us to count the cost before we embark on any project. But our government is doing its best to prevent us from seeing the real figures.

Isn't it time for the government to get honest with the American people about how much it's really asking us to pay for its programs?

April 20, 1992

Simple Sand
The Greatest Resource

"A new energy crisis?" asks *Nation's Business*. Is cheap oil "lulling the public into a false sense of security?" asks *National Journal*.

Yes, we are still hearing echoes of the energy crisis of the 1970s. Not long ago *Scientific American* warned that in thirty or forty years most of the earth's cheap oil and gas will be depleted. Some pessimists call for government price controls or even rationing.

But are we really facing a resource crisis?

What the doomsayers ignore is that there are really two sides to every resource: the physical material itself and the human ability to make use of it.

The natural resource and the human resource.

Take the example of oil. In the 1970s, we were told that the world was running out of oil. But today we have plenty. What happened?

Human creativity was applied to the problem, new sources of oil were uncovered, and new techniques were developed for extracting it. It turned out the world wasn't running out of oil, after all.

Of course, it's true that there's only so much oil buried in the earth. But our ability to find it, extract it, and use it are constantly changing as human technology advances.

In fact, human technology defines what materials qualify as a resource to begin with.

Take oil as an example. Before we had the technology to use it, oil wasn't even considered a resource. If you discovered oil on your land, you threw up your hands in despair.

Perfectly good farm land—ruined.

Then we developed technologies that use oil. And suddenly it became a valuable resource. Black gold, they called it. Discover it on your land, and you throw up your hands in joy.

You've struck it rich.

Of course, the day may come when we do run out of oil. But as that day approaches we will develop alternatives. Our stoves used to burn wood; they now run on gas or electricity. We used to make things from wood or metal that today we make from plastic.

What all this illustrates is the seminal role of human creativity in the debate over resources. Modern technology isn't limited by the starting materials; it's limited only by what human creativity can make of them.

That's what we should expect. After all, we were made in the image of a creative God.

And how did God create the world? By speaking. In Genesis each stage of creation begins with the words, "Then God said." In the psalms we read, "By the *word* of the Lord the heavens were made."

The word. In Greek: logos. It means knowledge, planning, design. That's how God created the world, and it's also how human beings create.

The crucial role of knowledge and design is perhaps best illustrated in computer technology. The silicon in a computer chip comes from ordinary sand. Yes, sand. What makes the chip so fantastically complex is the amount of human engineering and design that goes into it.

And consider the resources that are saved by computer technology. A fraction of an ounce of sand in a computer chip holds as much information as a library of books using tons of paper and ink. It performs the work once done by thousands of calculating machines made from tons of metal, using hundreds of reams of paper.

No, the doomsayers notwithstanding, we are not running out of resources.

We are just *beginning* to tap the greatest resource of all: the human mind, made in the image of God.

March 6, 1992

Are "Values" a Smokescreen?
Ethics and the Economy

The editor of a small-town newspaper recently wrote, "Family values are important, . . . but people want to hear about the economy right now."

It was a nice way of saying what other commentators are saying a lot *less* nicely. The major media are sneering at the values issue, calling it a smokescreen to take people's mind off the "real" problem, which is the economy.

Okay, let's talk about the economy. What are the factors that make for a thriving economy?

Well, for starters, people have to be willing to work hard; that's motivation and self-sacrifice. They have to be willing to honor contracts; that's honesty and fidelity. They have to invest time and effort in projects that pay off only in the future;

that's self-discipline and delayed gratification. People have to cooperate with co-workers; that's kindness and respect. Lawmakers have to pass bills for industry that are fair and consistent; that's integrity.

The conclusion is obvious. The marketplace depends on people holding high ethical standards. Values aren't peripheral to the economy.

They are its very basis.

The other side of the coin is that a *decline* in values leads to a decline in the economy. Bad ethics are costing society a lot of money.

Take health-care costs. Louis Sullivan, secretary of Health and Human Services, estimates that up to 70 percent of our health-care costs stem from behavior that people could control: smoking, drinking, violence, even eating junk food. These are issues of self-respect and self-control.

Moral issues.

The sexual revolution is costing society a great deal as well. Health costs are driven up by the epidemic of sexually transmitted diseases. Welfare costs rise sharply as men desert their families.

These are moral issues.

And remember the savings-and-loan bailout? Our economy still hasn't recovered from it. And all because some folks thought they could dip their hands in the till and take whatever they wanted.

That's a moral issue.

Historian Gertrude Himmelfarb, writing in *Forbes* magazine, says that a sound morality "is the precondition of a sound economy." People understood this more clearly in the past, Himmelfarb says. One hundred fifty years ago, Thomas Carlyle argued that if we want to raise the standard of living, we should not ask about people's salaries but about what he called their "disposition": their beliefs and attitudes, their sense of right and wrong, their motivation and purpose.

These are the central factors in a person's economic progress.

Columnist Ben Wattenburg puts it this way. Suppose you had a choice of giving your child a gift of $100,000 or instead instilling values like discipline and hard work.

Which one would you choose?

The answer is obvious. A child without self-discipline will soon squander the $100,000. But a child with good values will work diligently and succeed at virtually anything he puts his hand to.

So don't let the pundits tell you values are irrelevant to the economy. The truth is precisely the opposite.

Values are at the very *heart* of the economy.

September 23, 1992

Euphemistically Speaking
No-Fault Language

You've heard a lot over the past months about the recession with its massive layoffs and millions of people unemployed. Well, I have good news: No one's been laid off at all.

That's right. They've simply experienced what one Vermont firm called "a career change opportunity."

When General Motors closed one of its plants, the company called it a "volume-related production schedule adjustment." It didn't mention all the people who were adjusted right *out* of the production schedule.

When Chrysler closed a plant, it announced that it was initiating "a career alternative enhancement program." Bet those workers out pounding the pavements were grateful for the opportunity to enhance their career alternatives.

What we're seeing here is a rash of euphemisms—misleading verbiage designed to paper over life's harsher realities and to allow those responsible to sleep a little easier at night.

Business is not the only culprit. Education is one of the worst offenders. Students don't fail anymore. They "achieve a deficiency"—which sounds like something to be proud of. Tests are called "evaluation instruments." And they're not used to find out whether students can read but whether they can "construct meaning from the text."

If you like your child's teacher, you mustn't tell her she's great. You must say she has excellent "instructional delivery skills." Even the school bus driver has been gussied up with a new title. She's now a "certified adolescent transportation specialist."

Supporters of Prison Fellowship will be interested to learn that solitary confinement is now called "involuntary administrative segregation." And some states have renamed Death Row the "capital sentences unit."

Sounds so much more benign, doesn't it?

The Department of Defense is another fertile source of euphemisms. Today's soldiers are never surrounded or ambushed. Instead, they "engage the enemy on all sides." They're never outnumbered either. They simply "operate in a target-rich environment."

In the Persian Gulf War, killing the enemy was referred to as "servicing the target." Missing the target and killing people you didn't mean to hit was called "collateral damage."

At some hospitals patients never die, they just experience a "negative patient-care outcome." And governments never raise taxes, they "enhance revenues." I wonder if Benjamin Franklin's proverbs would be remembered today if he had said, "There's nothing certain in life but negative patient-care outcomes and revenue enhancements."

The examples I've listed are all genuine and documented in *The Quarterly Review of Doublespeak*. Some are just silly, but the overall trend reveals something profoundly disturbing. People invent euphemisms when there's something they don't want to face: a risk or a responsibility or a painful experience.

The explosion of euphemisms in our language today indicates an unwillingness to be honest and straightforward—to let our yeas be yeas and our nays be nays; to accept responsibility for our actions.

We refuse to face reality.

And so we clutter up our language with postconsumer secondary materials—excuse me, I mean *garbage*. And hope in that way to hide the negative net worth, I mean the *bankruptcy* of our ideas.

November 27, 1992

Saints and Bureaucrats
Is Government Crowding Out Charity?

If Mother Teresa came to your city, would it welcome her? Silly question, you say. Mother Teresa is a Nobel Prize winner, a world figure.

Well, New York City didn't. The city government there decided Mother Teresa just didn't have what it takes to run a proper charity institution.

What it takes, you see, is an elevator.

Mother Teresa is the ninety-pound woman who has such a powerful ministry to the sick and dying in India. Apparently, she decided that New York City needed her services as much as Calcutta. About one out of every hundred New Yorkers is homeless—which adds up to a staggering ninety thousand people huddling in shelters or living on sidewalks.

So Mother Teresa's Missionaries of Charity bought two crumbling town houses in New York City. Their plan was to renovate the houses and use them to care for the sick and the homeless.

Oh, yes, they found private funds to support the project. This wasn't going to cost the government one cent.

Still, the government found a way to stop them. These nuns were accustomed to facing the obstacles of disease and poverty. But they were completely unprepared for the obstacles that could be thrown in their way by New York City bureaucrats.

Buried deep in the fine print of some city ordinance is a regulation decreeing that facilities like the one proposed by Mother Teresa must have an elevator. The elevator in question costs about $50,000—a mere pittance, perhaps, to bureaucrats who are used to spending other people's money, but a fortune to nuns who are as poor as the needy people with they serve.

The nuns were bewildered. They didn't need an elevator. They promised to carry the sick to bed in their arms, just as they always had.

No good, said the bureaucrats. Rules are rules.

In the end, Mother Teresa's nuns had to give up the houses and return to India. There they can care for the sick and the poor without an elevator. New York City's homeless now enjoy neither the loving arms nor the elevator.

All this says a great deal about the bureaucratic approach to compassion. Government programs are often administered by men and women who have simply got themselves a job—not adopted a mission. They work on behalf of the poor and the homeless with all the moral passion of a computer. As Mother Teresa found out, the overriding concern is not helping the poor but keeping the rules.

And oh, how many rules there are! Government imposes endless regulations and standards on the exercise of compassion. The paperwork and policies eventually crowd out private charity. Like Mother Teresa, many simply can't afford to operate.

The end result is that the only people left in the field are the professional, government-certified, government-paid social workers—the kind who see the need for an elevator but are blind to the worth of Christian love and mercy.

Government charity may feed the body, but it is powerless to feed the soul. That is the realm of the church. The tragedy is when government fails to recognize its own inadequacy and jealously uses its power to drive out private and Christian charity.

If Mother Teresa came to your city, would it welcome her? Maybe not such a silly question after all.

January 27, 1992

6

Ideologies and Isms

Daddy's a Tyrant
Why Don't Westerners Understand?

A young woman accuses her father of being a tyrant. She wears clothes he disapproves of. She even rejects her father's last name.

But this is not a rebellious American teenager.

No, it's the thirty-four-year-old daughter of Cuban dictator Fidel Castro. She likes to wear a T-shirt with an American flag emblazoned across the front. Her name is Alina Fernandez Revuelta.

Cuba is a country where political dissent is a crime, punishable by prison. Yet lately Alina has taken to criticizing her father publicly. "I used to believe in socialism when I was very little," Alina says. "But now Cuban socialism is a dead-end street."

Castro has responded to his daughter's charges by bugging her apartment and assigning secret police agents to trail her. She says she'd like to leave Cuba. But think for a moment what she would find if she ever came to the United States: She'd find politicians and academics who want this country to embrace the same statist mentality that has ruined Cuba—the mentality that looks to government to control every aspect of life.

The difference is that in today's political climate these people aren't called revolutionaries. All across the globe people are shying away from terms like Marxist, communist, and even liberal.

Yet the same statist mentality is alive and well.

We see it when a Republican president presides over the largest increase ever in government spending and regulation. We see it when Democrats live up to their reputation as tax-and-spend liberals.

We see it in the knee-jerk reaction many of us have whenever something goes wrong: The government ought to do something, we say. There ought to be a law.

We see it most of all on the college campus, which pundits have described as one of the "last bastions of Marxism." One historian says, "Marxism is more strongly adhered to now than at any other time in U.S. academic history." Well-known French political writer Jean Francois Revel has even commented that, "Anymore, when we want a Marxist for a debate over here, we have to import one from an American university."

But wherever statism flourishes it leads to bureaucracy and the decline of private initiative—just as it has in Cuba. Theologian R. C. Sproul once asked Francis Schaeffer what was his "greatest concern for the future of America." Without hesitation, Schaeffer replied: "Statism"—the threat of an ever-expanding state.

Our defense against statism is the biblical teaching that government ought to be limited. The state's role is not to *control* the private sphere but to maintain public order so the private sphere can flourish. Protection by the state is meant to allow families, churches, and businesses to fulfill their own God-given roles.

The growth of statism is often deceptively slow: a new regulation here, a new restriction there. All in the name of doing some social good, of course. Back in the seventeenth century Jean Baptiste Racine wrote, "the face of tyranny is always mild at first."

Think of Alina Revuelta, who got her first glance at tyranny as a young girl when she looked up into the face of her father, Fidel Castro. It must have seemed like such a kind, fatherly face.

But today she knows better. Today she bluntly calls Castro a tyrant.

So the next time you hear government touted as the solution to every problem, remember Alina. Behind the mask of mildness may lurk the hidden face of tyranny.

January 3, 1992

Pro Patria
What Is Christian Patriotism?

Quick, what famous event do we commemorate on the Fourth of July?

Not sure? A little rusty on your sixth-grade civics? Well, you're in good company. A Gallup poll reveals that one out of every four Americans doesn't know that July Fourth commemorates the Declaration of Independence.

The same number can't tell you which country we declared independence *from*.

It's a poor patriotism that doesn't even know our national history and traditions. What does it mean, in the light of Scripture, to be an American citizen?

Patriotism used to be a simple matter. Most of America's traditions were rooted in a Christian heritage. To be a good Christian seemed to be synonymous with being a good American.

And no wonder. Through most of our history as a nation, Christianity was the dominant religion. At independence, the Founding Fathers declared a national day of prayer and thanksgiving—a holiday we still celebrate.

Many states used to require the Christian religion to be taught in colleges, prisons, and orphanages. Up to the 1960s many states required Bible reading and prayers in the public schools. Textbooks referred to God without embarrassment. Almost all Americans agreed that our law was rooted, as John Adams put it, in a common moral and religious tradition stretching back to Moses on Mount Sinai.

In a culture like this, it was easy for a Christian to be a patriot. Maybe too easy. Vibrant biblical faith often degenerated into mere civil religion, where the well-being of the country was equated with the expansion of God's kingdom.

But today the dominant culture is no longer Christian. Many of our cultural and intellectual leaders have come to reject the major values and institutions of American life—especially its religious values and institutions.

This movement is sometimes called the adversary culture. It criticizes the American system while praising other political systems. Some Western intellectuals and journalists even praised communism at the height of the Gulag. During the Vietnam War, actress Jane Fonda told a student audience that if they only understood communism, "you would hope, you would pray on your knees that we would some day be communists."

Well, it's quite a long step from the Founding Fathers declaring a day of prayer and thanksgiving all the way to Jane Fonda urging us to pray for the overthrow of the American system. Where along this range of attitudes is true Christian patriotism?

The Christian position is beautifully balanced. On one hand, we don't deify our country. We don't wrap the flag around the cross. Our spiritual citizenship is in heaven, and that's where we place our ultimate allegiance.

But the only place for *expressing* that allegiance is in the concrete loyalties God calls us to here on earth—including loyalty to country. We can't love mankind in the abstract; we can only love people in the particular, concrete relationships in which God has placed us—our family, our church, our community, and our nation.

So brush up on your civics, dust off your U.S. history books, and thank God that He has not only called us into His kingdom but that He's also allowed us to live in—and yes, love—this particular country.

July 3, 1992

Why Americans Hate Politics
The Biblical Task of Government

Last year a new book came out that asked, Why do Americans hate politics? The reason, says author E. J. Dionne, is that the federal government has reached its tentacles into more and more areas never before under its jurisdiction: most of them controversial social issues that tie the government up in endless political conflict.

As sociologist James Q. Wilson explains, before the 1960s the federal government was much more limited. The few tasks it did, it did well: It ended the depression, helped win World War II, built the interstate highway system, and established social security.

Americans took pride in their government.

But today the federal government has plunged into every area imaginable. It tries to control education, manage race relations, end sex discrimination, and even outlaw so-called hate crimes (as though the state could control people's motives). These are all issues over which the American people themselves disagree sharply. Which just about guarantees that the government will be tangled up in constant ideological warfare.

Maybe it's time to ask whether the government really *should* be taking on all these additional tasks.

What is the proper role and function of government?

Biblically speaking, the purpose of government is twofold: to promote justice and restrain evil. The first is a positive task: promoting harmony among people so they can live together in *shalom,* the Hebrew word for peace. Even if there were no sin in the world, societies would still need organization and leadership. Someone would have to work out procedural rules to maintain public order, starting with simple things like where to place traffic lights.

But after the Fall, a second task was given to government: restraining evil. Public order must now be maintained through coercion. The angel who drove Adam and Eve out of the garden with flaming sword in hand was the first cop on the beat. In Romans 13, Paul says God has given the state the power of the sword to punish evildoers.

We must remember that when Paul was writing his epistle, the idea that the state has specific, limited tasks was revolutionary. It meant government does *not* have ultimate or unlimited authority over its citizens.

Yet at the very time these words were penned, the Roman emperors were making a claim to exactly that kind of unlimited authority. They were setting themselves up as deities. It was a collision course that ended with Christians being thrown to the lions.

In our own age, Christians aren't faced with a Roman coliseum, but the biblical teaching is just as revolutionary. Our national government increasingly rejects any inherent limits. It keeps reaching deeper and deeper into social and moral issues that ought to be the province of churches, families, and local communities.

That may well be why Americans hate politics, as E. J. Dionne says. But the solution isn't to withdraw from politics. It's to regain the biblical teaching on the proper limits of the state.

September 10, 1992

The Political Illusion
Limits of Government

Congress recently shot down a constitutional amendment that would have required the federal government to balance its budget. In essence Congress said, We can't do it. We can't do what it takes to balance the budget.

It was a major admission of defeat.

Politicians have been promising to fix the deficit for years. In 1976 both presidential candidates made promises to balance the books. But today the debt is bigger than ever and growing.

And it's finally beginning to dawn on people that government is not able to deliver on a lot of its promises.

For most of us, that's a hard lesson to learn. We instinctively turn to government to solve our social problems. It's a habit reinforced from the time we're young.

Listen to these quotations from the teachers' edition of a fifth-grade social studies textbook.

"Today, when people lose their jobs," the textbook says, "they can get some money from the government." A few pages later the book says, "Today, families who do not have enough money for food can get money from the government." And a few pages later we read, "Today, families who cannot afford to pay their rent can get help from the government."

The message is obvious: Government is the solution to every social need.

Here's a remarkable quotation that sums it all up. Explaining why the national government has grown so large, a junior high civics textbook says that over time, "people were no longer content to live as their forefathers had lived. They wanted richer, fuller lives. *They wanted the government to help make their lives rich and full.*"

What is this book teaching kids? That *government* can make our lives "rich and full."

This goes far beyond the traditional philosophy of limited government, in which the state is given only certain specified tasks, such as operating a police force and regulating traffic. And it shows that Americans have fallen prey to what political writer Jacques Ellul calls "the political illusion": the idea that government is actually capable of creating the good life, the good society.

This is nothing short of idolatry, treating the state as a god.

But like all idols, the state inevitably disappoints those who worship at its shrine. A government that can't even manage the simple accounting task of balancing its budget is certainly not capable of making people's lives "rich and full."

And it was never meant to.

Biblically speaking, government is simply one of several social structures ordained by God, each with a specific task to do. The job of the state is to promote justice and restrain evil. The hope that it can do more than that—that it can make people happy or fulfilled—is doomed to failure and disappointment.

There's only one way to make life "rich and full"—not by turning to government but by turning to God.

The kingdoms of this world rise and fall, but the kingdom of God will rule in human hearts for eternity.

September 14, 1992

Little Platoons
Tending Families and Neighborhoods

The 1996 Olympic games will be held in Atlanta, Georgia, right next to one of America's poorest neighborhoods: Summerhill.

There's a story to tell about Summerhill—a story that shows how government policy sometimes hurts more than it helps.

Founded after the Civil War, Summerhill was once the proud home of freed slaves. Only a generation ago, it was still a bustling neighborhood, alive with block parties, church socials, and local businesses.

But in the 1960s and 1970s, the neighborhood began to show signs of aging and was targeted for urban renewal. The government promised to transform the neighborhood into a modern mecca, with new homes, schools, and community centers. Federal agencies poured nearly $200 million into the project.

Yet today Summerhill is a mere ghost of the vibrant community it once was, a place of boarded-up buildings, weed-infested vacant lots, and crack cocaine dens.

What went wrong?

Urban renewal was based on a political philosophy that looked to the state as the only instrument for meeting human needs. It ignored social groupings like family, church, and neighborhood—what the great British statesman Edmund Burke called the little platoons: the groups where we meet people face to face and form our most intimate relationships.

With total disregard for the little platoons, urban planners brought their bulldozers into Summerhill and razed houses and local businesses to the ground. They built a highway that cut right across the neighborhood. They built a stadium for the Atlanta Falcons that displaced some five thousand residents. After all that, they tried to build a new community from scratch.

It was an abject failure.

Today the area is such an embarrassment that Atlanta officials are groping for ways to spruce it up before the Olympics come to town.

Cases like Summerhill are forcing government to rethink its philosophy. A few years ago, a minor government official named James Pinkerton created a stir by calling for a "new paradigm." He said government must now decentralize power and return it to Burke's little platoons.

A similar approach was championed by Christian statesman Abraham Kuyper back at the turn of the century. Kuyper said that a biblically based political theory should give equal respect to all the social structures ordained by God. Family, church, school, business—each has its own distinctive task that no other group can do. The role of the state is to protect these little platoons so they can carry out their God-given tasks.

But instead the modern state tries to usurp those tasks. And the attempt has left behind broken families and shattered neighborhoods—like Summerhill.

Christians often talk about the principle of limited government, but the question is, where do we draw those limits? The answer is that the responsibilities of the state end where the responsibilities of the little platoons begin.

If we want to be a nation of vibrant, caring communities, we cannot look to government to solve all our problems. We have to tend the smaller structures where real relationships and real love can grow.

September 11, 1992

Voice of the People

Is America a Republic or a Democracy?

Is America a democracy? Of course it is, most people would say. But in the Pledge of Allegiance we recite a line that says "and to the *republic* for which it stands." The truth is that America is not a democracy but a republic.

So what's the difference?

There are significant differences between the two forms of government. To begin with, there's the role of public officials. In a democracy, Irving Kristol explains, the public official is a "common man, who has a mandate to reflect the majority." His duty is not to vote his own convictions but to be a mouthpiece for the people.

In a republic, however, the public official is not meant to be a common man but someone with special expertise and character. Someone who can rise above the clamor of the crowd. Someone educated in the historical concept of the common good. Someone who doesn't vote by public opinion polls but by constitutional principle.

This republican concept of representation is what the American founders intended when they set up our government. They distrusted pure democracy, where the will of the people reigns supreme. They knew the will of the masses is volatile and easily swayed.

The writings of Jean Jacques Rousseau were quite influential at the time, with his theory that the basis of government is the general will of the people. This was the vision of democracy that was to inspire the French Revolution.

But the American founders disagreed profoundly. They had escaped the tyranny of the monarch, and they adamantly wished to avoid the tyranny of the masses. They proposed that the basis of government is not the *will* of the people but their *rational consensus.*

It is summed up in the phrase "the *consent* of the governed." This was to be a system where popular passions were sifted through a process of reasoned and principled debate, until a consensus was reached.

That's why Americans do not vote directly on issues but go through representative bodies, like the Senate and the House of Representatives. The people vote for their representatives and in turn the representative bodies weigh and deliberate on the views of the people.

The American founders chose this system because they regarded it as consistent with the biblical teaching that all human beings are fallen. Rousseau had recommended a system based on the general will, because he viewed the will of the people as infallible. But the American system frankly recognizes that people often want what is wrong or harmful. It therefore constructs a series of barriers through which every idea must pass before becoming law.

What does this mean for us today? Since America is a republic, we have a responsibility to elect public officials who fit the republican mold. I mean republican with a small *r:* men and women of character, who can rise above the clamor of the crowd, who are firmly grounded in our constitutional and legislative history.

That's a tall order, I'll admit. But it's fully consistent with the biblical view of human nature.

And the only kind of leader our republic was made for.

September 18, 1992

A Tale of Two Revolutions
Why the American Revolution Was Unique

The last Fourth of July the *New York Times* ran a full-page reproduction of the Declaration of Independence. Readers could marvel at the loops and swirls of John Hancock's graceful handwriting.

But I wonder how many readers took time to marvel at what the document actually says.

The Declaration of Independence is unique in the history of revolutionary documents. It doesn't rally the masses to overthrow society, as most revolutionary manifestoes do. The tone is calm and reasonable. Nor is it an invitation to lawlessness, because the colonists believed their demands were lawful. They weren't destroying a legal order, they were demanding what they felt were legitimate rights *within* a legal order.

To understand how remarkable this really is, compare the American Revolution to the French Revolution, only a few years later.

The French Revolution was driven by a fanatical determination to destroy the existing social order. The leaders were disciples of Jean Jacques Rousseau, who believed that individual corruption is caused by a social corruption.

The solution, they said, is to raze the corrupt society to the ground.

The goal of the American Revolution was exactly the opposite: The colonists were revolting in order to *preserve* their society, not to destroy it. They were committed to their traditions and way of life and were determined to protect them from tyranny.

Another crucial difference: The French Revolution was avowedly atheistic. Alexis de Tocqueville wrote that, at the time, hostility toward religion was "fierce, intolerant, and predatory." The revolutionaries even introduced a new calendar, starting the first year not with Jesus' birth but with the revolution.

By contrast, many of the leaders of the American Revolution were devout Christians. A major impulse behind the revolution was a passion for religious freedom.

Another difference: The French revolutionaries were utopian. Just tear down corrupt social institutions, they said, and people's natural virtue will shine through. In their optimism, they placed no restraints on the new government they formed. As a result, it soon became even more corrupt than the government it replaced.

The American founders, however, held the biblical teaching that humanity is intrinsically prone to evil. In their words, man is "depraved." As a result, they wove a network of checks and balances into the new government to protect against abuses of power.

One final difference: In the end, the French Revolution devoured its own children. Many of its leaders fell before the guillotine. Order was finally restored by the iron fist of Napoleon.

But the American Revolution gave birth to a country both prosperous and free. Its leaders were elected to high office and later died peacefully in their beds.

No wonder Irving Kristol calls the American Revolution the only successful revolution in modern history.

Perhaps even *too* successful. Our own revolution was so unproblematic that its seminal ideas were quietly forgotten. Today almost no student of political science reads the literature of that period, like *The Federalist Papers*. Few really understand our revolutionary heritage.

And that ignorance could be a greater threat to America's freedom than any outside force has ever been.

September 17, 1992

Didn't We Throw the Rascals Out?
Reflections on Watergate

This year was the twentieth anniversary of the Watergate scandal, and retrospective articles flooded the media. I was swamped by a wave of interview requests asking for my perspective lo these many years hence. Everyone is probing for a lesson.

What can we learn from Watergate?

The conventional view is that Watergate was about a bunch of corrupt people who had taken over the White House. The solution, it seemed, was to throw the rascals out, write a few new laws, and clean up the whole system.

Henry Allen, a staff writer at the *Washington Post,* which broke the story twenty years ago, says many people at the time felt that once the perpetrators were brought to trial, "the innate goodness of the citizenry" would be aroused and government would be cleaned up for good.

Well, as we all know, the government *wasn't* cleaned up for good. Watergate was followed by Koreagate, Burt Lancegate, Irangate, the savings-and-loan scandal, and various congressional scandals.

Why? Because there *is* no "innate goodness of the citizenry."

The great myth of the twentieth century is that people are inherently good—that evil is just a result of external social causes. All we need is a little education and social restructuring and we can create a utopian society.

But the Bible teaches that things are not so simple. Evil is not something external; it's rooted deep within the human heart.

Instead of an innate *goodness* in human nature, Christianity teaches that there is an innate *depravity.* Every society needs strong moral restraints to keep sin from bursting forth and undermining the social order.

In America over the past few decades we've witnessed a dramatic weakening of those moral restraints. The process accelerated when religion was removed from public life, because religion is the basis for morality.

First, prayer was taken out of the schools. Then the Ten Commandments were taken off the walls of courthouses. Christmas crèches were barred from public property. In Zion, Illinois, a lawsuit was even brought to change the name of the town.

Today, if you argue any issue from a religious point of view, you're likely to inspire ridicule, whether you're on a college campus or on the Donahue show.

All this hostility to religion is having an effect. In 1963, the number of Americans who said that they believed the Bible is literally true was 65 percent. Today, the number has dropped to 32 percent.

And without a religious base, morality rapidly declines. A recent Gallup poll found that 70 percent of Americans no longer believe there's such a thing as absolute morality.

The result is that American society no longer places any strong restraints on human depravity. There are no absolute, immovable standards to curb our sinfulness.

The lesson of history is clear. Will Durant, who wrote the classic *History of Western Civilization,* concluded that there had never been a single society that successfully maintained morality without religion.

So what is the lesson for Americans as we mark the twentieth anniversary of Watergate? That the biblical teaching on human nature is true: We are sinners—and without an absolute moral code rooted in religious conviction, there is nothing to hold sin in check.

Watergate threw one set of rascals out, but others have simply taken their places. Why? Because Watergate was a manifestation of a deeper malaise within American society: the loss of absolute moral values.

June 17, 1992

True Confession?
Ted Kennedy and Morality

Mea culpa—I have sinned.

These are words rarely heard in politics. So people were startled when Edward Kennedy offered a public confession.

"I recognize my own shortcomings," Kennedy said, "the faults in the conduct of my private life. I realize that I alone am responsible for them."

Senator Kennedy has lived under a cloud since 1969, when he left a young woman to drown at Chappaquidick. Since then, he's earned a reputation as a womanizer and a heavy drinker. Then he was involved in his nephew's rape case.

In fact, Kennedy has so compromised himself in sexual matters that when the Senate grilled Clarence Thomas on sexual harassment charges, he hardly opened his mouth. Afterward, his negative rating was a steep 54 percent—twice that of anyone else on the Judiciary Committee.

Even friends and supporters began to murmur that Kennedy's personal life was interfering with his professional duties.

That's when he decided to come clean.

Some people say Kennedy's mea culpa was just political damage control. Perhaps so. It was delivered with about as much passion as if he were reading the stock market news.

Still the confession was a significant admission for American liberalism: the first time a major spokesman has acknowledged the link between personal morality and the public good.

The tendency in political liberalism is to treat social issues as the only issues with a moral dimension. Global warming and dwindling rain forests—these are topics of great moral import. But whether you sleep around and with whom—*that's* purely a matter of private choice.

There are even some Christians who fall into the same moral schizophrenia: who denounce racism and poverty as great evils but show endless tolerance for divorce and homosexuality.

They're more likely to comb their neighborhoods to register people to vote than to invite them to church.

What's the root of this strange moral dichotomy? It began two centuries ago with the Enlightenment, when philosophers rejected the biblical doctrine of sin and began to teach that people are basically good—that only social structures are evil. If that is true, then to eradicate evil you do not have to change individual behavior—only social structures. Moral effort was redirected away from personal ethics and toward economics and politics.

The idea became widespread in America through the counterculture of the 1960s. Recall that the sexual revolution went hand in hand with social activism. Sex, alcohol, drugs—whatever you did in your personal life was your own business. But great moral energy was poured into the peace movement, the civil rights movement, and the environmental movement.

That's why Kennedy's confession is so significant. Whether heartfelt or not, the fact that he felt constrained to make it reveals a crack in the old liberal code. It's a step in the direction of realizing you can't have social morality without personal morality.

You see, the man who will cheat on his wife will cheat in his professional life. The man who has no self-restraint in his personal life will have no restraint in his political life.

It's a matter of character. That's why Jesus said that the one who is faithful in small things will be faithful in big things.

Wouldn't it be ironic if Senator Kennedy—albeit unintentionally—were to bring America back to that great moral truth?

December 18, 1991

Private Morality and Public Policy
Yes, Virginia, There Is a Connection

"What people do in their private lives is their own business." Those words from erstwhile presidential candidate Ross Perot, when he said that he would not bar homosexuals from his cabinet.

The issue crops up in every major election campaign: Does a candidate's private morality have anything to do with his public life?

For years, liberals have said no. People can do anything they like in private, and it has no effect on their ability to govern. Some conservatives are now picking up the refrain. John O'Sullivan, editor of *National Review,* wrote that he'd rather be governed by a free-market rogue than by a socialist monk.

But the distinction between private life and public policy is not always so neat and simple. When a person regularly lives a certain way and habitually makes certain choices, over time that affects the way he or she thinks about issues.

And the consequences can be far-reaching.

Consider one historical example, the life and thought of Jean Jacques Rousseau. In 1762 Rousseau wrote the classic treatise on freedom, *The Social Contract,* with its familiar opening line: "Man was born free, and everywhere he is in chains."

But the freedom Rousseau envisioned wasn't freedom from state tyranny; it was freedom from personal obligations. In his mind, the threat of tyranny comes from smaller social groupings: family, church, workplace, and so on.

We can escape the claims made by these groups, Rousseau wrote, by transferring complete loyalty to the state. In his own words, we become "independent of all [our] fellow citizens" only by becoming completely "dependent on the republic."

This idea smacks so obviously of totalitarianism that one wonders how Rousseau came up with it. Historian Paul Johnson offers an intriguing hypothesis. At the time Rousseau was writing *The Social Contract,* Johnson explains, he was struggling with a great moral dilemma.

An inveterate bohemian, Rousseau had drifted from job to job and mistress to mistress. Eventually, he began living with a simple servant girl named Thérèse. When Thérèse presented him with a baby, Rousseau was, in his own words, "thrown into the greatest embarrassment." His burning desire was to be received into Parisian high society, and an illegitimate child—by a servant girl!—would be an awkward encumbrance.

So a few days later, a tiny blanketed bundle was left on the steps of the local orphanage. Over the years, four additional children were born to Thérèse and Jean Jacques; each one appeared on the orphanage steps.

Historical records show that most of the babies in that orphanage died; the few that survived became beggars. Rousseau knew that, and several of his books and letters reveal desperate attempts to justify his action.

At first he was defensive, saying he could not work in a house "filled with domestic cares and the noise of children." Later he became self-righteous. In handing his children over to a state orphanage, Rousseau argued that he was merely following the teachings of Plato. Hadn't Plato said that the state was better equipped than parents to raise good citizens?

Later, when Rousseau turned to political theory, these same ideas seemed to reappear in the form of general policy. He recommended that responsibility for educating children be taken away from parents and given to the state. His ideal state was one where impersonal institutions liberate citizens from all personal obligations.

Now here was a man who himself had turned to a state institution for relief from personal obligations. Were his own choices being transmuted into his political theory?

Is there a connection between Rousseau the man and Rousseau the political theorist?

In politics and in every other subject, ideas do not arise from the intellect alone but from the whole personality. They reflect our hopes and fears, longings and regrets. Once we choose a particular course of action, we feel pressure to find a rationale for it.

Consider a contemporary example. How many people who choose an abortion are afterward pro-life? Very few. With notable exceptions, most embrace a pro-abortion stance that soothes any lingering doubts about their decision.

When the Reformers talked about "total depravity," this is what they meant: that sin affects every aspect of our being, including our ideas.

The world has paid dearly for Rousseau's moral choices. Most of the tyrants of the modern world have knelt at the altar of Rousseau, from the leaders of the French Revolution to Hitler, Marx, and Lenin.

So can we really say that private behavior has nothing to do with public policy? Just ask the survivors of Hitler's concentration camps or the Soviet Gulag.

April 14, 1992

Russia's Real Heroes
Beyond the Media Spotlight

The photo in the *Washington Times* was startling. It showed Mikhail Gorbachev being carried away, lying on his side, his eyes glazed, his limbs stiff.

I looked closer and saw it wasn't the real Gorbachev. It was a statue from Madame Tussaud's Wax Museum in Amsterdam. Employees were removing it from the tableau of world leaders.

It was symbolically appropriate. Days later the red flag with the hammer and sickle of communism was lowered over the Kremlin, and Gorbachev resigned as leader of the Soviet Union.

Western leaders were quick to eulogize him. President George Bush praised Gorbachev for opening the gates to freedom. Former President Ronald Reagan saluted him. Former British Prime Minister Margaret Thatcher hailed his contribution to world peace. American universities began inviting him to join their faculties.

A writer for the *Washington Post* even compared him with Moses, leading his people out of slavery.

The irony is that these people are all praising Gorbachev for something he didn't mean to do. He never meant to end communism, only to reform it. As recently as the August 1991 coup, Gorbachev pronounced himself a dedicated communist.

No, Gorbachev didn't destroy the communist empire. It was cut out from under him. The real work was done by millions of individual men and women who have stood up to communism over the past seventy years—and whose reward, often as not, was a stint in the Gulag, where they were beaten and starved.

In 1990, when I traveled to the Soviet Union, I met some of them. People like Aleksandr Goldovich, a physicist who was caught trying to escape the Soviet Union by rowboat. For that he was sentenced to fifteen years of hard labor.

I met Goldovich in the notorious prison Perm Camp 35, in the Ural Mountains, surrounded by miles of frozen Siberian wasteland. His cell was something out of the Middle Ages—a dark concrete hole that looked more like a cave than a cell. Nothing in it but a wooden bench and a dim light.

Goldovich was gaunt and lean, but he had a radiant smile. Though the KGB insisted on filming our interview, Goldovich looked straight into the camera and fearlessly described years of torture and abuse.

I marveled at his courage.

Then I saw where it came from. Above the door, etched into the concrete, was a cross. A symbol of the spiritual power that had sustained Goldovich through all those years in prison.

Before I left that dank cell, I asked him to pray with me. And I knew that I had met one of the real heroes of the revolution.

Today, Gorbachev is being eulogized as though he personally ushered democracy into the old Soviet Union. In reality, he was nothing but a reforming communist—whose reforms got out of hand.

In fact, when he saw where things were heading, he fired the reformers in his inner circle and hired a group of hard-liners—the same group that later staged the coup attempt and tried to bring back old-style communism.

So I'd like to hear a little less about Gorbachev in the media and a lot more about men and women like Aleksandr Goldovich, who stood for the truth and were willing to pay the price. These are the people who undermined communism at its foundations. They're the ones we should be thanking.

They are the true heroes of the revolution.

January 6, 1992

The New Nazis
Ideas Can Be Idols

In the 1960s, rebellious young people grew their hair long and sang songs about love and peace. In the 1990s, rebellious young people are shaving their heads bare and singing songs about hatred and violence.

"Skinheads" they're called.

They wear black jeans, jackboots, and bomber jackets decorated with Nazi insignia. They carve swastikas on tree trunks and scribble white supremacy slogans on walls.

In Europe, skinheads are violent. They beat up foreigners, throw firebombs into their homes, and set their cars ablaze. Their slogan is "Foreigners get out!"

What's going on here?

The Nazi insignia and swastikas tell the story: The skinheads are resurrecting Nazism.

Nazism was not just about shouting "Heil Hitler" and erecting concentration camps. It was also a philosophy called fascism. Fascism denied all spiritual truth and idolized what is tangible and earthy: the nation, the race.

Fascist philosophy was not completely defeated after World War II. It simply went underground. Today we're seeing its reemergence in the skinhead movement.

And not just there. Fascism is even turning up on university campuses. The academic world is reeling from the discovery that two of the most influential scholars of modern times—Martin Heidegger and Paul de Man—were once Nazis.

Heidegger was a German philosopher who once dreamed of becoming the official philosopher of the Nazi state. De Man was a pro-Nazi journalist in Belgium. These men were later to shape many of the ideas taught on university campuses today.

But perhaps it should not really be so surprising that fascism is reemerging. Human beings are incurably religious. The Russian novelist Fyodor Dostoevsky once wrote that a person "cannot live without worshiping something."

Anyone who rejects the true God must worship an idol.

An idol is not necessarily a figure of wood or stone. It can also be an idea or a set of ideas put forth to explain the world without God.

An ideology.

You can often recognize ideologies because they end with "ism"—communism, socialism, nationalism, fascism. For many decades the most aggressive ideology was communism. A third of the world's population lived under communist rule.

The recent decline of communism has created an ideological vacuum. Fascism is rising to fill that vacuum. And no wonder. Fascism, with its emphasis on race, resonates with the exaggerated sense of race and ethnic identity emerging all around the globe today—the tendency to break into competing groups: Hispanics versus Jews versus blacks versus whites.

In polite company, we call it "multiculturalism." But it's really an expression of the same impulse we see in fascism— the impulse to identify people foremost by race and ethnic group.

So don't be surprised when you read that skinheads are the newest fad. As one idol, communism, is toppling and another idol, fascism, is being resurrected.

The rise and fall of idols has occurred ever since biblical times. And it will continue throughout the rest of human history.

As long as humans revolt against God and raise ideologies to take His place.

February 7, 1992

Opening the Files
Unveiling Life under Communism

One of the most oppressive aspects of life under communism is the ubiquitous network of informers. Secret police agents are everywhere. You never know when neighbors and co-workers are snooping on you.

You never know who you can trust.

These sharp truths are being brought home today in East Germany, where the files of the secret police are being opened to the public. Listen to some of the heartrending stories.

A husband-and-wife team were once leading dissidents under the communist government in East Germany. When the couple read their files, they discovered that over the years their mail had been opened, their apartment had been bugged, and a hidden camera had recorded every visitor to their home.

The wife learned that secret police agents had tried to break up their marriage by luring her into an affair. The husband discovered that the reason he lost his job was a campaign of false accusations planted by the secret police.

Similar stories are surfacing in German newspapers almost daily. A mayor discovered that for years his best friend had reported on him to the secret police. Athletes discovered that teammates were reporting their private conversations. A young man whose escape to the West was foiled discovered that the informer was his own father.

A leading dissident, now a member of parliament, opened her files to discover that the person who informed on her all her adult life was her own husband. Without knowing it, she had *married* a secret police agent.

A Protestant pastor who had suffered from prolonged depression discovered from his files that his doctor was a secret police agent who had given him psychoactive drugs in an effort to destroy him emotionally.

The same pastor also discovered that the secret police had sent young women his way hoping to seduce him. (When that didn't work, they sent young male homosexuals.) Even children were recruited to report on his kids.

For Christians perhaps the most appalling revelation is that the secret police had infiltrated deeply into the churches, especially ecumenical organizations like the World Council of Churches.

Stories like these ought to convince any remaining doubters that communism is an inhuman, oppressive political system. You notice I said *is* an oppressive system, not *was*. Since the fall of communism in Eastern Europe, many people have begun to treat the topic as passé, no longer worth serious discussion.

But communism remains a formidable presence in the world through its stranglehold on China, Cuba, North Korea, and other holdouts. A full quarter of the world's population still lives under a system as inhumane as the system coming to light today in East Germany.

The people of God dare not forget those suffering in the chains of political oppression. While we rejoice in the fall of communism in Eastern Europe, nevertheless we must remain vigilant in prayer for people who still live under communist tyranny around the globe.

August 13, 1992

Body Count

Who's an Absolutist?

I was recently invited to appear on a national talk show, where I discussed the role of values in public life. The host caught me afterward and said, "I don't understand why you religious people are such absolutists—why you want to impose your values on everyone else."

Sounds familiar, doesn't it? Many people assume that anyone who holds absolute moral principles must automatically be absolutist in mentality as well: rigid, inflexible, and hostile. Writing in the *New York Times,* historian Arthur Schlesinger went so far as to say a belief in absolute truth is responsible for war, slavery, persecution, and torture.

How can Christians respond to charges like these?

We can start by explaining to people that there are two completely different kinds of absolutes. For Christians, God Himself is the only absolute; truth and ethics are rooted in His character.

This keeps us from looking for absolutes anywhere in the created world. We should never deify any person, idea, or political system.

But nonbelievers will *always* end up deifying some part of creation. You see, all people are created to be in relationship with God; even when they deny His existence, they still feel the need to base their lives on something bigger than themselves.

As a result, they take some part of the created world and absolutize it. They turn it into an idol.

This explains why the modern world has become a battleground of ideologies. Bereft of religious faith, many people turn to a system of ideas—like communism or fascism—which becomes a secular absolute, taking the place of God.

With all due respect to Arthur Schlesinger, these secular absolutes are much more likely to produce an absolutist mentality than Christianity ever has. The twentieth century is witness to the worst slaughters ever committed in the name of absolutist ideas.

Take a simple body count. Christianity has on its record the Crusades and the Inquisition. But the crusading armies were tiny by modern standards, and medieval warfare consisted mostly of isolated battles between professional soldiers.

Compare that to World War II, when the Nazis plunged the whole world into war. Not to mention the millions they exterminated in concentration camps.

By modern standards the Inquisition was small potatoes, too. It's estimated that three thousand people were killed over a period of three hundred years. Of course, that's three thousand too many—but compare it to the 60 million killed during seventy years of communist oppression.

So when you hear people denounce Christians as absolutists, explain to them the two kinds of absolutes. Secular absolutes are often advanced by the power of the sword. But transcendent absolutes, when rightly understood, foster tolerance—because our ultimate allegiance is to the things above, not to any group or government deified here on earth.

When we contend for Christian moral absolutes, we're not pushing "our" morality on anyone. We're simply communicating God's transcendent law—a divine truth that sets men and women free.

November 9, 1992

7

Family, Fathers, and Feminism

The Family Gap
Parents As a Power Bloc

Political pundits have talked for several years about a gender gap—a difference in political opinions between men and women. But recently pollsters announced the discovery of a much larger difference.

They're calling it a family gap.

A *Reader's Digest* opinion poll shows that on cultural values, a deep split divides voters with children from voters without children—whether the latter are single or married.

Take, for example, the issue of abortion: Only 48 percent of parents favor abortion, compared to 64 percent of married couples without children and a whopping 72 percent of singles.

On the issue of working mothers: A huge 74 percent of parents approve of mothers staying home with young children, compared to 53 percent of the childless and 54 percent of married couples without children.

On homosexuality: Only 28 percent of parents believe homosexuals have a right to marry, compared to 46 percent of singles and 44 percent of married couples without children.

Asked to choose a political label, 64 percent of parents said conservative, compared to 45 percent of singles and 49 percent of married couples without children.

This striking gap holds across lines of age, gender, income, and region. The only factor affecting it is race. On several issues, black parents are even more conservative than white parents. On drugs, for example, 18 percent of white parents favor legalizing marijuana, but among black parents the number drops to 4 percent.

Political analysts typically consider a five- to ten-point gap in the opinions of population groups to be significant. But the *Reader's Digest* poll found that on several issues the family gap tops twenty points—much higher than the gender gap ever was.

How can we explain the family gap?

It seems that the experience of parenthood itself deepens and matures young adults. The responsibility, the sacrifice, the commitment, and the new sense of the future all combine to shape parents' attitudes on key moral issues.

Psychologists used to speak as though all our development took place in the growing-up years. Toilet training and thumb sucking seemed to set a person's character for life. But today psychologists view all of life as a series of developmental steps to maturity—from youth to marriage, to raising a family, and finally old age.

This doesn't mean everyone has to marry and have children in order to become mature, of course. Some of us have no choice in these matters. But generally speaking, those who follow the normal adult pattern are statistically more likely to develop mature character than those who choose a prolonged Yuppie adolescence.

Once again we see the wisdom of the biblical ethic, which upholds marriage and the family. Not only because it's the best arrangement for raising children, but also because it's a way for adults to build strong character.

We've heard a lot over the years about the silent majority and the moral majority. But the real untapped political power in America today may be held by the parent majority.

August 10, 1992

Politically Correct Television
Numbing Our Minds with Numbers

Political correctness—PC. First it hit college campuses. Now it's hitting television. The networks are using prime-time programming to promote politically correct issues.

In PC television, we're treated to programs like "The Torkelsons," a show about single-parent families. What a contrast to the 1950s, when millions of Americans gathered around their black-and-white television sets to watch Ozzie and Harriet Nelson and their two sons.

Ozzie and Harriet became a symbol for the traditional family.

But now we're told that the traditional family is gone. Television must portray what are called "new social realities." The executive director for "The Torkelsons" told reporters that, after all, only one in ten American families is traditional anymore.

One in ten?

Statistics can be used to prove anything, it is said. And this is a prime example. Because that statistic is as cooked as any I've seen.

Let's analyze it. According to the Family Research Council, the 10 percent figure is based on an artificially narrow definition of the traditional family: one where Dad works, Mom's a housewife, and they have two—just two—children at home.

But this definition excludes all kinds of people who aspire to traditional family values.

It excludes young couples, whose family is still in the planning stage.

It excludes families where the mother works part time.

It excludes people like President and Mrs. Bush, who are quite traditional but have more than two children.

It excludes grandmothers and grandfathers whose children are grown and married.

What about you? Does *your* family fall within the narrow definition of breadwinner, full-time homemaker, and precisely two children at home? If not, you and yours are lumped in the same category as homosexual couples, unmarried partners, and communes.

My own family suffers the same fate. I have three children instead of two, and they've married and moved out.

Since the sexual revolution of the sixties, the number of traditional families has declined. But it remains a lot higher than 10 percent.

So why was that statistic cooked up?

It seems almost deliberately contrived to make people *think* the traditional family is becoming extinct. There's no doubt that certain folks would *like* to see the family die out: gay rights activists, radical feminists, and sexual libertines. And if they can make it *look* that way, well, they've won half the battle.

People are less motivated to fight for a losing cause. If they *think* traditional families are only a fraction of the population, then government policy and public opinion will eventually become more accepting of alternative lifestyles. Even Christians may find it harder to sacrifice to do what's right if they think they stand alone.

So the next time you hear some expert cite that 10 percent statistic, don't be taken in. Remember it's based on an artificial definition of the family.

The truth is that a majority of Americans hold traditional values regarding family life. The good news is that this majority seems to be growing. *Fortune* magazine recently ran a computer analysis and discovered a burst of stories about the comeback of the traditional family. As the baby boomers mature, it seems they are rediscovering the wisdom of committed, stable family life.

PC television may be doing its part to help do the family in. And "The Torkelsons" may be showing on the screen. But the folks in their living rooms watching it are beginning to look more like Ozzie and Harriet.

October 1, 1991

How Do *You* Define "Family Values"?
Something to Aspire To

Family values—it's the latest slogan to emerge from presidential politics. And the media is going haywire over it. At the

Republican convention reporters scurried about asking people what *they* thought family values were—and then gleefully concluded that no two people gave the same answer.

It seemed no one could define what the phrase means. Even Barbara Bush seemed a bit confused, saying in her speech, "However *you* define family, that's what we mean by family values."

With all due respect, Mrs. Bush was way off the mark. Family values are simply those values and beliefs that support the family.

Scripture teaches that God created the family to be one man, one woman, living in faithful love and raising their children. Families are the first community we live in, where we learn the most basic values. If we look at history, this has been the pattern for all stable societies.

Of course, in a fallen world we all fail in some ways to live up to the biblical norm. All around us we see struggling families, loveless families, and broken families. But the fact that some people don't live up to an ideal doesn't mean we should throw it out.

That would leave us with nothing to aspire to.

And yes, most people still aspire to the model set by the traditional family. Parents who adopt children resolve to treat them just *as if* they were their biological children. Single mothers look for men to act as father figures for their children.

The truth is that the traditional family at its best is the ideal *all* families aspire to.

But, of course, in today's culture it is no longer polite to say so. Society has drifted so far from any absolute standards that many people refuse to commit themselves to any single ideal for the family. School textbooks teach children that a family is any voluntary group of people living together.

Holding to a single definition of the family is denounced as harsh, exclusive, and discriminatory.

In a way, holding on to biblical standards *is* discriminatory—not in the sense of discriminating against *people* but discriminating between *ideas*. The Bible teaches that it's good to be faithful to your spouse and wrong to be unfaithful. The Bible teaches that it's good to love and support your children and wrong to abuse or abandon them.

These are moral discriminations we *must* make in order to have healthy families. They are not optional. They are part of the moral order of the universe.

But they are exactly the kind of moral distinctions modern people resist making. They prefer a fuzzy sort of thinking that blurs all moral distinctions. One psychologist said, "Family values is the great Rorschach blot of American politics. . . . People bring their own meanings to it."

This is total relativism—much like Barbara Bush's comment that a family is whatever you define it to be. And there is no more potent prescription for moral and family chaos.

August 31, 1992

Candice Bergen's Family Values
Merely Personal Standards

I wager nearly half the country tuned into the season's opening of "Murphy Brown." We all listened as Candice Bergen looked straight into the camera and told us that there is no normative definition of the family, that all that matters is "commitment, love, and caring."

But the fascinating thing is that Candice Bergen herself is actually very much in favor of family values.

That's right. Listen to what Bergen told *TV Guide* in a recent interview. "As far as my family values go," Bergen said, "my child and my family have always been my top priority. . . . I don't see the point in having a child if you're not going to spend as much time as you can with that child."

These are strong words, but there's more. Bergen claims that during the filming of the notorious episode when Murphy Brown had her baby, she herself had warned the producer about the implicit message the show might send.

Let me quote again from the *TV Guide* interview: "I said we do have to be careful," Bergen said, "that we don't send out the message . . . to young women especially, that we're encouraging them to be single mothers."

And she ended by saying, "I myself . . . believe the ideal is that you have a two-parent family. I'm the last person to think fathers are obsolete."

When I read that I was bowled over. Wow, I thought, so Candice Bergen really believes the two-parent family is the ideal? *Then why is she so opposed to Dan Quayle saying exactly the same thing?*

The answer is subtle, so listen carefully. We live in an age of individualism, where it's OK to be in favor of family values and marriage and all sorts of wonderful things—just so long as you make it clear that these are only your own private opinions. When Candice Bergen tells us her family ideals, all she's doing is expressing her personal feelings.

But Dan Quayle and his fellow conservatives are saying something completely different. They're saying family values are part of a transcendent moral code that is binding on everyone. They're saying there are objective standards against which we can measure people's behavior.

That's the difference.

As long as you are merely expressing your own feelings, you are free to say whatever you like. But if you maintain the existence of a moral code that is objective and universal, you have committed a grave transgression against the reigning ethos of individualism.

That's why in the *TV Guide* interview Candice Bergen complains that Dan Quayle has become "arrogant," "aggressive," and "offensive." The reason is *not*, as we have seen, that she disagrees with him. She actually holds a lot of the same family values. His offense is that he actually holds these values as objective truths.

When we participate in the family values debate, we have to understand what the other side really thinks. The root of the debate runs deeper than family issues.

The real disagreement is over the very nature of truth.

September 25, 1992

They Just Don't Get It
The War Over Family Values

The "Murphy Brown" episode has come back to haunt us again. At the Emmy awards, the creator of the sitcom hailed single parents and urged them, "Don't let anyone tell you you're not a family."

Why has family values become such a disputed topic? Why were the media so quick to jump on a single line in a single speech by Dan Quayle?

The answer is that the family is at the heart of a major cultural divide in America today—a divide over the question of moral authority. It involves questions like: How do we justify saying there's only one model for the family? How can we say that some relationships are immoral?

How do we know what's right and wrong?

James Davison Hunter, in his book *Culture Wars*, says Americans hold two competing visions of moral authority. On one side is what he calls the orthodox vision. It sees institutions like the family as created by God. Moral standards are rooted in the structure of creation.

In this view, right and wrong are absolute, binding on everyone.

On the other side is what Hunter calls the progressive vision. It sees institutions like the family as a creation of human society to meet human needs. If people want to, they are free to experiment with other ways to meet those needs—other kinds of relationships.

Right and wrong are not absolute in this view, they are relative.

Once we understand these two competing visions we can make sense of the raucous debates on the talk shows and the nightly news. People who hold the orthodox view defend what we call traditional family values. People who hold the progressive view tend to reject traditional family values.

This doesn't mean all progressives are immoral or anti-family. There are plenty of progressives who live stable, caring lives, and are highly committed to their families. The point is that they have no transcendent *reason* for their commitment.

As Robert Bellah explains in his book, *Habits of the Heart,* many Americans have high ideals, but they have no transcendent principles upon which to base those ideals. Ask them *why* they are faithful to their spouses, ask them *why* they care about their kids, and all they can say is, "It feels right for me."

By the same token, they can't say why anything is wrong either. If values are what feels right to me, then I have to give *you* the freedom to do what feels right to you. Anyone who holds the orthodox vision—who says some things are right or wrong for everyone—strikes progressives as bigoted.

Francis Schaeffer used to say that Christians need to stop seeing issues in bits and pieces and start seeing the big picture. The big picture behind the family values debate is simple: Are morals absolute or are they relative? Are they God-given or do we make them up as we go along?

Christians ought to take the lead in moving the national debate away from clichés and simple sloganeering. We need to educate our neighbors on the real meaning of the "Murphy Brown" firestorm.

What we have in the family values debate is a fundamental disagreement between two world-views.

September 29, 1992

Crimes of Fashion
I'd Kill for That Coat

Seventeen-year-old Brenda Adams went to a party wearing a brand-new leather coat. But she didn't come back wearing the coat.

In fact, she didn't come back at all.

As Brenda was leaving the party, she was accosted by two tough-talking girls who demanded her coat. She was beaten, kicked, and dragged across the street. Then one of the girls pulled out a gun and shot her.

As Brenda lay dying, the girls ripped off her coat.

It's a tragic example of a crime wave that's hitting our cities—kids killing kids for their designer clothes. Reporters are calling them "crimes of fashion."

In some places a quarter of all armed robberies now involve clothing. In Milwaukee, an eighteen-year-old was shot for his San Francisco 49ers jacket. In Newark, a fifteen-year-old was shot by five youths who wanted his bomber jacket.

Schools are trying to control the violence by imposing stricter dress codes. The principal of a Brooklyn high school banned shearling coats and gold chains. The Detroit Board of Education imposed a new dress code after two students were killed for their Nike shoes and expensive jackets.

What's behind these bizarre armed robberies?

Since most of the violence occurs in low-income neighborhoods, it would be easy to pin the blame on poverty. Maybe these kids steal because they can't afford to buy their own designer items.

But teens who steal aren't taking just one for their own use. Police have arrested kids with four or five jackets hanging in their closets. Newark police arrested one boy with sixteen jackets.

No, the real reason for the robberies is that clothes have become potent status symbols. Wearing $150 shoes is a way of proving you're important; you're a big shot.

By the same token, stealing something is a way of striking at someone *else's* status. A Milwaukee district attorney says that the robberies are about "humiliation and power."

This is materialism run recklessly amuck. Where material things define the person. Where your jacket is more important than your life.

The young people who commit these murders must be held responsible, of course. But so must society at large. In the past, families, schools, and churches worked hard to teach children moral values, self-control, and respect for others.

But today, children are more likely to be on their own. They have less supervision, less input from adults who care about them. As a result, they are falling prey to the crassest of advertising and commercialism.

They literally believe clothes make the man.

We find the same attitude among children in our wealthiest suburbs. Teachers in posh Fairfax County, Virginia, report that even first-graders are acutely conscious of which kids are wearing designer clothes to school.

On every level, the problem is the same: People whose dignity is no longer rooted in being creatures made in the image of God are searching desperately for other ways to feel important, other ways to create a sense of significance.

As Christians, we must not merely condemn, we must reach out with the only source of genuine individual dignity: that the God of the universe made you and loves you.

Kids giving up their lives for fashion need to hear that there's something much bigger to give their lives to.

January 20, 1992

Dating Etiquette
What's Behind Date Rape?

A study of junior high students reveals some pretty startling facts about their dating etiquette. Half the youngsters said that when a man pays for a date, he has a right to kiss the woman. A fifth said that he has a right to sexual intercourse with her.

Is *this* sexual liberation? When a man buys sex by buying dinner? When a concert ticket is a ticket to sex?

And what if the woman thought the concert invitation was really *just* a concert invitation? A man who feels *entitled* to sex may end up using force. The result: date rape, currently one of the biggest issues on college campuses.

Date rape is a tragedy. The victim is shamed and humiliated. She becomes the butt of cruel jokes in the fraternity houses. And the authorities are likely to cover it up to protect the school's reputation.

Feminists are trying to change all that by drawing public attention to the problem. But they're ignoring the question at the heart of the issue: Why is date rape happening? Why have social restraints broken down so completely that young men feel they have a right to sexual favors—even by force?

The answer is in the old biblical principle: You reap what you sow. For years, our society has sown the seed of sexual permissiveness. Sex dominates movies, television, and popular music.

In some places a young man is handed a package of condoms in high school: a clear signal—from school authorities no less—that he's expected to be sexually active.

The old code of chivalry has been discredited. Remember the time when no man could claim to be civilized unless he showed courtesy and protectiveness toward women? Radical feminists have denounced that old code as oppressive.

But I wonder if women didn't prefer the so-called oppressive ideal of men opening doors for them to the *new* ideal some men have adopted in its place: That a real man takes whatever he can get sexually. That a real man doesn't take no for an answer.

What feminists seem unable to understand is that the loss of the older code puts women at risk. To state the obvious, there are biological differences between the sexes. It's easier to assault a woman than a man. When moral and social constraints are lifted, it's women who become more vulnerable.

Feminists say the solution to date rape is for men to respect women who say no. But that's not enough. The real problem is that sex has been stripped of its moral dimension. It's been reduced to a clash of personal desires.

The man says, "I want," and the woman says, "I don't want"—but they have no moral principles to support their decision, no common code of decency binding on them both.

It's one private will pitted against the other.

Add alcohol or drugs to the equation, and you have a classic setup for date rape.

America needs a recommitment to the idea that sex is more than a private choice. It's a moral issue. There are moral standards transcending what you or I may want at the moment.

The 1960s sowed the slogans of free sex. Today we are reaping a harvest of forced sex.

In sex as in politics, freedom without moral restraints leads to might is right.

December 17, 1991

Virgins Speak Out
Glamour Magazine Discovers Chastity

Glamour magazine just made a shocking discovery: Many of its readers are virgins.

It all started when the magazine asked its readers a question: "Are there any virgins left out there?" The response took the editors by surprise: two thousand women wrote in to say that *they* were virgins—and proud of it.

The magazine summarized the responses in a March 1992 article entitled, "2,000 Virgins: They're *Not* Who You Think." In other words, they're not ugly wallflowers. They're intelligent, "with-it" young women, who are articulate, who know what they want, and who read sophisticated magazines. Like *Glamour*.

They've simply chosen not to have sex outside marriage.

Judging by their letters, it is not an easy choice to make these days. The women told stories of being teased and humiliated, accused of being prudish, and made to feel like freaks.

Some women even sent in photos to prove that they're really just normal human beings.

In the face of such intense opposition, why are there still young people who stand against the current? The women who wrote in listed several good reasons.

Almost all of them listed AIDS and other sexually transmitted diseases as a good reason to remain chaste. Others said they didn't want to be pressured into sex by peer pressure and the media.

Many said that sex is too meaningful for a casual relationship. As one woman put it, "a lot of feelings, trust, and intimacy are put into a relationship once sex is involved." That's why she wants to save it for a relationship that's going to last.

Others warned that sex outside marriage loses its deep meaning. One woman told *Glamour* that sex is for expressing love—and you can't possibly love a new person every few months. Casual sex tears it out of the context of love and turns into selfish gratification.

What's interesting is that none of the women spoke of sex as something bad or dirty. Yet the standard stereotype is that people who abstain just don't like sex very much. *Glamour* itself quoted sexologist Sol Gordon saying that saving sex for someone you love implies that sex by itself is dirty.

But the virgins who wrote in didn't express a low view of sex. On the contrary, they saw it as something intensely meaningful—so special that it should be saved for a special context: for the committed relationship of marriage.

One letter writer said, "God doesn't forbid sex before marriage because He wants to put us in a box with a list of rules and no fun." No, it's because "He wants the best for us."

That hits at the core of the issue. God's laws aren't capricious or arbitrary. They tell us who we are and what is truly best for us.

The sexual revolution is running down and people are beginning to see that sexual morals make sense after all. The old moral laws aren't just for old fogies. They're for young people, too.

Even for sophisticated young women who read magazines like *Glamour*.

May 15, 1992

What's Wrong with Children's Rights?
Is It Really Good for Children?

A well-known Christian television show was dealing with the subject of Hillary Clinton. The tone of the show had been critical of Mrs. Clinton when one of the co-hosts spoke up: "But what about all the good things she does for children through the Children's Defense Fund?"

Well, what *about* that? Hillary Clinton has long been a ardent advocate of children's rights—and isn't that a good thing?

Well, it depends on what you mean by the term.

Most of us probably think of broad human rights, like the right to be treated honestly and fairly. But Hillary Clinton and the Children's Defense Fund are talking specifically about *legal* rights for children—rights that can be enforced by law or through the courts.

And legal rights for children would inevitably have the effect of intruding the state into family life and creating vast new government bureaucracies.

A legal right means nothing unless it can be claimed against someone. Legal rights for children will be claimed either against their parents or against the government.

In the first case, children could sue their parents over a disagreement concerning which school the children want to attend. Children's rights give minors a legal standing against their parents—treating them as mini-adults, capable of making their own decisions.

Hillary Clinton calls this "the presumption of competence"—referring to legal competence. She insists that children should have a legal right alongside their parents to make decisions about such issues as whether to attend school, whether to get a job, and whether to have an abortion.

This idea is more radical than it sounds, warns columnist Paul Gigot in the *Wall Street Journal*. If adopted by the Supreme Court, "the theory would give the state a wedge to pry into family decisions," Gigot says. "It's just what our lawsuit-happy society needs: Kids suing Dad over a job at McDonald's."

The other side of children's rights is that it would greatly expand state bureaucracy. Consider: If a child has a legal right to quality day care, against whom can that right be claimed? Not the parents this time, but the government. It is merely an inverse way of saying the government has a duty to provide day care. That's why Hillary Clinton, as chairman of the

Children's Defense Fund, worked passionately for federally funded day care.

A child's right becomes a bureaucrat's duty.

The election of Bill Clinton to the presidency has brought Hillary Clinton to the public eye and has raised an issue that will be with us for a long time: namely, what is the role of government in the lives of children?

Christians ought to be very cautious of anyone who recommends decreasing the role of parents and increasing the role of the state in family life. God created the family as the basic unit of society and planned that truth would be passed from parents to children, from generation to generation.

Children's rights theory claims to promote the welfare of children. But in reality it throws children into the arms of state professionals—who may be filled with big ideas but empty of the bonds of family love.

May 19, 1992

Kiddie Divorce
Should Children Divorce Their Parents?

America's divorce rate is a national scandal—but it could soon get much worse. If children's rights groups have their way, divorce will go beyond husbands and wives . . . to include the kids.

In a groundbreaking decision, a Florida judge recently ruled that an eleven-year-old boy named Gregory has the right to divorce his parents. Gregory charges his parents with abuse and neglect and wants to be adopted by his foster parents.

Now obviously a child should not have to remain in an abusive home. But remedies for cases like that are already available. Our legal system allows a state-appointed guardian or child welfare agency to petition for a change of custody.

Gregory's case could have gone through the normal channels. Instead, the judge decided to create a *new* right out of thin air. For perhaps the first time in our nation's history, a child was given legal standing to divorce his parents.

Children's rights advocates are ecstatic. One lawyer said the decision strikes down what he called "the old paternalistic mumbo-jumbo that says children have no rights."

But hold it a minute. No one ever said children have no rights. It's illegal to murder children—which means they have a right to life. It's illegal to kidnap children—so they have a right to liberty. It's illegal to steal from children—so they have a right to property.

But there's a big difference between universal rights like these and procedural rights, like voting or representing yourself in court. Procedural rights are limited to adults who are mature enough to understand the law. Children are traditionally represented by parents or guardians, a system that protects them from direct legal accountability.

What children's rights advocates want to do is rip away that protection and give them the same responsibilities as adults. Karen Adams of the National Child Rights Alliance says that she'd like to see kids have the right to go to court to decide things for themselves as soon as they learn how to talk. "We've had . . . children as young as three years old saying, 'I don't want to live here anymore,'" Adams says. In her ideal world, tots could sue in court before they're even big enough cross the street by themselves.

The rhetoric of liberation leads straight to litigation.

Of course, practically speaking, kids aren't knowledgeable enough to claim legal rights on their own. If they don't depend on their parents to represent them, they'll turn to other people—like lawyers and social workers.

As a result, the real effect of so-called children's rights is to take power away from parents and give it to outside professionals.

What's behind children's rights is a mentality that sees family bonds as narrow and constricting and views the state as a tool for liberating people from those bonds.

It's the Enlightenment worship of individual autonomy—extended down to youngsters.

Well, Gregory may win his case in court. But if he does, parents across America will continue to *lose* ground to an ever-expanding state.

August 4, 1992

The New Privacy Right
Now It's for Kids, Too

The right to privacy.

It's not mentioned anywhere in the Constitution, but in 1973 the Supreme Court decided it existed anyway—and that it guaranteed the right to abortion.

But privacy may soon be used to guarantee a whole slew of other rights.

Take a recent example. In Florida, a circuit judge threw out charges against two young men for violating the state's statutory rape law. Florida law makes it illegal to engage in sexual relations with a girl below the age of sixteen—whether she consents or not.

The idea is that some actions are so significant that young teens and adolescents shouldn't even be asked to consent to them before they're mature enough to understand the consequences.

Nevertheless, the judge threw the case out.

On what grounds? On the right to privacy, enshrined in Florida's state constitution.

The judge argued that if the right to privacy allows minors to choose whether to have an *abortion* without consulting their parents, then surely it must also allow them to choose whether to have sexual relations.

Now most of us thought it was bad enough for the state to intrude into the relationship between parents and children on the issue of abortion. But it turns out abortion was just the wedge that would pry open a floodgate for the whole so-called children's rights agenda.

The judge's ruling was one step in that direction. Consider: If abortion is interpreted to guarantee children the right to sexual relations, where does the reasoning stop? Can they make their own decisions about attending school? Guess that gets rid of compulsory education laws. Can they make their own decisions about whether to work? Guess that gets rid of child labor laws.

And how far down the age scale does this privacy principle extend? What about ten-year-olds? Or five-year-olds?

Behind the judge's decision is a theory that denies the reality of developmental stages in childhood and adolescence that warrant adult protection. The theory was expressed by Hillary Clinton, an advocate of children's rights, in an article that shrugged off the idea of adolescence as sheer "invention." And it was expressed in another recent court case, where a judge said that there's nothing "magic" that happens to kids when they reach "the age of maturity."

Well, I don't know if maturity is "magic," but as any parent knows, it's real. There are genuine developmental differences between a six-year-old, a twelve-year-old, and an eighteen-year-old. It's only common sense to acknowledge those differences in law—by placing young children under their parents' protection.

By denying those differences, children's rights advocates are busy removing parental protection. The statutory rape ruling is just one example. The ACLU tipped its hand when it praised the ruling as one step toward giving children the same rights as adults.

The case gives us a glimpse into the kind of world that children's rights folks really want: a world without parental authority and without childhood innocence.

August 6, 1992

Beating Up on Dad
Images of Fathers in Children's Literature

It looks like a charming children's story—three little bears on a scouting escapade. But who's this? Papa Bear is coming along. And at every step of the way, Papa makes a complete fool of himself.

If Papa suggests the direction to take, the path is sure to end up in a swamp. If he makes the campfire stew, it's sure to taste awful.

Just what is this book teaching kids about fathers?

The story I just described is from the highly popular Berenstain Bears series. In several of the books, Papa Bear is portrayed as a bumbling oaf. The sensible one in the family is Mama Bear.

In the story on junk food, Papa is the worst offender. It's Mama who enforces the switch to a healthy diet. In the story on manners, again, Papa is the worst offender. It's Mama who enforces politeness.

Isn't there anything Papa does best? Well, yes, he's given one distinction. In a book on fitness, the children outdo Papa on every skill except one: Sister Bear can run the fastest, Brother Bear can jump the farthest, but when the exercise session is over, Papa Bear can sleep the longest.

Ha, ha. Let's all have a good laugh at Papa's expense.

This treatment of fathers is, sad to say, not the exception but the rule in children's books. In a recent issue of *Newsweek* a young father complains that he has a terrible time finding books for his children that show fathers in a positive light.

Or finding books that even show fathers at all. Remember Babar the elephant? When Babar's mother is killed by a hunter, the baby elephant is pronounced an orphan. But wait a minute: Why is he an orphan? Doesn't he have a father? Doesn't his father care?

The same bias against dads carries over into books for teens. A survey of contemporary teen literature found that the majority portray mother-headed families.

Even when fathers are part of the story, they're much more likely than mothers to be cruel and abusive. The few times fathers are portrayed as good, they're nice but weak: They stand aside with a smile and let the teenagers decide for themselves what to do.

What will happen to a society where children's imagination is filled with images of fathers who are oafs and fools? And it's no good saying this is all "just" fiction, the way people said recently about Murphy Brown. When children read story upon story with absent or abusive fathers, that can't help but shape their expectations.

Psychologists recognize the emotional impact of books—so much so that there's even a branch of counseling today called "bibliotherapy," which uses storybooks to change children's attitudes.

And if stories have the power to do good, then clearly they have the power to do harm.

That's why the women's movement has worked so hard to change the image of women in children's books. And the civil rights movement has worked to root out negative images of black people.

Maybe it's time to start a movement for fathers.

June 19, 1992

Father Hunger
The Men's Movement

Seven hundred men gathered recently in Austin, Texas, to squat around campfires, pound drums, and howl and sweat together. It was the First International Men's Conference, and participants were hoping to rediscover their true manhood.

Yes, just as the sixties gave birth to the women's movement, so the nineties promise to give birth to a movement for men.

It's easy to poke fun at the drums and the feathers. Yet two books on the subject—*Iron John* and *Fire in the Belly*—have been on the *New York Times* bestseller list for nearly two years.

Obviously, underneath the silly stuff, the movement is touching some kind of nerve. What is it?

Robert Bly, author of *Iron John,* says that American men suffer from "fatherlessness"—boys growing up without their fathers. If you think back to colonial times, life was much different. Fathers worked alongside their sons on farms and in family industries, passing on the skills *their* fathers taught them. The Industrial Revolution changed all that. It tore fathers out of the home to work in factories and offices. For the first time in history, women became the primary parents.

Today, boys spend most of their growing years around women—with their mothers at home and with female teachers at school and at Sunday school. They grow up with only the haziest notion of what their fathers do all day.

According to the Family Research Council, the average father spends only eight minutes a day in direct conversation with his children. In families where the mother works, too, it drops to four minutes.

No wonder many boys suffer from what Robert Bly calls "father hunger"—a longing for a man's love, an insecure sense of masculine identity.

Signs of the malaise were everywhere at the First International Men's Conference. In workshops men openly wept and railed against fathers who had neglected or abandoned them. Grown men talked of the need for father figures to overcome the pain they still carried inside.

Well, like most secular movements, the men's movement may pinpoint some valid problems, but its solutions are woefully inadequate. You don't mend a wound in the heart by squatting in tents and banging on drums.

The real solution is found in Psalm 27:10—"My father and my mother have forsaken me, but the Lord will take me up." It is the Lord who is a Father to the fatherless. He can heal emotional wounds and give the kind of love the human heart longs for.

Over the next several years, the problem of fatherless men is likely to grow worse. We're just beginning to see the fallout from the rise in divorce rates since the sixties. Only a few years after a divorce, most fathers lose contact with their children.

In addition, there's an increase in children who never *had* contact with their fathers—whose parents never married. Boys growing up yesterday may have suffered neglect from fathers who were too busy, but many boys growing up today suffer from having no father at all.

The church needs to be praying and planning how it will minister to these fatherless men—with Big Brother programs, mentoring relationships, and classes to teach fathering skills.

Reach out to young men *before* they head for the hills and the tom-toms. Point them toward the heavenly Father—the only person who can really satisfy their "father hunger."

March 12, 1992

Daddy, Come Home
The Epidemic of Absent Fathers

Ask a typical government bureaucrat what the problems facing our nation are, and you're likely to hear a lot of abstract talk about economic trends and trade deficits.

But ask Louis Sullivan, secretary of the Department of Health and Human Services under the Bush administration, and he'll tell you that the greatest challenge of our generation is the flight of men from family life.

Since the 1960s, America has seen a staggering increase in broken families. Liberal social scientists don't like to use phrases like "broken families"; they glibly describe them in neutral terms like "new family forms" and "single-parent homes."

But in the eyes of a child, what's nearly always happening is the loss of a father.

And statistics show that the results of that loss are devastating. While the national poverty rate is 6 percent, the poverty rate for female-headed households is 30 percent. Among black female-headed households, it jumps to 50 percent.

The blunt fact is that poverty is not going to be eradicated from our black communities so long as nearly 70 percent of black children are born out of wedlock.

And with no-fault divorce, poverty is rapidly making inroads into the middle class as well. Half of all new welfare recipients are recently divorced women and their children. Today the most reliable indicator of whether a child is poor is whether or not he lives in an intact family.

But a missing father means much more than a missing paycheck. A father's love and discipline are crucial to character formation. And for children growing up without that love, the statistics are grim.

Fatherless children display more antisocial behavior, do worse in school, and are twice as likely to drop out than children from intact families. They are more likely to use drugs and become sexually active at an early age. More than half the teenagers who have attempted suicide live in single-parent homes.

Most children who run away from home are leaving fatherless homes. And approximately 70 percent of juveniles who end up in long-term correctional facilities grew up without a father at home.

Even health rates are affected. A recent study by the Department of Health and Human Services found that after controlling for age, sex, race, and socioeconomic status, children from broken families are twenty to forty times more likely to suffer health problems than children living with both parents.

The numbers are overwhelming. Our nation can no longer afford to be morally neutral about family forms. For the sake of our children, we must begin to design social policies that support and encourage intact families.

Which is to say, we need programs that encourage *men* to take their family responsibilities more seriously.

Most of our national dialogue on family issues, most of our parenting classes, most of our social supports for parents focus on mothers. But it is not women who are abandoning or neglecting their children, says Secretary Sullivan. It is men.

The time has come to shift our attention to the issue of male responsibility and the indispensable role fathers play in family life.

There's a reason God created the family the way He did. Children need fathers as well as mothers in order to thrive.

And even more important, in order to learn to trust God as their *heavenly* Father.

August 18, 1992

Granny Dumping
The Costs of Family Breakdown

In a hospital in Tampa, Florida, an elderly woman was recently dropped off—and never picked up again. She was found at the door of the emergency room, slumped in her wheelchair. A note pinned to her purse read, "She's sick. Please take care of her."

When the hospital staff looked around for the woman's family, all they saw was a pair of taillights disappearing into the distance.

This is just one story in a growing trend that's been dubbed "granny dumping." Staff at Tampa General Hospital say that only two years ago they almost never saw elderly people abandoned on their doorstep. Now, they say, it happens two or three times a week.

What we're seeing here is a coming together of demographics and moral breakdown.

America's population is aging, and the baby boom generation is moving up the age curve. Our birthrate has gone down, and our survival rate has gone up. The result is an expanding population of elderly people—with a shrinking base of younger people to care for them.

That in itself would have produced a tremendous strain on the younger generation trying to care for aging relatives. But making things worse is a flight from family responsibilities that has plagued American society since the 1960s.

For example, ever since the sixties larger numbers of people are remaining single or *becoming* single again through divorce or separation. These people have a harder time caring for aging parents, just as they have a harder time caring for young children.

The fact is it takes two people to care for dependents—one to earn an income, another to give care and nurture. Yet one study found that nearly half the people who care for elderly relatives today are single.

Another factor making it harder to care for the elderly is an increase in the number of families that are raising children at the same time. One study found that four out of five families caring for elderly parents still have children under sixteen years of age living at home. Demographers call this group the "sandwich generation"—squeezed between caring for two kinds of dependents at the same time.

This, too, is often a result of the flight from family. For many years the cultural message to young women has been that having a career is more important than having a family. As a result, women began putting off childbearing. Today the average age of childbearing is in the low- to mid-thirties, much older than a generation ago.

Many of these late families end up taking care of baby and granny at the same time.

Late families can also be the result of divorce and remarriage. It's not unusual today for parents to have a set of teenagers and a set of toddlers from a second marriage. The second-time-around family is prime for becoming part of the sandwich generation.

Americans like to think it's their own business whether they marry, whether they have children, and whether they divorce. But private choices always have public consequences.

The family is God's basic unit for health, education, and welfare. When people make choices that weaken the family, it threatens the health, the education, and the welfare of our entire society—leaving some people out in the cold.

Maybe out on a hospital driveway.

May 26, 1992

The Revolt Against Feminism
Susan Faludi's Backlash

A new word is entering the political vocabulary. It's "backlash" and it's being popularized in a new book on the bestseller lists entitled *Backlash: The Undeclared War Against American Women.*

The most potent weapon in this "undeclared war," says the author, Susan Faludi, is the myth that feminism has failed. As Faludi sees it, everywhere—from Hollywood to Madison Avenue to the nightly news—people are conspiring to make women believe that feminism is dead, conspiring to drive women out of the workplace and back into the kitchen.

Well, Faludi is right in saying there's a trend against feminism—but her interpretation of this trend is dead wrong.

It is *women* who are moving away from ideological feminism. They are rethinking the knee-jerk commitment to outside careers. A poll by *Time* and CNN finds that 63 percent of women today do not consider themselves feminists.

Faludi would have us think this is all due to an ugly, coercive backlash, concocted by reactionary forces to keep women subordinate. Faludi, who is not married and has never had any children, can't conceive that intelligent, adult women would actually choose to spend a major portion of their lives caring for children and creating a rich family life.

It *must* be some outside conspiracy.

But the idea of a backlash is contradicted by the enormous attention Faludi's own book is getting—culminating in a cover story in *Time* magazine.

No signs of a backlash there.

The truth is that the rejection of feminism is no conspiracy being foisted upon women. It's a change welling up from within the minds and hearts of women themselves.

And it's happening even within the feminist movement itself. Betty Friedan, who helped launched the movement with her book *The Feminist Mystique*, later wrote *The Second Stage*, where she worried that feminists had denied the importance of family life. Germaine Greer, who condemned marriage and motherhood in her book *The Female Eunuch*, later wrote *Sex and Destiny*, which celebrated children and family.

Reporter and novelist Sally Quinn recently rocked the readership of the *Washington Post* with a biting critique of feminism.

Clearly, it's not just so-called reactionaries who are critical of feminism. Even women weaned on feminist ideology are rethinking their views.

What's really happening is quite simple: The baby boomers are having babies and raising families of their own.

And that's changing their values and perspectives.

Listen to the poignant story told by feminist Erica Jong. Shortly after she had her first baby, Jong was invited to a poetry reading. It was her first public appearance after giving birth, and Jong decided to read several poems expressing the deep feelings she experienced in becoming a mother.

An audience of radical feminists booed her off the stage. Jong was devastated. Today she writes articles on the failure of feminism—rooted, she says, in its unwillingness to recognize the central fact in the lives of 90 percent of American women: the fact that they have children and that they resent being made to feel guilty about it.

So Faludi is wrong. There is no outside conspiracy. Just a spontaneous change as a generation of men and women, made in the image of God, grow up and discover the normal joys of family and children.

April 8, 1992

Coming Home
The New Traditional Mothers

The group of women meeting in the living room of a Washington, D.C., home was remarkably diverse. The only thing that seemed to unite them was a common commitment to being home with their young children.

On one side of the room were the traditionalists. Crisply coifed and conservatively dressed, they represented a national Christian organization called Home by Choice.

Then there were the countercultural types: no makeup, long hair, babies toted in slings across their shoulders. These women represented Mothers at Home, one of the country's first advocacy groups for mothers.

Across the room sat a group of highly professional women—women who had agonized over leaving well-paying, successful careers when they decided to stay home with their children. They formed a support group called Mothers First.

Then there were women from a group called Lawyers at Home, there being enough lawyers in Washington to form a group just for themselves. These women had a tough look about them and spoke in the aggressive manner of the courtroom lawyer. But they, too, had come to support mothers who want to take time out from their careers to raise their own children.

What drew this amazingly diverse group of women together was the sense that the tide is changing. For the first time in decades, there is a renewed respect for mothers who choose to stay home.

After the rise of militant feminism in the sixties, many women felt that being a mother and a homemaker was a trivial job, second best—that they really should be doing something better with their talents.

Lonna Wilkinson, a dancer and choreographer, describes the feeling well. "For women of my generation," she says, "motherhood really got a bum rap." There was a sense that there were more important things to do in life than be a mother.

But women still feel the age-old tug to nurture new life. Last year, the annual number of births in America jumped to 4 million for the first time since the end of the postwar baby boom. This was a steep increase in the number of births, and it appears to have taken place among both younger women and older women, who had postponed childbearing.

Motherhood is becoming popular again.

The change set in when women who had delayed childbearing couldn't put it off any longer and began having children. They discovered that having a baby was far more fulfilling than they'd been led to believe.

Carlie Dixon was thirty-five when she became pregnant with her first child. Carlie had practiced law for nine years and was a partner in a Washington, D.C., law firm. She fully intended to return to work after the birth of her child. But when her child was placed in her arms, her whole value system turned upside down.

"I was completely unprepared for the emotional attachment I would have with this child," Carlie says. "I didn't realize how much I would want to spend time with him."

Carlie is not alone. A recent article in *U.S. News & World Report* notes that for the first time in decades there has been a slight but statistically significant drop in the number of mothers in the work force.

More women are staying home—and enjoying it more. A 1989 survey by the Roper Organization found that 66 percent of women described having children as "very satisfying." Only 35 percent described their jobs in the same terms.

Yes, after decades of getting a "bum rap," to use Lonna Wilkinson's phrase, motherhood is coming back into its own.

April 27, 1992

Family Time Famine
Giving Parents More Time

American families are spending less time together than ever, says a well-known sociologist. She calls it the "family time famine." Statistics show that today's parents spend 40 percent less time with their children than their parents did.

That's a staggering decrease in adult investment in children.

The good news is that some parents are trying to reverse the trend. A recent story in the *Washington Post* announces that fast-track professionals are slowing down. They're exploring things like part-time work and flexible schedules to create more family time.

Lynn Myers is a pediatrician who began working part time when her first son was born. Today her children are older, but she still restricts her work to school hours, so she can help with homework or drive to soccer practice.

Driving a kid to soccer may not sound as glamorous as working in a prestigious medical practice. But it can be much more important. Lynn Myers says, "I find my kids share a lot of their successes and hurts" during that time together.

Today one of the fastest-growing options is home-based work, integrating family and work. Caroline Hull is a computer specialist who started her own business at home when her children were born. Jeannie Herbert is a nurse who holds childbirth education classes in her home.

But it isn't just women who are working to solve the family-time famine. Bob Hamrin was economic adviser to a national political figure when he decided he wanted more time with his growing family. Bob left a promising political career to start a home-based consulting firm. Now he can adjust his work schedule around his family, taking time off to attend a child's school function or sports event.

Stepping off the fast track when your children are young isn't easy. As I think back on my own life, my biggest regret is not spending more time with my kids.

Really making family the top priority means standing against a culture where materialism and workaholism are rampant. It means realizing you may not advance as fast in your career as some of your colleagues—at least for a few years. It means being willing to accept a lower standard of living.

Call it the "Parent Penalty."

In today's high-powered career world, parents who really invest in family life pay the Parent Penalty. But the trade-off is knowing you're doing the right thing for your children, giving them the emotional security they'll draw on for the rest of their lives.

There's a professional trade-off, too. People who enjoy a healthy family life make better workers. The Association for

Part-Time Professionals says part-time workers invest more productive effort into the hours they do spend on the job.

Good parents make good workers.

Unfortunately, it's not always easy to persuade businesses and corporations of that. Even Christian ministries can fall into the trap of workaholism. In one Christian ministry, workers were told that if a job could be done in a normal forty-hour week, then management hadn't put enough workload into the position.

But we should expect Christian businesses and ministries, of all people, to uphold the importance of the family. They should be taking the lead in creating family-friendly work strategies: things like part-time positions, flexible hours, and home-based work.

Encouraging a healthy family life is not only a biblical principle. It also happens to be good business.

June 26, 1992

8

Justice for All

Paying the Bill for Atheism
Do We Need Another Study on Crime?

Thomas Jefferson once wrote that disagreements over religion never hurt anyone. If my neighbor says there is no God, he said, "it neither picks my pocket nor breaks my leg."

Well, with all due respect, Jefferson was wrong. Atheism *does* pick my pocket—and yours, too.

As a case in point, Harvard School of Public Health is gearing up for a new ten-year study that will cost upward of $80 million. Researchers will study children across several age groups to identify the causes of crime.

Eighty million dollars is a pretty hefty price tag—and all to search for something we already know.

That's right. If we're Christians, we already know what causes crime. The Bible teaches that human beings are morally responsible, capable of choosing between right and wrong.

Choosing to do wrong is what the Bible calls sin.

So if we believe God's Word, we don't need another multimillion-dollar study on the cause of crime. As the Book of James puts it, people sin when they give in to their evil desires.

This biblical principle used to be widely accepted. But Western society has moved away from its biblical moorings and devised a new, humanistic theory of human behavior. Humanism denies the reality of sin; instead, it says, human nature is inherently good.

And if human nature is good, then the cause of evil and crime must be something *outside* the individual—something in the environment: Crime must result from ghettos and poverty.

Human beings aren't morally *depraved* in the humanistic view, they're just economically *deprived*.

This was the vision that underlay the effort to solve crime by a massive War on Poverty. But the War on Poverty has not solved crime—as the Los Angeles riots so recently proved— and in recent years a more biblical view is reemerging.

Psychologist Stanton Samenow and psychiatrist Samuel Yochelson spent seventeen years studying criminals. They discovered that criminal behavior could not be tied to any environmental causes—not ghettos or poverty or any of the other conventional explanations.

Instead, they found that crime results from a conscious decision. People commit crimes when they make wrong moral choices. Whether the street thug or the white-collar criminal, both make exactly the same choice.

Samenow and Yochelson ended their study with a startling conclusion: The only way a criminal can change, they said, is by a conscious shift to a new way of thinking—what they called a "conversion."

It's an apt description. At Prison Fellowship we've seen thousands of offenders turn from a life of crime through a conversion to Jesus Christ.

So I have a proposal for Harvard—one that might even save $80 million. Walk through prison hallways with some of our Prison Fellowship volunteers and talk to inmates who have experienced that conversion.

They'll be happy to tell Harvard researchers exactly how they were drawn into a life of crime—and then to explain the real solution: a conversion to a new life by the power of God.

August 19, 1992

What the Church Can Do
The Lesson of History

What causes crime?

Ask that question and you're bound to hear a litany of familiar responses: poverty, racism, social alienation, lenient judges, not enough prisons. The remarkable thing is that, according to recent studies, none of these is the real cause. Contributing factors, yes, but not the root cause.

Criminologist James Q. Wilson researched the history of crime in America. He wanted to explain why crime decreased in the middle of the last century and then, after some fluctuations, shot up dramatically in the 1960s and has been climbing ever since.

Wilson checked all the standard explanations of criminal behavior. But he found that none of them correlated with the patterns he was seeing. Take poverty, for example. If poverty causes crime, it's very difficult to explain why crime was low during the Depression, when over a quarter of the population had no income at all. Or why crime rose during the affluent sixties and seventies.

Then Wilson stumbled on a historical fact he had not noticed before. The decrease in crime in the last century followed on the heels of a widespread religious revival known as the Second Great Awakening. Repentance and renewal spread across the country. Church membership rose steeply. Christians formed voluntary associations devoted to education and moral reform.

American society came to respect the values of sobriety, hard work, self-restraint—what sociologists call the Protestant ethic.

As the Protestant ethic triumphed, the crime rate plummeted.

But then the trend shifted. Beginning in the 1920s and 1930s, the Protestant ethic began to fall out of favor among the educated classes. Following in the footsteps of Sigmund Freud, social scientists began to teach that self-restraint is not good but harmful. The educated classes began to view ethical principles as oppressive.

Their cause was no longer freedom *for* religion—a classic American liberty—but freedom *from* religion.

The attitudes of the educated classes percolated through to popular consciousness in the 1960s. The ideal of self-restraint and community responsibility was out; the ideal of personal liberation was in. When the hippies demanded freedom to do their own thing, they were expressing a wider cultural shift away from a shared moral consensus and toward individual choice.

The result was a sudden and dramatic increase in crime.

The lesson of history is clear: When Christian belief is strong, the crime rate falls; when Christian belief weakens, the crime rate climbs. Widespread religious belief creates a shared social ethic that acts as a restraint on the dark side of human nature.

Without the internal restraint of a shared ethic, order has to be imposed externally by force. That's what Mao Zedong meant when he said morality begins at the muzzle of a gun. As leader of the bloody revolution that imposed communism on China, Mao was not speaking abstractly.

There are only two ways for a society to survive. Either its civic order will flow from a shared social ethic rooted in spiritual commitments . . . or order will be imposed by the muzzle of a gun.

That is the choice facing America today.

October 30, 1991

What's a Sheriff to Do?
Overcrowded Prisons

If it weren't tragic, it would be funny.

A California sheriff was ordered by a federal judge to reduce overcrowding in prisons. He complied by cutting sentences and letting prisoners out early.

The hapless sheriff was then sentenced by *another* judge to jail. The charge? That he was releasing prisoners early!

What's a sheriff to do?

Prison overcrowding is a real problem. But the solution is not just cutting sentences. And the solution certainly is not *adding* to the prison population by throwing law-abiding sheriffs in with the criminals.

A real solution is alternative sentencing for nondangerous offenders.

The people who need to be incarcerated are violent offenders, who are a direct danger to the public. But nearly half the people in prison today are there for nonviolent offenses. Simply reducing sentences across the board means many violent criminals are released back onto the streets to make room for nondangerous ones.

This is ludicrous. Violent offenders are unleashed on the public, while nonviolent offenders lie in their bunks all day at public expense.

The nonviolent criminal has bilked the public once when he committed his crime: theft or fraud or whatever. Then we let him bilk it again: to subsidize his idleness behind bars.

A much better use of public money—and human resources—is to sentence nondangerous offenders to community service. Assign them to clean up a ghetto neighborhood. Work in a street mission. Prison Fellowship conducts two-week work projects using furloughed inmates to rehabilitate run-down housing.

Nondangerous offenders can also work at paying jobs and use the income to pay back the people they have wronged. That's called victim restitution.

When I speak on this subject, people sometimes come up to me and say, "Victim restitution—what a great idea. Where did you get it?" And I say, "Do you have a Bible? Dust it off and read it." That's where the concept came from.

Alternative sentencing programs are good for the victim, good for the community—*and* good for offenders. Time and again the response to Prison Fellowship's work programs is gratitude: gratitude for the chance to do something positive for society rather than vegetate in a prison cell.

Of course, programs like these can't be accomplished by the criminal justice system alone. They require the cooperation of local churches and communities. Quincy, Massachusetts, has one of the best victim restitution programs in the country. Several local businesses have agreed to accept offenders as employees. They are required to use their salaries to pay back their victims.

The relationship works out so well that businesses often keep offenders on staff permanently when their sentences are over.

When I was convicted in the Watergate scandal in 1974, I was sentenced to prison. When Oliver North was convicted for his role in the Iran-Contra scandal fifteen years later, the same judge sentenced *him* to two years of community service, working with inner-city youth in Washington, D.C.

Was I upset at the discrepancy in sentencing? No—I applauded the judge's decision. Just consider: A nonviolent offender put behind bars costs taxpayers about $20,000 per year. Put him on probation and the supervision costs are a fraction of that. And the benefits are incalculable.

So come on, California. Start using alternative sentencing to solve your prison overcrowding.

And by all means, stop sending your hard-pressed sheriffs to jail.

November 19, 1991

Getting Tough on Crime
Will It Work?

A recent study finds that federal judges are sentencing criminals to longer prison terms. Sentences imposed last year averaged more than twice as long as terms imposed two years earlier.

The change reflects a get-tough-on-drugs policy, which has resulted in mandatory prison terms for drug offenders and harsher terms for repeat drug offenders.

As Christians we applaud tough measures against crime. Or *do* we?

May I suggest that what looks tough on paper doesn't always get tough results in the prison yard or on the street. Longer terms do not necessarily keep people behind bars any longer. They are not a stronger deterrent to crime, either.

Here's why: The simple fact is that the U.S. prison system is so overcrowded it simply cannot absorb longer sentences. Some prisons have resorted to setting up tents to house minimum-security inmates. But what most prisons do is simply shorten the terms and let inmates out early to make room for new ones.

Recently, a county judge in California sentenced a man to jail for one month. But when the man reached the jailhouse door, he was told to go home. It turned out that because of overcrowding, everyone's sentence was being reduced by thirty days. This man's sentence was exactly thirty days, so it was reduced to zero.

He signed in and then walked right out again.

The fact is that overcrowding is so severe and the cost of building new prisons so high that early-release policies are going to continue, in spite of judges who order longer sentences. Restructuring sentence terms is an exercise in futility.

The hope, of course, is that the *threat* of longer sentences will at least deter crime. But criminologists agree that harsher penalties don't deter criminals if they have good reason to think the penalty will never be imposed. And that's exactly what criminals do think today.

Consider the statistics. Only one out of three crimes is even reported to the police. Of those, only one in five leads to an arrest. Which means that for every hundred crimes, there are only seven arrests.

Of those seven arrests, less than half are convicted. And of those, only half are incarcerated. (The rest are put on probation.) In short, for every hundred crimes committed, only two people end up in jail or prison.

The seasoned criminal knows this. He knows the odds are that he will never have to pay for his crime. So he's not going to be deterred by talk about tougher sentences.

Punishment deters only when criminals know they will be caught and that punishment will be swift and sure. Milder sentences actually deter as effectively as tough ones—*if* the criminal knows they will actually be imposed.

We all want to stop crime. But simply putting longer sentences down on paper isn't going to accomplish much. About the only beneficiaries of longer prison terms are the politicians who can claim a good law-and-order record come election time.

Real reform would be the development of alternative forms of sentencing for nonviolent offenders: community service, house arrest, and victim restitution. Put them to work serving their community and restoring their victims. This is the biblical concept of reconciliation, and it works.

If prison space is reserved for keeping really dangerous offenders off the streets, the problem of early releases would be solved. And a tough sentence would be more than just a number on a piece of paper.

January 13, 1992

Lessons from Los Angeles
Breakdown of the Moral Order

The smoke has cleared over the skies of Los Angeles, but the political fires will burn for a long time to come as policy makers debate the cause of the riots and ways to prevent their return.

The riots may have started with the Rodney King case, but they quickly grew into much more than that. The looting and murder we watched on our television screens was the result of unfettered human depravity—what the Bible calls sin. One black shopkeeper, surveying the looters' wreckage, said, "This has nothing to do with Rodney King. This has to do with greed."

That's a more honest assessment than we're likely to hear on the evening news.

Every political order rests on a moral consensus. In order to live as a community, we must all accept certain objective principles—obligations that transcend our personal desires— such as respect for the property of others. Without that moral order, there's little government can do to maintain civil order.

We could post National Guardsmen on every street corner, and chaos would still erupt.

This is the real lesson of Los Angeles: that a democratic government cannot be sustained unless its citizens first practice *self*-government. When they give in to their impulses, the law of the jungle takes over.

And that can happen anywhere, not just in the inner city. Looting is looting—whether it's done by gang members in T-shirts or by white-collar bankers in three-piece suits. We saw it in the savings-and-loan fiasco, which is still being sorted out. Instead of smashing windows in the ghettos, these men were quietly writing figures in a ledger book. But the moral content of their act was exactly the same: By dipping into other people's savings, they were just as culpable as the looters in Los Angeles who robbed their neighbor's shops.

Take away the restraints of conscience, and people grab whatever they can.

The riots in Los Angeles reveal in a microcosm what can happen anywhere in America when the moral consensus that holds a free society together breaks down. And that moral consensus depends in turn on a strong religious faith.

Our Founders understood this. Two hundred years ago, John Adams said, "Our constitution was made only for a moral and religious people. It is wholly inadequate for the government of any other."

And historians Will and Ariel Durant, after studying two thousand years of Western civilization, concluded, "there is no significant example in history . . . of a society successfully maintaining moral life without the aid of religion."

I wish we all had heard one of the black residents of Los Angeles interviewed on television. He gestured toward the looters storming the shops and cried out, "This is *stealing*. Don't these people have any morals? Don't they believe in God?"

Those simple questions hit right at the heart of the issue: As our nation turns away from God, we are losing the only sure basis for a moral order in society—an order that applies to all people, black or white, in ghetto neighborhoods or in corporate boardrooms.

It's good to see the smoke clearing over Los Angeles and to hear the sound of hammers rebuilding the stores and businesses. But unless we work just as hard to rebuild the bonds of our moral consensus, those walls will surely tumble down again.

Not only in Los Angeles but across the rest of America as well.

May 12, 1992

Blind Justice
The Tyson Rape Case

We know sex sells movies, and now, it seems, sex sells news. Coverage of the Clarence Thomas harassment case, the Kennedy rape case, and the Clinton adultery case have left us wondering if news programs shouldn't be R-rated.

And now there's another rape case. But this time, there are much deeper questions at stake—questions about the very purpose of the courts.

The case involved former heavyweight boxing champion Mike Tyson, who was convicted of raping a young woman on a date. No sooner was the verdict announced than all sorts of groups rushed to predict what the social fallout would be. Women's groups celebrated the conviction, eagerly forecasting its impact on future rape cases.

Other groups bemoaned the conviction and spoke out strongly against a jail sentence. They argued that putting Tyson behind bars would achieve no social good at all—that it would even be harmful. A group of ministers even circulated a petition saying Tyson is one of the few "modern-day African-American heroes." The petition urged the court to consider the devastating effect it would have on young blacks to see their hero languishing in jail.

Well, no matter which set of predictions turns out to be right, both sides missed the most important point. At issue here is foremost a question of justice: Is the man guilty of a crime? And since the court has said yes, what is a just form of punishment?

But these questions aren't even being asked.

The groups interviewed on the nightly news aren't concerned about justice *inside* the courtroom; they're concerned about the impact *outside* the courtroom—on people in the streets. Will it help women or hurt them? Will it help young black men or hurt them?

I'm certainly no prophet and I don't know what effect Tyson's conviction might have. What concerns me is this attitude that what *really* counts is the social effects a court decision has. What various interest groups are asking of the court system is not justice but results.

Justice is being sacrificed to social engineering, with the courts used as tools to produce preselected social outcomes. We don't want judges to read the law; we want them to read our petitions. We don't ask them to interpret and apply legal opinion; we demand that they interpret and assuage public opinion.

It was much the same kind of legal pragmatism that led to the crucifixion of Christ. Pontius Pilate wasn't thinking about justice, he was thinking about keeping the political peace in Jerusalem and assuaging the mob outside his window.

With that in mind, he sacrificed Jesus to pacify the crowds.

But true justice is like the statue that adorns many courthouses, personified as a woman wearing a blindfold. The blindfold means she doesn't look to see *who* is being sentenced or what the social outcome will be. She simply metes out what is due.

Mike Tyson deserves better than to be used as a political pawn by various interest groups. What he deserves, and what the rest of the country needs, is a bracing dose of blind, impartial justice.

March 19, 1992

Cleaning Up Charleston
Making Sure Crime Doesn't Pay

Charleston, South Carolina, can boast a unique accomplishment: It has reversed its crime problem. While crime continues to escalate in most other American cities, Charleston has actually reduced burglaries, armed robberies, auto thefts, and larcenies.

What's their secret? In a recent issue of *Policy Review*, Charleston's chief of police, Reuben Greenberg, tells the story.

The first target, Greenberg says, was street-level drug dealing. Open-air dealing—with its fights, assaults, turf wars, and drive-by shootings—was turning some areas of the city into wastelands.

The standard approach, arresting dealers, wasn't working. Literally within hours, the dealers were out on bond or bail and back on the streets selling again.

So the Charleston police hit upon another strategy that proved to be simple, economical, and highly effective. They simply put a uniformed cop on a dealer's street corner—and scared off all his customers.

The effect was immediate. With a policeman standing forty feet away, no one came near the drug dealer. A car would slow down, then drive on by.

The strategy worked even better when the police added a weapon to their arsenal—a Polaroid flash camera. If potential customers drove by a second time, the officer would take their photograph. And that's the last he would see of them.

Critics of the policy said dealers would just move to another street corner and keep on selling. But they didn't. They couldn't move far beyond their initial base or they'd lose their customers. And risk getting killed for invading another dealer's turf.

Then critics said that the police would have to guard the corners twenty-four hours a day. That fear turned out to be unfounded as well. Police learned that if they covered the drug market areas during the high-demand period—from Wednesday through Saturday—that sufficed to cut off most sales and drive the dealers out.

The next step was to spruce up the area, make it look like a neighborhood again. That's important in making residents feel good about their homes again and bringing businesses back into the area. So Greenberg got prisoners out of jail and put them to work picking up trash, mowing weeds, painting over graffiti.

The plan turned out to have an unintended benefit. Some of the prisoners had once been drug dealers—some even dealing in the very neighborhood they were now cleaning up. Young boys who had once seen these men loaded down with gold chains and flashy rings now saw them wearing orange jumpsuits that said "County Jail" on the back.

It was a sobering lesson.

So where did the drug dealers go? About a third simply went out of the drug-selling business altogether, reports Police Chief Greenberg. Of course, it would be nice to be able to report that they *all* did. But a third is not bad when you realize it was accomplished without a massive increase in manpower or money and without overburdening the jails or the courts.

All it took was treating crime as a business—and reducing the profit margin until the business was no longer worthwhile to operate.

As Christians, we know that crime doesn't pay on a spiritual level—that wrongdoing kills the inner spirit of a man or woman.

But what Police Chief Greenberg did was make sure that on an economic level, crime didn't pay either.

May 25, 1992

The Lost Generation
Blacks in the Criminal Justice System

The media recently reported a startling new crime statistic: On any given day in the District of Columbia a full 42 percent of young black men are entangled in some way in the criminal justice system.

The statistic comes from a new study covering black men between the ages of eighteen and thirty-five. It found that 15 percent are in prison, 21 percent are on probation or parole, and 6 percent are out on bond or being sought by the police.

No study has reported such high numbers before. Of all black men living in Washington, D.C., 85 percent are arrested at some point in their lives.

Eighty-five percent! How can we explain such a tragedy?

Jerome Miller, author of the report, thinks he knows. "We're using the criminal justice system to deal with a wide range of problems that are primarily social," Miller says.

Many kids enter the criminal justice system through minor offenses: truancy, vandalism, shoplifting, petty drug use. Troubles that often stem less from criminality than from social problems. They may be the result of school failure, family breakdown, peer pressure, or emotional instability.

Now if a youngster is from a middle-class family, there's a good chance that his resources will be mobilized to help him out. Teachers intervene, parents are notified, tutoring is arranged, a church youth leader sets up a discipling relationship.

Everything is done to divert the youngster *away* from the criminal justice system.

But if the youngster is from a poor family, living in a ghetto, he doesn't have these resources. Minor infractions are likely to draw him into the criminal justice system. If he doesn't straighten up, he's likely to be packed off to a juvenile detention facility.

But using the criminal justice system to solve social problems only makes things worse. The kid who is labeled a criminal often acts more and more like one. And a stint in detention usually leaves him schooled in more advanced techniques of crime.

What's the answer?

The real solution is to recreate the social networks that can rescue these kids early on. And that begins with the church.

Sending a child to reform school costs the District of Columbia about $60,000 per child every year, Miller reports. So he offers a daring suggestion: "Suppose we gave all . . . that $60,000 to, say, the men's group at a church near where the youngster lives and said, '*You* keep him out of trouble.'"

Just imagine all the creative solutions a group of godly men could come up with if they had anything close to $60,000 to help one boy or girl.

Of course, whether the government ever agrees to reforms like that, the people of God are still called to lead the way in helping these youngsters. We can't just sit by and criticize the police for not reducing crime when churches are not reaching out to help kids *before* they fall into a life of crime.

A famous pastor once wrote, "There is something very pathetic about the efforts . . . to restore by police coercion what has been lost by the decay of moral and cultural traditions. The church cannot recoup *its* failure by giving advice to the police department."

Those are the words of a pastor speaking in crime-ridden Germany in the 1920s. But they apply just as well to crime-ridden American cities in the 1990s. Christians today are likely to want to "give advice to the police department" in terms of voting for tougher laws and tougher sentences.

But what we really should be addressing is "the decay of moral and cultural traditions."

July 2, 1992

Christianity in the Public Square
Why Bad People Do Good Things

Last year I met with the minister of internal affairs in the Soviet Union. He was surprisingly candid about his country's crime crisis—a 38 percent increase in a single year.

The Soviet people, he told me, are being driven to crime by political and economic hardship. No, I told him, that's not it. Your problem is not economic or political, Mr. Minister; it is spiritual.

You only need to read your own Russian writer Fyodor Dostoevsky, I told him. Dostoevsky wrote a brilliant novel called *The Brothers Karamazov,* a story about three brothers who debate the source of evil in the world. Finally one brother cries out, "If there is no God, then everything is permitted!"

That's your problem, I told the Soviet minister: seventy years of atheism. The Soviet state has pounded it into the people's heads that there is no God . . . and the people have concluded that therefore everything is permitted.

Without God, there is no restraint on our baser impulses. Crime becomes inevitable.

Then I told the Soviet official about Prison Fellowship, and the way it brings the Word of God into the prisons. He looked across the table at me and he said, "Mr. Colson, You're right. That's what we need in the Soviet Union."

The Soviets have watched a civic order based on atheism collapse. Today they understand the need to restore religion to public life.

Ironically, Western society is moving in the opposite direction: Many people are trying to *remove* religion from public life. Under the banner of pluralism, cultural and political leaders are seeking to push all talk about God out of the public arena. We're told we can't publicly espouse a Christian view of crime or abortion because America is a pluralistic nation.

The answer we should be giving is that it is precisely because we are a pluralistic nation that we *can* espouse a Christian position on these issues. In the traditional sense, pluralism means *every* group has a right to argue its own case in the public square and try to persuade the populace.

If people understood the social impact of Christian faith, they would welcome its contribution. According to a recent study, Christians give more money per capita to charity—even to secular charities—than any other group in America. They are also much more likely to volunteer their time to charitable causes.

And the church's record was even stronger in earlier eras of history. Church historian Marvin Olasky studied the history of charity in America and found that in the middle of the last century there was a remarkable flowering of Christian compassion. A huge wave of migration to the cities had resulted in America's first real problems with slums and city crime. But Christians responded, opening their homes to deserted women and orphans, offering employment to rootless men, and founding societies to combat drunkenness and other social evils.

The result was a widespread uplift in morals and a decrease in crime. Crime rates fell and remained relatively low until the 1960s, when the Christian social ethic was undercut by a pervasive secularism.

I was once asked to give a lecture on ethics at Harvard Business School with the suggested title of "Why Good People Do Bad Things." I replied that a much better title would be "Why Bad People Do Good Things." The real question facing our society is how we can motivate inherently sinful people to do good.

And the answer is that we must teach them the biblical basis for ethics, rooted in God's law. The only compelling reason for ethical rules is the conviction that they are not the creation of our own minds—that standards of right and wrong are enduring, unchanging principles based on the character of a holy God.

This is a truth the Soviets have had to learn the hard way. And a truth we ignore to our peril.

October 31, 1991

The Difference It Makes
When Hearts Are Handcuffed by Love

Prisons are not very pleasant places. After fifteen years in prison ministry, you might think I'd get used to it. But I haven't. And prisons in Third-World countries are indescribably worse. Primitive, crowded—a shock to North American eyes.

One of them, however, is different.

It's Humaita Prison in Brazil. When I visited Humaita, I was struck by the clean courtyard with its whitewashed patios and crisp blue trim. Inside, the rooms are orderly and the beds neatly made.

A sign on the wall says, "It's not enough to stop doing evil; you must also do good." Another reads, "All honest work is blessed by God."

From those lines perhaps you can guess what makes Humaita different: It's run by Christians. For the past eighteen years, Humaita has been operated by a group of Christian volunteers, who are now members of Prison Fellowship Brazil.

After the volunteers took over Humaita, the number of inmates returning to prison dropped to a mere 4 percent. Yet the average worldwide rate is 75 percent—an astounding difference.

What's the secret to Humaita's success? Higher walls? More guards? Just the opposite. Humaita has no guards. When an inmate enters Humaita, his handcuffs are taken off and he is told, "In this prison, your heart is handcuffed by love, and you are watched over by Christ."

Humaita has developed an innovative system that allows inmates to earn their freedom in stages. At each stage, they are given greater access to the outside world. In the final stage, they live at home, work at outside jobs, and merely report every day to prison.

But the heart of Humaita's program is that it introduces inmates to Christ. During my visit there, I attended a chapel service where several inmates told how they had converted to Christ. In remorse for their crimes, many had made restitution to their victims.

After the chapel service, the inmate who was acting as my guide asked if I would like to see the punishment cell. It's a dark, narrow cell once used to subdue unruly prisoners, he explained. At times in the past, so many inmates were crowded into the tiny cell that they suffocated.

But now, I was told, the cell holds only one prisoner.

As we walked over to the prison's high security area and stopped in front of a heavy steel door, I braced myself for the worst. And yet when the door swung opened, what hit me was not the stench of sweating bodies but the aroma of fresh flowers. An altar graced one end of the room. Above it hung a carving of Jesus on the cross, with a banner that read "We are together."

The prisoner in the cell was Jesus.

In that dark, narrow cell is the secret to Humaita's success. There criminals learn of a savior who, like them, was branded a criminal—who can truly say to them: *We are together. I bore the punishment for your sins; I served your sentence.*

There is no question I'm asked more frequently than this one: Does Prison Fellowship's ministry really work? Are prison conversions real? Do they last?

I've decided that the next time I'm asked that question, I'm going to suggest that the person buy a ticket to Brazil. See firsthand the difference it makes when criminals understand that Christ is there with them—that He was a prisoner, too, and that He went to the cross in their place.

That's a lesson we Westerners could learn from a scruffy bunch of convicts in Brazil.

December 26, 1991

Mr. Owen's Neighborhood
When a Prison Moves Next Door

If state officials decided to build a prison near your town, how would you feel? Worried? Anxious?

That's exactly how the residents of Limestone County, Alabama, felt when they heard about plans to build a correctional center there. Several citizens raised their voices in protest.

There was one man, though, who raised his voice not in protest but in prayer.

Bert Owen was a retired engineer, a thin, white-haired man. When the bulldozers and jackhammers arrived, Bert rode his bicycle down to the construction site. As he watched the prison walls go up, he prayed for the prisoners who would be coming to live there. And when the cells were finally filled, Bert immediately signed up as a volunteer.

It was a brave step: He'd never done anything like it before. And the first day he stood hesitantly wondering where to begin. Then he noticed a group of men standing in a circle. He walked over and discovered they were Christians.

God had led him straight to a group of believers!

Things couldn't have worked out better, Bert thought. The group welcomed him and eagerly agreed to attend a Bible study.

The next step, however, was not so easy.

When he returned, Bert discovered that twenty men— about half white and half black—had signed up for the Bible study. "Good, let's open with prayer," he said, and routinely asked the men to hold hands.

Instantly, the room was charged with tension. The inmates scowled and stepped back. What was wrong? Then Bert saw: The whites and blacks were refusing to join hands with one another.

Quickly, Bert switched gears. Today's lesson, he decided, would be about Christian unity. "Men," he said, "if you're going to form a church behind bars, you've got to start by loving each other."

But the message was not well received. And before Bert had finished, half the class had walked out.

That day, he left the prison discouraged. But he had prayed over these inmates for months, and he wasn't going to give up now. When he returned the next week, there was a pleasant surprise: All the men who had walked out were back again.

Yet he knew the big test was still to come. Taking a deep breath, he said, "OK, men, let's join hands and pray." Then he waited. Slowly, awkwardly, the men held out their hands— blacks and whites together.

It was a small miracle, the first of many Bert was to witness over the years.

Today, Bert works with Prison Fellowship, still riding his bike over to visit inmates and lead Bible studies. The funny thing, Bert says, is that for years he had asked God to send him to the mission field. But instead God sent a mission field to him—in the form of a prison.

So if state officials decide to build a prison near *your* town, remember Bert's story. It may well be God's way of calling you to a mission field.

August 17, 1992

9

Signs and Science

Even the Wind and Waves Obey Him
How Science Supports the Bible

Talk about the Bible being historically true, and the first thing you hear is, What about Jonah and the whale? Noah and the flood? The parting of the Red Sea?

These stories are held up as so preposterous that no one could possibly take the Bible seriously. People even make jokes about them.

But scientists who study these events say they are not as impossible as they might seem. Sometimes they are just special cases of perfectly normal laws of nature.

Take, for example, the parting of the Red Sea.

The biblical record says God used the east wind, blowing all night to push the waters back. Recently, two oceanographers decided to see if they could describe the process in greater detail. Their results were published in the *Bulletin of the American Meteorological Society*.

It's a well-known scientific fact that a steady wind blowing over a body of water can change the water level. It happens frequently during winter storms on Lake Erie, for example, where steady winds have changed the water level as much as three feet. The two oceanographers decided to see if the same thing could happen on the Red Sea—to be precise, on the narrow sliver of the Red Sea reaching up into the Gulf of Suez where, many scholars believe, the Israelites crossed when they were escaping from Pharaoh's army.

The scientists analyzed the topography of the area, using sophisticated computer calculations. They concluded that a moderate wind blowing constantly for about ten hours could very well have caused the sea to recede a mile or two. The water level would drop ten feet, leaving dry land for the Israelites to cross.

"The Gulf of Suez provides an ideal body of water for such a process because of its unique geography," said one of the scientists. The gulf is more than two hundred miles long but only twelve to eighteen miles wide. Winds channeled between the mountains on each side of the gulf could exert a powerful force on the surface of the water and push the water back from the shoreline.

Later, an abrupt *change* in the wind could cause the water to return rapidly—in a sudden, devastating wave. It could easily have trapped Pharaoh's troops, just as the Bible describes.

The study doesn't prove that the crossing of the Red Sea happened exactly this way, of course. It merely shows that there are perfectly normal forces that God could have used to perform His miraculous deliverance.

Now a skeptic might argue that if there's a natural explanation, then it wasn't a miracle after all. That's how the *Boston Globe* interpreted the recent study.

But if it was only a natural event, isn't it strange that the sea parted *just* when Moses held out his staff? And that it fell back *just* when Pharaoh's soldiers were in hot pursuit?

No, God may use a natural process to accomplish His goals, but it's still a work of His hand, in His timing, and for His purposes.

So the next time someone tells you the Bible stories are just too unbelievable to be real history, give them a little science lesson on the laws of nature.

And then tell them about the God who *created* the laws of nature and directs them for His purposes.

The One whom "even the wind and the waves obey."

May 11, 1992

Big Ruckus over the Big Bang
Origin of the Universe

The press has been full of stories about NASA's latest discovery, which scientists say might help confirm the big bang theory. A scientist interviewed on "Nightline" said the finding gives new proof that the Genesis account of creation is false.

But, of course, it proves nothing of the sort.

According to the big bang theory, the universe began as a tiny, densely packed ball that exploded with a blinding blast of energy. Tiny bits of matter were sent hurtling outward in a smooth cloud of gas. Eventually the gas coalesced to form the first stars and galaxies.

But there's always been a serious problem with this scenario. If the universe began as a smoothly expanding cloud of gas, what caused it to coalesce into galaxies? Newton's laws of motion tell us that an object will continue moving straight ahead unless some force acts upon it. What force existed after the big bang to cause matter to *stop* moving straight out and *start* clumping into stars and galaxies?

Scientists used to say the force was gravity. But gravity is very weak. You yourself exert gravity on everything around you, but it's too weak to produce any noticeable effect. A body has to be quite large before gravity becomes a significant force.

That means there has to be a crucial first step after the big bang when molecules somehow gathered into a lump dense enough for gravity to take over.

For the past two decades, cosmologists have been searching for evidence of this first step. It's been dubbed the missing link of the big bang theory. Some astronomers were even beginning to wonder whether the big bang was really a viable theory of the origin of the universe.

That's why the recent discovery was hailed with such enthusiasm. It might mean scientists have found the missing link needed to salvage the big bang theory.

What scientists actually detected is a kind of radiation they believe is a residue from an early stage of the universe. It is marked by very slight temperature variations, indicating differences in density, like vast ripples out in space. Scientists think it may represent the initial clumping of matter they've been searching for.

If it is, does that disprove Genesis? Not at all. In many ways, the big bang theory is highly compatible with Genesis—much more compatible than earlier theories were.

From ancient times the Genesis account has been unique in teaching that God is a real Creator, who began with nothing. Creation *ex nihilo*. In other religions, creation stories always start with some sort of preexisting material, which is itself eternal.

In ancient Greece some of the pagan religious stories were secularized and became the earliest forms of philosophy. Here, too, matter was regarded as eternal, a teaching that Christians did battle against all through the early church period and the Middle Ages.

Finally, in the nineteenth century, scientists formulated the law of conservation of matter—that matter can neither be created nor destroyed—and it seemed science itself taught that matter is eternal.

The biblical doctrine of creation out of nothing was mocked as hopelessly unscientific.

Then about sixty years ago, scientists came up with the big bang theory. Matter is not eternal after all, the theory says. It came into existence at a particular time in the remote past—just as Genesis says.

After centuries, secular theories correlated with biblical revelation.

Of course, the big bang theory leaves one important question open: If the universe is not eternal, what caused it to come into existence? That's something science cannot answer. For obviously the *cause* of the universe must be something *outside* the universe. And isn't that just what Christians have been saying all along?

Yes, the heavens do declare the glory of God. And today they seem to be speaking louder than ever.

April 30, 1992

A Tailor-Made Universe
Created for Life

The big bang theory of the origin of the universe has been infused with new life these days—ever since scientists discovered those "ripples" out in space that may have started it all. Scientists once thought the universe was eternal, but with the big bang theory, science is now on the side of Genesis.

It seems the further science progresses, the more it supports the biblical view of the world.

Let me give you a few other examples. Many scientists have noted that the universe is remarkably well suited for life. Everywhere science is uncovering what one physicist calls "cosmic coincidences."

For a familiar example, take water. When water freezes, unlike most other substances, it expands and floats. If water didn't have this unique property, then in cold weather, lakes and rivers would freeze down to the bottom, and all fish would be killed.

Or think about the position of our planet in the solar system. If the earth were only slightly closer to the sun, it would be too hot for life. We would all burn up. But if the earth were further away from the sun, it would be too cold to support life. We would all freeze.

Isn't it a marvelous coincidence that the earth is just where it is in the solar system?

The strength of gravity is another cosmic coincidence. If the force of gravity were just slightly stronger, that extra tug would long ago have pulled the cosmos together and caused it to collapse in on itself.

If, on the other hand, the force of gravity were just the tiniest bit weaker, then it wouldn't be strong enough to maintain the stars and galaxies and our own solar system.

The fact that gravity has just the right strength is, in the words of one scientist, "a gigantic fluke—or divine intervention."

The same could be said of the electrical force. Every tree, every blade of grass is made of atoms containing electrons and protons. The electron has an electrical charge that balances the charge of the proton exactly.

What would happen if the two charges were not precisely balanced? If the electron carried more charge than the proton, every atom in the universe would be negatively charged. Since like charges repel, the atoms would repel each other and the universe would explode apart.

In a previous century coincidences like these were seen as evidence of God's design. If the universe appears to be tailor-made for life, people said, that's because it *is* tailor-made for life. God created the universe to be a suitable home for His creatures.

But today many scientists shy away from any suggestion of the supernatural. They have come up with a rather odd alternative called the Anthropic Principle, which says that in some strange way these cosmic coincidences didn't just happen. They were meant to be. The universe somehow has its own purposes.

John Wheeler, a prominent physicist, says that the universe "must have known we were coming."

This is strange language for a physicist—to speak as though the universe itself were a quasi-intelligent being that could foresee the future and plan ahead.

And it just shows that those who reject Christian truth often come up with explanations that require even more faith than the Bible does.

May 1, 1992

A Christian and a Scientist
Bringing the Gospel to Eastern Europe

When the walls came tumbling down all across Eastern Europe, people in those countries begged Westerners to come in and share their ideas. One of the first Christians to respond was a scientist named Charles Thaxton.

Thaxton is co-author of a book on the origin of life, entitled *The Mystery of Life's Origin*. At the core of life is the DNA molecule—a twisted strand of chemicals that functions like a coded message. DNA is the command center of the cell; it tells each part how to function.

The tiny molecule packs in as much information as all the volumes in a typical library.

According to evolutionists, life originated when chemicals floating in a pool of water linked up to form the first DNA molecule. But Thaxton argues it couldn't have happened that way. To begin with, there is no laboratory evidence that something as complex as the DNA molecule could form by itself—with all the right chemicals linking up in just the right pattern.

What's more, the theory doesn't make sense logically. Consider: DNA is a message. Do chemicals have the power to write messages?

As an illustration, let's say we walk into a classroom and find the words "Chuck Colson, call your wife" written on the chalkboard. You ask me how it got there. And I tell you the chalk itself wrote the message—that the calcium carbonate in the chalk wrote the words.

You wouldn't accept an answer like that for a minute. After all, the information in the message is not contained in the chalk chemicals.

What if we wrote "Chuck Colson, call your wife" in ink instead of chalk? Would that change the meaning? How about finger paint? What if we took a stick and wrote it in the sand? We could even hire a skywriter to fly overhead and spell it out in smoke.

The message would remain the same no matter what material we used to write it. So the message cannot be located in the material itself. It is *imposed* on the material from outside.

When evolutionists say that the original DNA molecule formed when the right chemicals linked up, in essence they're saying the chemicals wrote the message. But that's exactly like saying the calcium carbonate wrote the notice on the blackboard. The truth, of course, is that the message was imposed on the calcium carbonate by the same person.

Everyday experience tells us a message can only be created by person, a mind. By analogy, the DNA code could only have been created by a powerful mind—what we Christians call God.

This is the argument Charles Thaxton presents to scientists when he travels through Eastern Europe. Everywhere he is met with open astonishment, because the standard evolutionary theory on the origin of life *came* from the Soviet Union.

Charles Darwin had speculated that life began in what he called "some warm little pond," but the first scientific theory specifying how it might have happened was devised by a Soviet scientist named Oparin.

Oparin's underlying motive was to promote communism. Communism rests on atheism—and for atheism to be persuasive, it has to give a complete and consistent world-view. For decades, communist propaganda used Oparin's theory to persuade people that atheism can explain everything—that we don't need God to explain life or anything else.

Today Eastern Europeans are hungry for alternatives to the atheism they were force-fed so long. They are amazed to hear Thaxton say that science itself points to God.

In Rumania, a university professor followed Thaxton back to his hotel room. With tears in his eyes the professor said, "It's a miracle. Never before have I seen a Christian and a scientist in one body."

The heavens do indeed declare the glory of God—and so does the tiny DNA molecule.

September 24, 1991

Give a Hand
The Origin of Life

Scientists have come up with a new explanation of birth defects. And it also has dramatic implications for theories about the origin of life.

Remember the Thalidomide tragedy? In the 1950s, this synthetic drug was prescribed as a sedative for pregnant women. It caused hundreds of children to be born with birth defects. A recent report in the *New York Times* says chemists think they've finally figured out why it happened.

Molecules come in two forms that are mirror images of each other, just as your right and left hand are mirror images. Scientists even call the two forms right- and left-handed. But the cells in your body can use only *one* form of each molecule. The wrong form doesn't fit the cell's metabolism—just as a right hand doesn't fit into a left glove.

What's worse, the wrong form of molecule sometimes acts as a poison that damages or kills the cell.

Scientists believe this is the key to many birth defects. When drugs are synthesized in the laboratory, nature has no way to discriminate between the two forms of molecule. As a result, what scientists end up with in their test tubes is a fifty-fifty mixture of right- and left-handed molecules.

The two can be separated, but the process is complex and expensive. So when you take a synthetic drug, most of the time you are taking both forms of the molecule. Since your body can only use one, it simply eliminates the alternate form.

But in some cases the second form is harmful. In the case of Thalidomide, chemists now believe one form of the molecule acted as a sedative, while the other caused the birth defects.

This is important news for the field of medicine—but think what it also means for the origin of life.

Scientists have tried for decades to prove that life began in a chemical soup. There was a big hoopla about forty years ago, when scientists first succeeded in producing amino acids, the building blocks of proteins.

It was hailed as compelling evidence for evolution.

But that early excitement has died down. And one reason is this thorny problem of right- and left-handed molecules. Synthesized amino acids have the same results as synthesized drugs: fifty-fifty mixtures of right- and left-handed molecules. Nature doesn't discriminate between the two when it makes amino acids.

But life can only use one form. The amino acids in proteins, for example, are all left-handed. A protein may consist of thousands of amino acids strung together—and *every one* has to be left-handed, or the protein will not function.

What this means is that nature cannot produce a protein. It can produce only fifty-fifty mixtures of amino acids—which are as useless for life as no amino acids at all. The origin-of-life experiments to date do nothing to prove that life could have evolved by natural processes.

Now, as I said earlier, there are *artificial* means of separating right- and left-handed molecules. But they are highly complex and represent the application of considerable scientific intelligence and expertise. So what the experiments really prove is that the creation of life requires intelligence and expertise.

Despite all the hoopla about proving evolution, origin-of-life experiments actually provide experimental evidence that the first appearance of life on this planet required an intelligent agent—which is just what Christians have always believed.

Remember, we're not even talking about anything very complicated here—not DNA or protoplasm or cell walls. We're talking about the simplest, most fundamental step in the reconstruction of life's origin. Even at this basic level, living things show an order, a selectivity, that comes only from intelligence and design.

The tiny right- and left-handed molecules have become one more voice in a crescendo of solid scientific evidence that this world came from the hand of God.

July 1, 1992

The New Neanderthal
Changing Views of Human Evolution

In a campaign speech former President Ronald Reagan once dared to say he harbored "doubts" about evolution. Immediately, the American Association for the Advancement of Science went apoplectic. It insisted that the 100 million fossils in the world's museums constitute "100 million facts that prove evolution beyond any doubt whatever."

Whoa, steady there. A fossil is just a piece of bone. It doesn't tell us where it came from or how it got there. Those things are matters of interpretation.

And even scientists disagree on interpreting the evidence.

For example, in recent months, major newspapers and magazines have carried serveral articles on the Neanderthals. The standard theory of evolution places Neanderthals as an intermediate step between humans and apelike ancestors. How many of us remember as children seeing full-color illustrations of "Neanderthal Man," stooped over and hairy?

Those pictures probably did more to persuade people of evolution than any purely scientific evidence ever did.

But today the status of the Neanderthals is being hotly debated. A group of geneticists have proposed that Neanderthals and humans evolved separately. In this theory, early humans arose relatively recently in Africa and then migrated across the globe, wiping out less-developed forms like the Neanderthals.

This debate is still raging among scientists. And the lesson for all of us is that confident words about evolution being proved "beyond any doubt whatever" are sheer bluster.

The fact is, this isn't the first time scientists have debated the Neanderthals. The standard picture of Neanderthals as shuffling, apelike creatures came from the work of a famous anthropologist around the turn of the century.

But fossils discovered later didn't show the same apelike characteristics. To solve the puzzle, in the 1950s two scientists reexamined the original fossil. They discovered it was from an old man who suffered from bone disease.

Healthy Neanderthals, it turns out, walked as upright as you and I.

A newspaper headline at the time announced "Neanderthal Man Straightens Up!" The Field Museum of Natural History in Chicago had to rework its wax models. The display had shown a mother and father Neanderthal and two kids—all hunched over. The models were redesigned to stand up straight.

Regardless of the conflicting interpretations scientists give to the origin of Neanderthals, today most agree that the Neanderthals were not much different from human beings. Their brains actually measured larger than our own. Recent research on their bone structure shows they could speak. Their culture was identical to that of early humans.

Neanderthals did have a distinctive skeletal structure, with thick bones and heavy jaws. But that's easily explained as a result of genetic variation. In *Genesis and Early Man,* Arthur Custance notes that within historical times Eskimos have undergone a similar change toward thicker skeletons as a genetic response to living in a harsh environment.

So take away the extra hair and the thick lips painted on by artists, and the Neanderthals were just another race of human beings.

Christians need never be intimidated by dogmatic pronouncements that science proves this or science proves that. Many of the accepted theories in science were shaped by a bias against religion—like the original picture of the Neanderthals. But over time, as more data come in, those theories often change.

If we are patient, we will always find that there is no final conflict between science and Scripture.

July 9, 1992

Origin of the Specious
Darwin on Trial

Several months ago, a small but prestigious group of scientists met privately on an Ivy League campus. Their agenda: to discuss the manuscript of a new book critiquing evolution.

And to set the author straight.

The author is a Berkeley law professor named Phillip Johnson. The theme of his book is that Darwinism is really philosophy dressed up in scientific garb. Underlying all the talk about genes and mutations is the philosophy of naturalism—the belief that there is no supernatural, that nature is all that exists.

Of course, Darwinism is presented as pure science. But Johnson invites us to ask what's *behind* the theory. How do scientists *know* natural selection can explain the origin of all life's structures?

Do they know because they've seen it happen? No, says Johnson—not in breeding experiments and not in the laboratory. For example, using radiation, geneticists can make fruit flies grow crumpled wings or deformed bodies. But they can't make them change into a new kind of insect—or even grow a new organ.

Then, perhaps, scientists can construct a *hypothetical* course for evolution? No, again, says Johnson.

Take the origin of wings. What possible steps could turn a foreleg into a wing? Shortly after starting to evolve, the limb would no longer function as a leg. But it would not yet function as a wing either. The poor creature could neither run nor fly.

Any animal unfortunate enough to evolve very much at all would simply die out.

Well, then, is evolution confirmed by the fossil record? There least of all, says Johnson.

Darwin's theory says we should find a continuous chain of fossils linking one life form to the next. But what we actually find is just the opposite. New creatures appear fully formed, without any intermediary links leading up to them.

The truth is that the scientific evidence contradicts Darwinism across the board. The central reason many scientists still hold the theory, says Johnson, is that they are committed to the philosophy of naturalism.

The scientist who believes nature is all there is simply has no other option. He *has* to find some purely natural process to produce complex life forms out of simpler starting materials.

He has to accept Darwinism.

So, you see, the deck is stacked. The scientist who believes in naturalism is biased in favor of Darwinism even before he examines the evidence.

If you'd like to read Phillip Johnson's arguments for yourself, his work is no longer just a manuscript passed around on university campuses. It was recently published as a book under the title *Darwin on Trial.*

Johnson writes that he became interested in the subject when he noticed that evolution has always had a religious dimension: From the days of Darwin, it has been advanced by people interested in undermining the Christian faith.

Many scientists see evolution as the key weapon in a war against religion—or, as they would say, against superstition and myth.

So Christians don't need to question their faith just because someone confidently claims that evolution is scientifically proven. That's not true, as Johnson has shown.

But we should also remember that ultimately, as Ephesians tells us, the battles we face are spiritual. Not against scientific theories but against principalities and powers, against spiritual forces in high places.

April 22, 1992

Can This Fish Be Saved?
The Environmentalists vs. the Dams

In recent years the Northwestern United States has been racked by environmental controversies, which show no sign of becoming extinct. One of the fiercest debates raging today is over the Columbia River system and the sockeye salmon.

And in that controversy we get a glimpse of two conflicting forms of humanism at war in our culture.

The young sockeye salmon have been making their way downriver from their spawning grounds to the sea every spring for millennia. But today the Columbia River and its tributaries have been harnessed by a string of hydroelectric dams. The reservoir pools slow the salmon down, and thousands perish before they reach the sea.

What can be done to save the salmon?

On one side of this controversy are businesses and industries that depend on the dams, from hydroelectric plants to barge companies to farmers who use the water for irrigation. They don't want any tampering with the dams because that would hurt their industries.

To accommodate their concerns, authorities have built waterways for the salmon alongside several of the dams.

On the other side are environmentalists, who insist the waterways are not enough. The only way to save the salmon, they argue, is to lower the water in the reservoir pools behind the dams in the spring, which would increase the speed of the current and wash the salmon out to sea.

To accommodate *their* concerns, authorities tried lowering the water level in several dams. But the results were disastrous. The retreating water left behind great piles of fish to perish in the mud—exactly what the environmentalists were trying to avoid.

What we're seeing acted out in the Columbia River controversy is a battle between an optimistic and a pessimistic form of humanism—both of them hopelessly inadequate.

Humanism is a philosophy that exalts the ability of human reason to solve our problems apart from God. It started out as an optimistic philosophy. The Industrial Revolution persuaded many people that science and technology would conquer nature and make it serve human needs.

Biologist David Ehrenfeld labels this the "arrogance of humanism": It ascribes godlike qualities to human reason, promising to give us the ability to control our own destiny.

But today that claim is starting to ring hollow. It is becoming painfully clear that we cannot control all the consequences of our actions.

Consider: When Henry Ford produced the first cheap automobile, he had no idea what kind of pollution cars would one day create. When Einstein calculated $E = mc^2$ he never dreamed what would happen to Hiroshima. And when engineers dammed the Columbia River, they never intended to wipe out a species of salmon.

Control our own destiny? It's turning out to be an empty boast.

But that doesn't mean we should rush to embrace environmentalism. It is merely the flip side of humanism—the pessimistic side. For the tree huggers and salmon savers still seem to think human reason can save the planet. And their policies have equally unforeseen consequences: in this case, great stinking piles of desiccated fish.

The lesson is clear: Humanism in any form is not only arrogant but mistaken. We are *not* God and we cannot control all the variables—or even foresee them.

The solution to our environmental problems must be found elsewhere: in the biblical teaching that God made human beings to be stewards over creation. That means that God intended us to develop the potential in creation through industry and technology. But it also means creation is not ours to misuse for our own purposes. We are responsible to someone higher than ourselves for how we treat creation.

In today's clash between two forms of humanism, Christians can offer a balanced alternative.

April 29, 1992

Politically Correct Barbie
The Language of Animal Rights

Have you seen the new Barbie doll? She carries a panda bear, and tiny giraffe earrings dangle from her ears.

It's Barbie as an animal-rights crusader.

Support for animal rights has become trendy. But in some cases it borders on fanaticism. Activists want to outlaw zoos and pet shops. They vandalize laboratories where animal research is conducted. They kidnap animals, demolish equipment, and torch labs.

These are extreme tactics—and they signal a fervid, even religious, commitment to the cause.

Some people think animal-rights activists are just sensitive people who love animals. And no doubt some of them are. But the extreme measures tell us there is also something much deeper: a commitment to an underlying world-view.

The basic assumption behind much of the animal-rights movement is that nature is all there is, that there is no God. The philosophical label for this is naturalism. In naturalism, humans are not unique: We are just another part of nature, along with birds and bears and polliwogs.

As one animal-rights leader put it, "In the scheme of life, we're all equal."

Of course, naturalism is nothing new. It's been the reigning orthodoxy in biology ever since Darwin. Animal-rights activists are just saying, Let's be consistent: If humans are really no different from the birds and the beasts, what gives us the right to control nature for our own ends?

One of the movement's most popular slogans is, "A rat is a pig is a dog is a boy."

What that means was spelled out graphically in a recent ad by a group called People for the Ethical Treatment of Animals. The ad compared the slaughter of cows and chickens for food to the multiple murders committed by Jeffrey Dahmer—as if killing animals and killing humans were morally equivalent.

What people consider "moral" depends on their philosophy. The biblical world-view starts out with the existence of God. It teaches that humans are unique, created in the image of God to be stewards over the rest of creation.

This basic biblical insight is confirmed daily by common experience. Modern technology proves that humans are unique: that they have a power over nature—for good or for ill—that no other creature has.

Our calling, of course, is to use this power for good. The earth doesn't belong to us; it belongs to the Lord, who made it. We are stewards, accountable to God for everything we do.

Historically, Christians have often crusaded to treat animals humanely. Saint Francis of Assisi is the best-known example, living his simple life among the creatures he loved. In the 1800s, one of my heroes in the faith, William Wilberforce, took a public stand against cruelty to animals. Not in the name of animal rights but in the name of stewardship.

This difference in words signals a vast difference in worldview. The animal-rights movement is not just about being kind to animals. It's about a radically naturalistic world-view that denies any special status to humans.

Animal rights may sound appealing because it promises a naturalistic utopia—a future when we will live in harmony with nature, when the lion will lie down with the lamb.

But this is a secular substitute for heaven—a secular second coming. Not when Christ comes down to earth, but when humanity comes down to the level of the animals.

March 27, 1992

Carl Sagan's Got Religion
The Use and Misuse of Biblical Language

Do you remember the immensely popular television series "Cosmos," hosted by astronomer Carl Sagan? Sagan wasn't just a scientist, he was an evangelist. His religion was the worship of the universe itself—the Cosmos, which he spelled with a capital *C*. His most famous line was, "The Cosmos is all there is, or was, or ever shall be."

But now, Sagan says, he wants to join hands with Evangelical Christians. In a recent issue of *Parade* magazine, he calls on Christians to work with scientists on environmental issues.

Up until now, Sagan has never shown any regard for Christianity. In one of his books he mocks the biblical conception of God, describing Him as "an outsized, light-skinned male with a long white beard, sitting on a throne somewhere up in the sky."

But now Sagan seems to have had a change of heart. He piously speaks of the biblical teaching that "the natural world is a creation of God, . . . deserving respect and care." He throws around Christian words like "stewardship."

Apparently, when it suits his own purposes, Sagan finds it easy to mouth the biblical language.

In his books Sagan has often argued that Darwin's theory of natural selection makes God unnecessary. He says we evolved from the Cosmos, and it is our only home.

But now Sagan makes free use of biblical imagery. In the *Parade* article, he talks about seeing ourselves as tenants on Earth, caretakers accountable to "the Landlord."

In his books Sagan has preached that our planet will be saved by more advanced life forms. He is part of a group of scientists devoted to searching for radio messages from extra-terrestrial intelligences. He writes that "the receipt of a single message from space" is all it would take to help us overcome our problems, from war to pollution.

But these days, Sagan isn't talking so much about extrater-restrials coming to our rescue. Instead, he's trying to harness the forces of religious faith here on earth. In the *Parade* article he describes several international conferences drawing to-gether rabbis, priests, Hindus, Buddhists, Native Americans, and Evangelical Protestants.

Sagan is not convinced that any of these religions is *true.* But he does recognize that religion has, as he puts it, "a pow-erful influence" on people—an influence he wants to channel to his own purposes.

What Sagan writes about Christian stewardship is biblical, of course. The Bible does teach that we are caretakers of cre-ation, accountable to its Creator.

But what I find galling is Sagan's cynical turnabout. Having attacked and mocked religion all these years, he now wants to coopt religious groups for the sake of his own goals.

I have nothing against working together with secular groups on common goals like protecting the environment. But let's do so with our eyes open. The danger is that when people like Sagan use conciliatory language, we may forget that they still hold a world-view that is absolutely hostile to our own.

A wolf is a wolf even when he comes in sheep's clothing.

Christian groups that decide to work with Carl Sagan need to remember that his previous record reveals nothing but contempt for the things we hold most sacred.

March 20, 1992

Building Paradise
An Unscientific Experiment

Several months ago in the Arizona desert, eight people in red jumpsuits stepped into another world—a huge, futuristic greenhouse where they've vowed to live for the next two years, cut off from the rest of the world. Funded by Texas billionaire Ed Bass, the project is called Biosphere 2, and it's touted as a great scientific demonstration of how humans will colonize other planets.

But if you look closely, you'll find a lot less science in the project than religion.

The huge greenhouse of Biosphere 2 is designed as a miniature Earth. It is supposed to be a closed, self-sustaining ecosystem, with its own rain forest, savanna, desert, and even a small ocean. Its inhabitants are supposed to grow their own food and breathe the oxygen given off by the plants.

Only weeks after its initiation, however, word leaked out that the greenhouse wasn't a closed system after all. For example, instead of growing all their own food, the Biosphere group had stored up several months' worth of food ahead of time. And the supposedly balanced ecosystem ended up being off balance, so that fresh air had to be pumped in from outside.

Various scientists associated with Biosphere 2 have recently *dis*associated themselves, saying there's been too much fudging for the project to qualify as truly scientific.

But that hasn't deterred the participants. Because as I said, their motivation isn't so much scientific as religious. Biosphere 2 is the outgrowth of a philosophy concocted years ago in a countercultural commune of the 1970s. The leader of that commune used to preach that Western civilization is dead, that the world is coming to an end, and that an elite group of people would flee to Mars, where they would evolve into a superior race. The commune eventually disbanded, but many of the members stayed together. They have now made a reappearance as the core group in Biosphere 2.

They have even revived the commune's doomsday philosophy, disseminating it through literature available to tourists who visit the project. You can now read all about the elite group destined to colonize Mars, living in structures similar to Biosphere 2.

From their literature, it appears that the former commune members see themselves as a key link in a vast cosmological saga that began with the Big Bang, went on to the evolution of the planets, the emergence of life, and is now about to take a giant leap forward in the evolution of a race of intelligent superhumans.

As one of their books puts it, the Biosphere group is part of a new race who will "transform themselves from localized planetary lifespans to cosmic immortality."

Human beings evolving to cosmic immortality? This is not science, it's religion. In fact, it has the ring of Satan's promise so long ago in the Garden of Eden: "You shall be as gods."

It's the ancient temptation dressed up in modern scientific trappings.

The media are treating Biosphere 2 as a tourist bonanza, with its flashy greenhouse windows and space-age jumpsuits. But the message it teaches to anyone who picks up the literature is a philosophy of cosmic humanism: that evolution will soon produce a race of immortals, "citizens of the world of science."

Well, thanks anyway, but I'm already a citizen of a heavenly city. And that heavenly city is going to be a lot better place to spend eternity than any green glass box on the planet Mars.

May 14, 1992

The End of Ideology?
South Africa and Social Darwinism

Last month apartheid in South Africa was put to the vote—and lost. In a national referendum, an overwhelming 70 percent of whites voted to continue the reforms of President F. W. de Klerk.

And with that vote, the death knell may well have sounded for yet another twentieth-century experiment in social engineering. Within this century we have witnessed the rise and fall of Nazism and communism. Now we may be witnessing the fall of apartheid. What many people don't realize is that these three political systems are kin to one another.

As historian Paul Johnson explains, Nazism, communism, and apartheid were all derived from a philosophy called Social Darwinism, which itself was derived from the theory of evolution pioneered by Charles Darwin. His famous book, *The Origin of Species*, was subtitled *The Preservation of Favored Races in the Struggle for Life.*

Social scientists were quick to pick up those phrases—"favored races," "struggle for life"—and apply them to human beings. What emerged was Social Darwinism, which sees human societies in endless competition for evolutionary advantage.

The Nazis located that competition between races, with the Aryans as the superior race. For communism, the competition was between economic classes, with the proletariat as the ultimate winner. For apartheid, the competition was between whites and blacks, with whites on top.

All three political philosophies have led to brutal repression. We all know about the gas chambers of the Nazis and the prison camps of the communists. And anyone who reads firsthand accounts of life in a South African township—like the book *Kaffir Boy*—will recognize essentially the same ideology at work.

Until de Klerk began his reforms, there was nearly absolute control of the black population through work permits, residence permits, and internal passes. Nighttime raids carted adults off to work in prison camps and left their families to beg or starve.

It is a tribute to the people of South Africa that they have finally voted to right these terrible wrongs. But while we rejoice, the country has to be careful that it doesn't reel backward from one totalitarian ideology and fall right into another—namely, communism.

The leading black organization that hopes to gain power when apartheid falls is the African National Congress, which includes a powerful communist element. And it shows no willingness to lay down its ideological arms—or its fighting arms, either.

The goal of the ANC seems to be to turn South Africa into a one-party, communist state, similar to many of the surrounding nations that champion so-called African Socialism. Ironically, as Paul Johnson shows, many of these nations use exactly the same methods of social engineering that South Africa uses—work permits, internal passes, and prison work camps.

If anyone needed evidence that communism and apartheid are offshoots from the same root, there it is.

It is sobering to realize that some of the worst horrors of the twentieth century—the brutalities committed in the name of Nazism, communism, and apartheid—all have their roots in a profoundly anti-Christian philosophy: in Social Darwinism.

The lesson is that science is no ivory-tower pursuit. It profoundly affects the way we see ourselves and our societies. Scientific theories often spill over into sociology and political theory.

And when scientists turn away from God, that has profound effects not only on science but also on all our politics and history.

As philosopher Richard Weaver said, "Ideas have consequences."

April 28, 1992

Friend or Foe?
Religious Roots of Science

Are science and Christianity mortal enemies?

Many people think so. They point to the classic controversies over questions like: Did humans evolve? How old is the earth? Are there miracles?

There are even people who think science disproves Christianity.

Well, there's a simple answer you can give these people: Tell them that without Christianity, we wouldn't even *have* science.

The case was made in a recent article in a journal called *First Things*. If you think back, most of the early scientists were Christians: Copernicus, Kepler, Galileo, Newton, Pascal. They believed the world had an orderly structure that could be scientifically studied, because it was created by an orderly God.

This alliance between faith and reason endured for more than three hundred years. It was only about a century ago that a new slant crept into the history books. People who wanted to discredit Christianity began to write books that pictured faith and science as enemies locked in mortal combat. The most influential was Andrew Dickson White's book, *A History of the Warfare of Science with Theology*.

The warfare image is one we've all grown up with.

But in recent years, there has been a remarkable reversal among historians of science. The more they study the historical record, the clearer it becomes that science could never have developed were it not for Christianity.

For example, Loren Eiseley, a well-known science writer, says that many civilizations developed great technical expertise—Egypt with its pyramids, Rome with its aqueducts—but only one produced the experimental method we call science. That civilization was Europe at the end of the Middle Ages—a culture steeped in Christian faith.

The reason science developed within a Christian civilization, says Eiseley, is the biblical teaching of a rational God. In his own words, "Experimental science began its discoveries . . . in the faith . . . that it was dealing with a rational universe controlled by a Creator who did not act upon whim."

In fact, the very idea that there are "laws" in nature is not found in any other culture. Science historian A. R. Hall says that the idea comes from "the Hebraic and Christian belief in a deity who was at once Creator and Lawgiver."

And sociologist R. K. Merton, in his famous thesis, says modern science owes its existence to the Christian notion of moral obligation. Since God made the world, Christians taught, it is not to be despised. Instead, we are under an obligation to study it and use it to the glory of God and the benefit of mankind.

The interesting thing is that the scholars I just quoted are not Christians. Yet what they are expressing is a new consensus among historians that Christian faith actually propelled the development of modern science.

So the next time you get into a discussion about whether science disproves the Bible, remind your friends that without the Bible, science wouldn't even exist.

It's true that God Himself can't be put in a test tube or studied under a microscope. But it is God who created and sustains the natural laws that scientists appeal to in their theories.

Scientists who reject Christian faith are actually cutting off the branch on which they're sitting.

June 3, 1992

10

Pressing the Hot Buttons

Window on the Womb
Seeing Is Believing

"Informed consent." It means explaining how an operation is performed and what its risks are. It means treating the patient as a free and responsible agent.

It's a way of maintaining the patient's dignity in medical care.

The most frequently performed operation in America today is abortion. Yet, strangely, some people are opposed to applying informed consent to abortion. Abortion activists have even lobbied to strike down informed-consent laws.

This is a sharp departure from the classical liberal tradition of treating the individual as a responsible agent. Why are abortion activists so *illiberal* on this issue?

Informed consent in abortion would mean telling mothers and fathers the basic facts of pregnancy and fetal development before they decide whether to get an abortion. Why shouldn't they benefit from the most up-to-date medical facts like any other patient does?

For centuries, the growth of a child in its mother's womb was shrouded in mystery. But today medical technology has opened a window on the womb. One of the most exciting forms of technology is ultrasound. Using reflections of sound waves, ultrasound projects a moving picture of the baby wiggling and waving its arms inside the mother's uterus.

Ultrasound has revealed that babies in the womb are much more aware of the outside world than anyone had previously imagined. If a bright light is placed near the mother's abdomen, the baby inside is startled and turns away. But if a soft light is used, the baby is attracted and turns toward it.

A loud buzzer will make the baby jump. But if a soft rattle is shaken, the baby takes its thumb out of its mouth and looks in the direction of the sound. A baby in the womb even learns to recognize the voice of its own mother.

Ultrasound makes a fetus seem more human. In fact, the word *fetus* no longer seems fitting once you've seen a movie of that moving, responding little person. "Fetus" sounds too technical, too abstract.

We instinctively call it *baby*.

That's why abortion activists are adamantly opposed to informed consent. The practice of abortion depends on *dehumanizing* the fetus. It's just a pile of cells, we're told. Just fetal matter.

But the fetus revealed by ultrasound is emphatically human.

What happens when a mother and father see ultrasound movies of their baby? Let me tell you a true story. A young woman—I'll call her Brenda—discovered she was pregnant. The pregnancy was unplanned, and when Brenda announced it at the office, she was noticeably glum.

But a few weeks later, Brenda came bouncing into the office full of excitement. In her hand were ultrasound photos. Proudly she passed the photos around among her co-workers. "Do you want to see my baby?" she asked. "Look how big she is."

Seeing her baby on ultrasound helped Brenda begin bonding with her baby even before birth.

Debates have raged in Congress over whether clinics should counsel mothers about abortion. I say *let* them give the facts about abortion. But let them give *all* the facts.

Let clinics give mothers the most up-to-date information revealed by ultrasound—how babies respond to light, to sound, even to the sound of their mothers' voices.

In fact, I have an idea. Why don't we *require* that every mother who visits a clinic see an ultrasound of her baby before she decides to have an abortion?

I wonder: How many would have the heart to carry it through?

June 1, 1992

Selling Abortion
How Abortion Clinics Market Their Services

Last May, the Supreme Court banned the use of federal money for abortion counseling. "An assault on free speech," abortion activists howled. How can women make "informed decisions?" they fumed.

Let's look at this sudden passion among pro-abortionists for informed decisions. Because if there's one thing abortion clinics *don't* encourage, it's informed decisions.

In a survey of women who had abortions, some 90 percent said the counseling they received gave few facts and was heavily biased in favor of abortion.

Take Kathy Walker; her story is not unusual. Kathy became pregnant when she was thirteen. Her parents took her to a Planned Parenthood clinic where abortion was presented as the only viable option. The doctor even warned Kathy in ominous tones that if she kept the baby, she'd end up a perpetual welfare mother.

Well, Kathy "chose" an abortion—but it could hardly be called an informed choice.

The truth is that abortion has become an industry. And what passes as abortion "counseling" is really marketing.

Carol Everett, who once owned and operated four lucrative abortion clinics, tells how the system works from the inside. If a girl decides to carry her baby to term, Carol explains, clinics don't make any money. They make money only if she gets an abortion.

So, inevitably, clinics put pressure on women to abort.

It starts with the first phone call. Nita Whitten, who once worked in an abortion clinic, says she was trained by a professional marketing firm in how to sell abortion over the phone. When a girl calls, Nita says, the object is not to help her; it's to "hook the sale."

The main tactic is fear. The phone operator asks the girl how late her period is and then tells her, "You're pregnant." Not "You might be pregnant," but "You *are* pregnant."

Once the girl comes in, the tactic is to present abortion as the ideal solution. Is the girl afraid to tell her parents? "They don't need to know," she's told.

Is she worried about school? "An abortion will let you stay in school."

Is she afraid she can't get the money? "Baby food and diapers cost a whole lot more."

And *after* the girl undergoes an abortion, there's even a marketing strategy to turn her into a repeat customer: Give her free birth-control pills.

That's right. A girl on the pill is more likely to be sexually active. But since she's too young to remember to take her pills consistently, it's a sure bet she'll come back. Pregnant again.

As Carol Everett puts it, birth control sells abortions. So when you hear debates over funding of abortion counseling, put that word *counseling* in quotation marks. Because in an abortion clinic, women aren't counseled. They're manipulated, pressured, and hoodwinked into thinking they have no other choice.

Yes, abortion is a business. A big business. One that uses all the slickest tools of marketing and sales.

March 24, 1992

When Abortion Is Fatal
What Pro-Choicers Won't Tell Us

Pro-life demonstrators were picketing a Chicago abortion facility not long ago when a thirteen-year-old girl named

Deanna Bell arrived for her appointment. The demonstrators tried to persuade her to consider alternatives. But Deanna was adamant, and they watched her disappear into the facility.

They never saw her alive again.

A little later an ambulance roared up to the facility, lights blazing, sirens blaring. But it was too late. The ambulance left empty, and its place was taken by a police wagon. Moments later, police officers emerged from the clinic, carrying a stretcher with a still body wrapped from head to foot.

The next day the newspapers told the story: Deanna Bell was dead. During the abortion, some of the amniotic fluid surrounding the baby leaked into her bloodstream, causing sudden heart failure.

Abortion activists say they want to keep abortion safe and legal. Well, it *is* legal, but it's far from safe.

Deanna's story is not unique. For example, in a single year (1989), in a single suburb of Washington, D.C., three women died following legal abortions.

Erica was a sixteen-year-old girl who had an abortion without telling her parents. During the procedure her uterus was perforated, and she died on her way home.

Gladys was a twenty-eight-year-old woman who died when an abortionist failed to diagnose an ectopic pregnancy. She believed the abortion had been successful and didn't even know about her life-threatening condition until it was too late.

Debra was thirty-four years old when she went into cardiac arrest during an abortion. She was rushed to a hospital, but it was too late.

All three of these cases were reported in the newspapers and received wide publicity throughout the state of Maryland. Yet here's a strange fact: When the Centers for Disease Control reported abortion-related deaths for that year, it listed none for the state of Maryland.

In fact, for the entire country, the CDC listed only one confirmed death from abortion.

How come? How did officials overlook three known cases? There are several possible reasons. First, in most states abortion reporting is completely voluntary—which means the official data collected are just about worthless.

Second, autopsy reports often cover up the true cause of death. For example, when Erica died, the autopsy report listed her death as an accident.

And third, when a woman develops complications from an abortion, where does she seek medical help? From the abortionist? Not on your life. She goes to her regular doctor. As a result, abortion clinics rarely have to deal with their mistakes.

Before abortion was legalized, says Dr. Bernard Nathanson, a former abortionist, he and his colleagues used to exaggerate the number of deaths resulting from illegal abortions. Today it looks like abortion activists are covering up the number of deaths from *legal* abortions.

The case for abortion is based, from beginning to end, on lies and deceit.

So yes, abortion *is* safe—but not for the woman. It's safe only for the abortionist, who is never forced to confront his mistakes.

Even when his patient's life is at stake.

November 24, 1992

Squandering a Heritage
Pro-Life Feminism

This is the Year of the Woman we were told all during the last campaign. Yet the elections ended on a troubling note: All the women elected to the Senate and the House of Representatives this year are pro-choice.

Why should this be any surprise? you ask. Because at the state and local level, there are hundreds of women officeholders who are pro-life.

Why weren't any of them elected to national office?

The answer is simple: feminist fund-raising organizations like Emily's List and WISH List refuse to support pro-life candidates—even if they are feminist on all other issues.

Yes, there *are* women who are both pro-life and feminist. In fact, the pro-life position has a rich heritage within feminist history. The nineteenth-century feminists uniformly opposed abortion.

Susan B. Anthony, for example, once wrote, "I deplore the horrible crime of child murder." And Elizabeth Cady Stanton compared abortion to the oppression of women. "When we consider that women are often treated as property," she wrote, how can women turn around and "treat our children as property to be disposed of as we see fit?"

The early feminists didn't treat abortion as a purely women's issue, either. On the contrary, they held men responsible for most abortions—realizing that in many cases abortion is a desperate response to male abandonment.

Back then, abortion was generally sought by young women who had been seduced with promises of marriage—then callously dropped when they became pregnant. Even today, most abortions are sought by single women—often pressured by boyfriends who don't want to face the responsibilities of fatherhood.

This is what Susan B. Anthony had in mind when she wrote: "The woman is awfully guilty who commits the deed; but oh, thrice guilty is he who drove her to the desperation which impelled her to the crime."

The solution to abortion, Anthony felt, lies in stressing male responsibility. And here we see the starkest difference between traditional feminism and the contemporary version. Today's feminists take male irresponsibility as a given—as a fact of life that can't be changed. The underlying reasoning seems to be that since we can't trust men, the only solution is to take matters into our own hands: Childbearing and abortion shall henceforth be purely a woman's decision.

What a defeatist view this is.

The early feminists passionately believed they could *reform* men. Their goal was to encourage family formation: to change social mores so that every man would feel morally obligated to marry and support the mother of his children.

But modern feminists have given up on men. They're so sure the brunt of the responsibility for children is going to fall on them anyway that they angrily demand the right to make a unilateral decision from the start.

But, of course, that will only exacerbate the problem. Defining childbearing as purely a women's issue is guaranteed to erode men's sense of responsibility still further—leaving even more women in the lurch.

So the next time someone says pro-lifers just want to oppress women, tell them about Susan B. Anthony and about feminism's pro-life history.

What a shame modern feminists have lost that proud tradition.

December 4, 1992

Who Stands for Women?
Abortion and Sexual Harassment

Capitol Hill is reeling under the shock of sexual harassment charges brought against Oregon Senator Bob Packwood by several women lobbyists and office workers. The irony is that Senator Packwood has been a champion of the feminist agenda from the Equal Rights Amendment to abortion.

Feminist leaders are devastated by the charges. Several have appeared on television nearly in tears, asking how anyone with such a sterling record of respect for women's rights could display such crass *dis*respect for the women with whom he worked.

Several feminists have actually admitted they knew the senator had a reputation for harassing women. Why didn't any of them report it sooner? The answer is they covered up for him because they didn't want to discredit a political ally.

Mary Heffernan, director of a women's foundation in Oregon and one of Packwood's accusers, said, after all, "Abortion rights were on the line." She describes his behavior as a "deep violation of what he stands for"—a "severe contradiction" to his entire career.

But is it really such a contradiction? Stop and think for a moment. It's true that Packwood labored hard for abortion. But does support for abortion necessarily signal respect for women?

I hate to be the one to say it, but a man just might support abortion because it's to his *own* benefit. We'd have to be blind not to see that abortion lets a lot of men off the hook. It allows them to avoid unpleasant things like paternity suits, shotgun marriages, and child-support payments.

Anyone who has worked in a crisis pregnancy center has counseled women pressured into an abortion by a lover. Anyone who has picketed an abortion facility has seen weeping women hurried along by a boyfriend.

There's no way around it: Abortion should not be labeled a woman's right but a man's retreat—from responsibility.

In the past, if a man caused a pregnancy, he felt at least some responsibility to help support the child. But today there are men who feel positively noble if they put up a couple hundred bucks for an abortion.

If the woman doesn't accept his offer, well, then, the pregnancy is her own problem, not his. In his eyes, he's done his part.

So I make no judgment of Senator Packwood personally. But I urge you to take this opportunity to show people that the feminist assumption is simply unsound. When a man favors abortion, that does not necessarily mean he is concerned about women.

It could mean he is looking for a way to legitimize irresponsibility for men.

December 2, 1992

People Aren't the Problem
Why Abortionists Aren't Pro-Choice

A quiet knock sounded at the door of a small apartment in China—the home of a young Christian woman I'll call Ling Tao. It was her brother with bad news: His wife was pregnant.

Normally that would be good news. But in China the government restricts the number of children a couple may have. If the wife gets pregnant again, she's hauled off to a clinic and forced to submit to an abortion.

Currently, the legal limit in China is one child. Ling Tao's brother already had their one child. Now his wife was pregnant again, and he was afraid for the baby's life. "What shall we do?" he whispered.

As a Christian, Ling Tao knew exactly what to do. She persuaded her brother and his wife to continue the pregnancy. And she promised that if the government ever found out about the second child, she would take it and raise it herself.

And so quietly, bravely, three people took a stand for human life against a government that throws people out on the garbage heap like so many empty cans.

Thank God it doesn't happen in America.

At least, not today. But maybe tomorrow. America has an active and well-funded population control lobby. The prestigious magazine *Science*, published by the American Association for the Advancement of Science, has printed articles recommending coercive measures to control the population. Birth licenses so only selected adults can reproduce. Compulsory sterilization for those deemed unfit. Heavy taxation of couples with more than the legal number of children. Fertility-control drugs added to the water supplies.

All this puts a new light on the so-called pro-choice movements. Here in America, groups like the International Planned Parenthood Federation (IPPF) use *choice* as a slogan, only because it's come to mean a legal right to abortion. But in places like China they show their true colors. There IPPF supports forced sterilization and forced abortion.

The real goal is not choice. It's population control—no matter how coercive.

Many abortion promoters see people as the problem. They think the more people there are, the less there is to go around: less money, food, whatever. Each person gets a smaller slice of the pie.

But what they fail to understand is that a person is not just another mouth to feed. A person is also two hands and a mind—which he can use to bake a *new* pie to slice and share with others. Over an average lifetime, an individual actually produces more than he consumes.

In modern technology the creative input of human hands and minds has become even more important than what nature provides as raw resources. Take the silicon chip, for example. It's made out of sand. Common sand. What turns it into computer chips is an incredible amount of creative human energy.

No, humans aren't the problem. When God created Adam and Eve, *His* pronouncement on the human race was that it was "very good." And God's first recorded words to them in Genesis 1 was a command to "be fruitful and multiply and fill the earth." When God promised Abraham descendants as numerous as the stars in the sky, that was meant as a *blessing*.

So the solution to poverty and pollution is not restricting the number of children born; it's calling all people to become children of God—to respect and care for the world God created. A change not in population size but in the human heart.

And if that happens, Americans will never have to fear a quiet knock on the door.

July 20, 1992

A Beautiful Choice
Commercials for Life

Picture this: A Yuppie couple comes home from work and relaxes on the couch to watch a rerun of "thirtysomething." They're young and sophisticated, and what they see on the show reflects their own secular and politically correct worldview.

Then, during a commercial break, a vivid message breaks through with a completely different world-view. Schoolchildren laughing and tumbling down steps. A father helping his son tuck in his shirt. Tots in Halloween costumes.

"All these children have something in common," says an announcer. "All of them were unplanned pregnancies . . . that could have ended in abortion. But their parents toughed it out . . . and discovered that sometimes the best things in life aren't planned."

It's a commercial extolling *life*.

The commercial is one of two produced by the Arthur S. De Moss Foundation. The foundation says that its primary goal is not to change the law but to change people's minds.

And that's exactly what these commercials do. They are attractive and engaging. They counter the standard media portrayal of pro-lifers as fanatics and woman haters. The decision not to abort is presented as courageous and life affirming.

The De Moss Foundation has hit upon a crucial aspect of pro-life strategy. Many of us who are opposed to abortion have focused our energies on the legal side of the battle: passing laws that limit abortion or challenge *Roe v. Wade,* the 1973 ruling that legalized abortion.

These are worthy efforts. But winning the legal battle is a far cry from winning the war against abortion.

If the Supreme Court reverses *Roe v. Wade,* that will push the question back to the states, where it will be decided by the democratic process. Which is to say, by the people.

And that's where the ultimate battle lies: in the hearts and minds of people.

The De Moss commercials are an excellent model of how to win that battle. In a gentle, engaging style, they nudge people to reconsider how to respond to a problem pregnancy. They hold people up as admirable if they carry their babies to term. They remind the audience that there are millions of couples ready to offer a loving home for those babies.

The De Moss Foundation's decision to air these commercials during prime time is nothing short of brilliant. Right during "thirtysomething," no less, when the audience consists of just those middle-class, single women statistically most likely to abort.

No wonder pro-abortionists are howling.

Many pro-lifers have already started using the commercials in a wider context. They're recording them for use at pro-life counseling centers or to show their friends.

That's a good idea for all of us. Why don't you watch for these commercials and record them on videotape. Then invite some friends over who are undecided about abortion or who even favor it.

It may be a slow process, but remember: That's how the battle for people's hearts and minds is waged.

One person at a time.

May 8, 1992

Why Bother with Sex Ed?
Norplant for Teenagers

Medical science has just offered a way out for parents and educators who can't be bothered with training kids in moral character. It's called Norplant, a synthetic hormone implanted under the skin that prevents pregnancy for five years.

Public health professionals are heralding the implant as a great boon for the inner cities, where teen pregnancies are high. The Baltimore health commissioner is quoted as saying that the implant "will cover [girls] during their school years, which is what you want."

I beg your pardon, but I thought what we wanted during their school years was to *teach* them. Teach them citizenship, responsibility, and a high moral code. Teach them to take their lives and their choices seriously.

Norplant does just the opposite: It trivializes their sexual choices. Sexual relations are no longer weighted with moral significance, no longer dignified as the means of family formation, no longer anything but a form of recreation. Nevertheless, Norplant is being backed by several professional organizations, from Planned Parenthood to government family-planning programs. The Baltimore health commissioner has even put together a professional association called the Norplant Consortium, an alliance of public health

administrators, hospitals, private doctors, and local philan-
thropic foundations.

This should really come as no surprise. When you think
about it, most of the radical ideas that have gained a foothold
in our society have come in under impeccable professional
auspices.

Take abortion. As the late Francis Schaeffer pointed out,
the abortion movement has its most powerful allies in the
medical community.

Or take euthanasia. Doctor-assisted suicide is the brain-
child of, you guessed it, doctors.

Take value-free sex education, promoted by groups like
the Sex Information and Education Council of the United
States (SIECUS). SIECUS guidelines treat abortion as just another option and recommend that teachers tell kids homosexual relations can be "as fulfilling as heterosexual
relationships."

The SIECUS guidelines have been officially endorsed by
the Centers for Disease Control, the National School Board
Association, and the American Medical Association.

All impeccable professional organizations.

Remember the brave new world described by Aldous
Huxley in his famous novel? Huxley predicted that the government would give its citizens birth-control drugs to allow
them to enjoy completely unfettered sexuality. The idea was
to distract people through perpetual sexual excitement so the
state could control them.

When Huxley wrote his novel, this was regarded as a
frightening scenario. Today completely unfettered sexuality
is being promoted by the most respectable professional
groups.

Christians need to fight back by forming our own professional organizations. We can't afford to let our foes paint us as
uneducated reactionaries. Christians need to realize the power
of associations, titles, and letterhead stationery.

The Norplant Consortium is in Baltimore, but similar organizations will be coming to your community. So be ready: Let's

make it our goal to establish alternative professional groups that treat youngsters as real moral agents.

Not as pawns in a brave new world.

December 16, 1992

Reverend Death
Euthanasia Plays the Religion Card

Dr. Jack Kevorkian—the infamous "Dr. Death" with his suicide machine—recently had his medical license revoked. Comedian Jay Leno turned it into a joke. "A suicide doctor practicing without a license?" he quipped. "That's dangerous. Someone could get killed."

It's a grim joke because, of course, Dr. Death's whole purpose is to help people kill themselves. And unfortunately there's a growing movement to allow people like Dr. Death to operate.

Last November, Californians voted on a death-with-dignity initiative, which would have allowed doctors to help people take their lives. That initiative was defeated, but similar bills have been introduced in four other states.

To help the movement along, euthanasia activists are enlisting the aid of religion. The Reverend John Pridonoff, an ordained Congregational minister, was recently named executive director of the Hemlock Society, a major lobby group for legalized euthanasia. Pridonoff says euthanasia is okay because a loving God wouldn't want people to suffer.

Even the secular world finds this a little hard to swallow. A Christian minister advocating death? A local reporter asked Pridonoff how he justifies that. After all, the reporter asked, isn't suicide against the Bible?

It is, Pridonoff admitted. "But"—and these are his exact words—"there are a lot of things in the Bible we've grown beyond as a society."

Grown beyond? I guess the reverend thinks we're too enlightened to need the old biblical ethic of care and compassion anymore. The Hemlock Society wants to replace those outdated notions with sparkling new ideas like death with dignity and doctor-assisted suicide.

They make it sound so modern, as if death itself ought to be a matter of individual choice. But the hard fact is that *voluntary* euthanasia inevitably opens the door to *involuntary* euthanasia.

Just look at Holland, where euthanasia has been unofficially tolerated for several years. According to a 1991 report by the Dutch government, nearly half of all euthanasia cases are involuntary. Doctors make unilateral decisions about whose lives to terminate without ever talking to the patients or their families.

So much for individual choice.

The real travesty is the attempt by the Hemlock Society to coopt religion into supporting all this. The United States is still a strongly religious nation. More than 90 percent of Americans believe in God, and more than half attend religious services regularly. Euthanasia activists are well aware of this, and that's why they're playing the religious card by enlisting folks like Pridonoff in their cause.

They had their "Dr. Death"; now they have "Reverend Death."

Will people be taken in by this shameless appeal to religion? It's up to you and me to make sure they won't be. We need to explain to people why death-with-dignity bills are wrong—morally and biblically.

Expressing God's love means helping people *work out* their problems, not helping them escape their problems through suicide.

In God's eyes, every life is valuable, no matter how depressed or sick or handicapped the person may be.

And that life ought to be just as valuable in our eyes.

October 14, 1992

Just Let Him Die?
Deciding to Save Lives

Times were when you did something wrong and were dogged by guilt for years afterward. Well, I want to tell you about a time a doctor did something *right*—and was dogged by guilt for years afterward.

What he did was save a man's life.

The year was 1968, and Kenneth Swan was a young army surgeon, just arrived in Vietnam. When a nineteen-year-old soldier was brought in on a stretcher, Dr. Swan immediately got to work. The soldier had been blown up by a grenade, losing his eyesight and both his legs. Swan labored seven hours at the operating table to repair the injuries.

He was sharply criticized the next day by his fellow surgeons. For not doing a good job? No, for doing the job at all.

"That kid was so badly mangled," the other doctors told him, "you shouldn't have even bothered to treat him. He would have been better off dead."

Those words burrowed their way into Swan's mind, and for the next twenty years he wondered whether he had done the right thing. Had he condemned the soldier to a life of helplessness? Was the man rotting somewhere in a VA hospital, his body covered with bed sores, his mind destroyed by pain-killing drugs?

Finally, Swan decided to settle the question. He began a search for the soldier he had patched up so many years ago in a Vietnamese jungle. It took more than two years, but in the end he found him.

And *what* he found is nothing short of astonishing.

Yes, the man was blind and in a wheelchair. But he was not languishing in any hospital. He was married and has two daughters. He attended college, learned to scuba dive, and is now training to help others cope with debilitating injuries.

At the age of forty-three, the former soldier has a zest for life and a faith in God. When a reporter asked him about his success in life, he responded simply, "I give the credit to God."

What a testimony.

The debate between Swan and his colleagues twenty years ago is still being waged in the medical community. Swan is of the old school. He says, "I was taught to *treat* the wounded—not leave them to die."

His colleagues represent a new philosophy. They practice selective medicine—weeding out the wounded who, they decide, do not have a life worth living.

It's an attitude that dogged even the soldier whose life Swan saved. When he flew back to the United States for rehabilitation, medical workers acted as if his case were hopeless. He overheard one doctor ask, "Why did they let this guy live?"

Swan knows now that he did the right thing in letting this guy live. And the issue that confronted the doctors on the battlefields of Vietnam still confronts doctors in the hospitals and clinics of America today. Advocates of abortion and euthanasia are urging doctors to weed out the infirm and the handicapped.

We can only hope the story of the young soldier blown up in Vietnam will stand as a powerful lesson to medical workers that all life should be treated as a gift from God.

And let's hope the Dr. Swans of this world will never feel guilty again—for doing the right thing.

March 2, 1992

Gays in Combat
Why It Won't Work

President-elect Bill Clinton was hoping to roll into Washington under a full head of steam, but already he's hit a few rocks on the tracks. The first was a near mutiny over his plan to open the military to homosexuals.

Newsweek magazine found that public support for gays in uniform has dropped precipitously—from 59 percent in August 1992 to 48 percent in December. That's lower than it's been in fifteen years.

Why are the numbers dropping? The standard media line is that opponents are diehard bigots bent on discriminating against noble-minded gays who just want to serve their country. But keeping gays out of the military has nothing to do with being bigoted or hateful.

Those of us who follow Jesus know we are all sinners; we all fall short of the glory of God. Even though homosexuality is morally wrong, still the homosexual is my neighbor, and I am called to love him. For Christians, opposition to gays in the military should never stem from hostility toward individual homosexuals.

Yet there *is* a principled case to be made: a case that starts with a biblical view of the calling and function of government.

In Romans 13 we read that political authorities are established by God. Their purpose is to act as "God's servants," to "bear the sword . . . to bring punishment on wrongdoers."

In other words, the government has a divine mandate to protect its citizens from wrongdoers. That means the government maintains a police force as a defense against *internal* threats, to protect law-abiding citizens from criminals. And we have a military to counter *external* threats from other nations.

People like myself who have served in the military know how demanding this kind of work can be. It means living in extremely close quarters, sleeping and showering together. It means learning to act as a cohesive unit under grueling conditions. It means trusting your buddies enough to put your life on the line in combat.

When you throw sexual attraction into the equation, these intense relationships can become skewed. Any time there is what military people call "emotional favoritism," unit cohesiveness is broken. And when that happens on the battlefield, the bottom line is that people may get killed needlessly.

This is the heart of the issue. The purpose of the military is not primarily to advance anyone's career or to promote civil rights. It is to defend our nation in time of war.

Gay groups may label this discrimination, but so be it: The fact is that the military already discriminates against all sorts of folks—people who are too short or too heavy, people who can't see well enough, people with flat feet. The military should not have to accept *anyone* into the ranks who will compromise its ability to fulfill its function.

Its *God-given* function, Christians would say.

This is the case we should be presenting in the public arena. Restricting gays from military service is not a matter of bigotry.

We stand on a set of principles: We believe government is not merely a human institution to be tinkered with at will.

It is an institution with a divine mandate—and *that* gives a standard against which *every* policy should be judged.

December 3, 1992

Gays at Work
"Diversity" Training

Today when AT&T says, "Reach out and touch someone," you might wonder what kind of touching they have in mind. According to a recent article in *Fortune* magazine, AT&T is one of several American corporations that support homosexual rights in the workplace.

Only they don't call it gay rights; they call it "workplace diversity."

It typically begins with support groups for gay employees. Apple Computers and Digital Equipment were among the first whose gay employees came out of the closet to form support groups. Today some companies, like Xerox, maintain computer bulletin boards for gays and are listed by gay student groups as a good place to find work.

If they really want to show their support, corporations offer so-called diversity training, aimed at making heterosexuals more open to gay co-workers. AT&T, for example, gives workshops on homophobia—a term applied to any form of opposition to homosexuality, no matter how principled. At US West, all top managers have attended diversity programs.

Some companies even make these programs mandatory. At Pacific Gas & Electric, all employees are required to attend sensitivity workshops on diversity. And at Levi Strauss, managers are evaluated partly on the basis of their support for workplace diversity.

Which means if you're a Christian and believe homosexuality is morally wrong, you're going to have a hard time rising through the ranks.

But it isn't just Christians who are affected. Everyone is, at least indirectly—because these programs don't come free. At Levi Strauss, the bill for diversity education is in the millions of dollars.

That's a cost passed on to consumers in the form of higher prices.

Gay groups are also lobbying for employee benefits for their partners and, if they succeed, that's another cost that will be passed on to the public. Since the incidence of AIDS is so high among homosexuals, everyone will be forced to pay higher insurance premiums. Lotus Development recently became the largest corporation to offer homosexual partners the same benefits as husbands and wives.

Homosexuals in the top echelons of a company can even affect the way it donates money. In recent years, companies such as AT&T and American Express have donated thousands of dollars to the Gay Men's Health Crisis, which raises funds for AIDS research and for workshops on safe sex—like one entitled "Eroticizing Safer Sex" and another called "Men Meeting Men."

Fortune magazine defends the gay-rights movement within corporations. It claims that when gay people are openly welcome in the workplace, then they are more productive.

But this grossly misinterprets the roots of productivity. Productivity stems from a high moral character—self-control, self-discipline, delayed gratification. But these virtues are rejected by doctrinaire homosexuals. They want to be free to indulge any and every glandular impulse. And judging by the steep promiscuity rates reported among gays, they have little concern for self-control or self-discipline.

The workplace that promotes gay rights is promoting the very character traits that will destroy American business.

Real productivity is not a result of homophobia workshops and diversity training. It's a result of a sound moral character, inspired by a Christian work ethic.

June 8, 1992

Homosexuals and the Home
Is Marriage Anything Special?

The citizens of San Francisco are going to the polls to vote today whether to repeal a domestic partnership ordinance—an ordinance that allows homosexual couples to register with the city.

But the issues at stake go far beyond whether City Hall should keep a registry of homosexuals. They go to the heart of what kind of society America will become.

Domestic partnership laws extend various benefits to homosexuals—health benefits, joint tax returns, property and life insurance, inheritance and pension rights—all of which were previously limited to married couples.

What's more, domestic partnership laws are not limited to homosexuals. Any two people who wish to may register as domestic partners and gain the rights and privileges once reserved for those willing to make a marriage commitment.

San Francisco's domestic partnership ordinance passed last year partly because it was translated into Chinese as *"family partnership,"* which slipped it past the highly traditional Chinese immigrants who make up a third of the city's population.

But domestic partners are *not* families. And to equate them with families has the effect of stripping *real* families of their proper recognition, denying them a place of special importance in society.

Christians know marriage and family are part of God's structure for creation. But that spiritual truth must be expressed in culture, in economics, and in the law.

Traditionally, of course, marriage has always conferred a number of special benefits. It qualifies a couple for the rights and responsibilities of an ongoing sexual relationship. It is the route to having and raising children. It confers membership in a kinship network that provides financial and emotional support.

But what happens when the law no longer respects these traditional privileges of marriage? When the law grants them to unmarried people—to domestic partners?

To answer that question, all we have to do is look at Scandinavia. In Scandinavia, social mores no longer restrict sexual relations to marriage; any combination of people may live together without incurring social disapproval. Neither is childrearing restricted to marriage. Cheap, state-run nurseries enable anyone to raise a child regardless of marital status. And the wider kinship network has been replaced by an extensive welfare system that kicks in when there is a health crisis or personal crisis—things that used to bind people to their extended families.

The result of all this is that people in Scandinavia simply aren't getting married anymore. Why bother . . . if you can get the same benefits *without* the hard work and commitment? The majority of children in Scandinavia today are born to unmarried women, something happening in America only in the inner city.

And I've seen what that leads to. I was in Scandinavia last year, and it's not the happy place it's held up to be. Scandinavia struck me as cold, spiritually dry, and morally bankrupt. It has the highest suicide rate in the world.

This is a vivid illustration of the way law can affect society as a whole. Make no mistake about it: The law is a moral teacher, influencing people's attitudes and choices. Will American law continue to recognize marriage and family as deserving special status and respect? Or will it make these benefits available to anyone for the taking?

Let's hope the voters of San Francisco realize they are not voting on a single, isolated issue. They are voting today on the broad question of what sort of families America will have.

And what sort of society we will be.

November 5, 1991

Condoms on Campus
A "Right" to Be Bailed Out?

For Texans the Alamo signifies a historic test of courage. But at the University of Texas at Austin there has been another test of courage for the heirs of the Alamo heroes.

A test that some passed, while others failed pathetically.

It all started when medical surveys found that students at the university exhibit a higher-than-normal rate of HIV infection. Students panicked. The threat of AIDS seemed to loom over them.

They demanded that the administration *do* something.

The governing body of the university duly met and came up with a predictable solution: They would encourage safe sex by selling condoms in vending machines across the campus.

Now stop right there. Remember we're not talking about minor children here; we're talking about young adults. And the trouble they've run into—the threat of AIDS—stemmed from their own behavior.

But did they respond as mature people who realized they'd created a problem for themselves? Did they say, OK, let's take stock and see what we can do to change our behavior and solve this problem?

No, they went running to the administration and insisted that the university bail them out.

The students couldn't even be bothered to take the minor responsibility of going down to the corner drugstore to buy their condoms. No, they demanded condom vending machines right on campus.

So now students at the University of Texas can buy condoms alongside Snickers bars and Tootsie Rolls. They can buy them in the dormitories, the gymnasium, the libraries, and even the dean's office.

The importance of this story is that it is a microcosm of what's happening in our larger society. People are demanding the right to make any moral choices they like. And if their choices create any problems, why, they turn to the powers that be and demand to be bailed out.

The prevailing mentality is that people have a right to any lifestyle they choose—and still be as healthy and happy as those who live by principled moral standards.

Not all the faculty at the University of Texas concurred in the condom decision. A group of thirty-one professors petitioned the university council to reconsider. They wrote that students are "created in the image of God," capable of examining the consequences of their behavior and making intelligent choices.

The role of the university, these professors said, should be to challenge students to think, not just to capitulate to their demands.

But when the dissenting professors offered their petition to the university council, the student representatives on the council were incensed. How dare anyone stand up to their wishes? The students strode up to the podium—and lectured their professors. We have to face reality, they railed. "We cannot legislate morality at our university."

When the vote was taken, the students had won. No one is legislating *their* morality, that's for sure. Or even challenging them to think seriously about it.

By giving in to the students' demands, the university authorities sanctioned a mind-set that says everyone has a right to make bad moral choices and then demand that the rest of us rescue them from suffering any consequences.

Or even suffering a minor inconvenience.

The dissenting professors were right. This is a mind-set demeaning to people made in the image of God.

April 6, 1992

Truth and Love
A Christian Response to AIDS

Two years ago Sue Seel learned that her brother Richard was dying of AIDS.

Sue hadn't even known he was a homosexual. Deciding how to respond to Richard proved to be the biggest spiritual challenge she had ever faced.

The first time Sue flew to San Francisco to see Richard, he met her in a public place. He wouldn't even invite her into his home. Still, she continued to see him every few months, little by little learning what life is like in a gay subculture.

The homosexual communities of the 1990s are sad, sordid places, overcast by death and despair. Virtually everyone there has watched friends die from AIDS—and knows that eventually they will succumb to the disease as well.

One might expect people in such deep need to be ripe for the gospel. But Sue discovered an intense, pervasive hostility among homosexuals against the Christian faith. They know only too well that the Bible condemns "The Lifestyle," as they call it.

As Richard grew more and more ill, Sue was haunted by a decision she knew she would one day have to make. The day would come when Richard would be too sick to care for himself. What should she do when that happened?

Should she care for him in San Francisco? That would mean being separated from her husband and children. Or should she bring him to her own home?

Sue agonized over the question. If she did bring an AIDS patient into her home, how would her friends react? What would the neighbors say? Would her children be teased or ostracized? Sue sought the advice of Christian groups that work with AIDS patients. Finally, she and her family decided they would care for Richard in their home.

The day came when Sue flew her brother home from San Francisco. For Richard, it was a whole new world. Sue's two boys played on the floor around his bed and read stories to him at night. Neighborhood children came over to play. Church friends dropped by to welcome him and pray with him.

In the last few weeks of his life, Richard was surrounded by a living testimony of God's love. Before he died, he committed his life to the Lord. His favorite verse was, "in His presence there is fullness of joy"—words now etched on his gravestone.

As Christians, we often find it difficult to respond to the AIDS epidemic in the spirit of Paul's injunction in Ephesians: to "speak the truth in love." We find it hard to achieve a real balance between the two.

Our culture preaches love—but equates love with tolerance, with passing out moral blank checks. As Christians we know that love sometimes means telling people they are wrong, that they are violating God's law.

But the question is, How can we couch that kind of hard truth in concrete demonstrations of love?

Through his sister, Richard had the opportunity to learn of a God who hates sin but loves the sinner. Thousands of Richards live in San Francisco, in Key West, in New York City.

How many Sues are there, willing to enter their world and convey both God's truth and God's love?

December 27, 1991

11

Religion in Life

The Real Rhett
The Story Behind Gone with the Wind

They say truth is stranger than fiction.

A case in point is the book *Scarlett,* a sequel to the classic novel *Gone with the Wind.* People lined up to buy *Scarlett* by the thousands. Nine hundred thousand, to be precise. At least, that's how many advance copies of the book were ordered.

For five decades readers have sighed over *Gone with the Wind* and dreamed about what happened next. Now one reader has written her dreams down in a book—one that appeals to today's soap-opera tastes.

What many people don't know is that the original novel *wasn't* just dreams. It was based on real people who lived pretty much the lives described in the book.

Yes, there was a Rhett Butler, though his real name was Rhett Turnipseed. And there was a Scarlett O'Hara, though *her* real name was Emelyn Louise Hannon. And yes, Rhett really did walk out on her and join the Confederate army.

The history of what happened next has been kept by Rhett's family, the Turnipseeds, a fine old South Carolina family. It was recounted recently in a column by Wesley Pruden, managing editor for the *Washington Times.*

I'm telling you where the story comes from because it's so improbable you may find it hard to believe.

After the Civil War, Rhett Turnipseed became a drifter and gambler, eventually ending up in Nashville. There his life was turned around. On Easter morning 1871, Rhett attended a Methodist revival meeting. He was moved by what he heard and converted to the Christian faith.

Soon after, Rhett attended divinity classes at Vanderbilt University. Eventually he became a Methodist preacher, riding a circuit in rural Kentucky.

Did Rhett and Scarlett ever cross paths again? Yes, they did. The Turnipseed family historians tell the following story. Reverend Rhett was worried about a young woman in his flock. She had run away, and rumor had it she was working in a house of prostitution in St. Louis. Reverend Rhett rode off to look for her.

Well, he found the young woman, but he was told the madame of the house had no intention of letting her go. Asking to speak with the madame, Rhett discovered that she was none other than his former love, Scarlett. Excuse me—Emelyn Louise Hannon.

Reverend Rhett challenged the madame to a game of cards. If he won, the young girl he had come to fetch would be free to leave. And win he did: with a royal straight flush—an ace, king, queen, jack, and ten of spades.

The story ends well for all concerned. The young girl married well and became the matriarch of a leading family in the state. After her encounter with the reformed Rhett, Emelyn left prostitution, converted, and joined the Methodist church. Eventually she opened an orphanage for Cherokee children.

She died in 1903, and her grave is marked to this day.

The true sequel of Scarlett and Rhett is more astonishing—and more moving—than any fictional account could be. It's a story of God moving in the lives and hearts of a man who was a drifter and a gambler and a woman who lived off the proceeds of prostitution.

If God can save the likes of *these,* surely He can work to save people in our world today.

Too bad the author of *Scarlett* didn't give us the real sequel. Perhaps the publishers are afraid that in today's market a true story like that wouldn't sell nine hundred thousand copies.

But to my tastes, it beats a soap-opera novel any day.

November 15, 1991

The Scarlet F
Are You a Fundamentalist?

Last year the *New York Times* pegged a certain Charles Colson as a leader in a movement that is driven by sadistic urges, that is given to apocalyptic visions of the end times, that denounces good literature as lies, that thinks journalists are out to get them.

In short, the paper said I was a Fundamentalist.

Fundamentalists have received a lot of bad press lately. In the 1970s, many Christians came out of their spiritual enclaves for the first time and entered the political arena. They began to fight publicly for their convictions about abortion, homosexuality, education, and family issues.

And they scared a lot of liberals—who had complacently pronounced America a secular society.

Now liberals are fighting back with all the ammo they can find. One of the sharpest weapons in their arsenal is that handy label "Fundamentalist." In current lingo, a Fundamentalist is a reactionary, unthinking, anti-intellectual thug who hates the modern world.

It isn't just Christians who are called Fundamentalists. Anyone perceived as fanatical and close-minded can be tarred with the same brush. The word conjures up images of the likes of Ayatollah Ruhollah Khomeini.

Call someone a Fundamentalist and the argument is over: Your victim is hung without trial.

But what does the word *Fundamentalist* really mean? The term started out as a perfectly good description of someone who holds to the fundamental doctrines of the Christian faith.

Back at the time of the Reformation, nearly everyone in Western society was a Christian of one brand or another. The only disputes were over different *understandings* of the Bible. But by the nineteenth century, the ground of debate had shifted. Various scholars began to question the truth of the Bible itself.

The philosopher Georg W. F. Hegel came along and said that everything is in a process of historical change—even our ideas about God—so how can the Bible be true for all times? Then Charles Darwin said living things evolve, so why invoke God to create life? Psychologist Sigmund Freud said belief in God is simply a neurotic illusion—a father figure in the sky.

And on it went. Taken together, it was a massive assault upon the Christian faith.

Christian leaders reacted to the assault in one of two ways. Some abandoned the classic doctrines of miracles, revelation, and the divinity of Christ, reinterpreting Christianity in terms of existentialism or Marxism or whatever other "ism" was handy. This is what we call liberal theology.

But other theologians stood strong for the historic doctrines of the faith. In 1910, they published a series of books entitled *The Fundamentals*, which argued that Christianity is defined by certain fundamental biblical doctrines: that the Bible is without error, that Christ is God, that He died to pay the penalty for our sins, that He rose from the grave, and that He will return.

These were the fundamental doctrines of Christianity in 1910—and they still are today. Believing them still makes you a Fundamentalist, whether you are Lutheran, Baptist, Presbyterian, Catholic, or Eastern Orthodox.

The sad thing is that "Fundamentalist" has become a all-purpose label for close-minded fanaticism. But we should not allow people to twist the term that way. Instead, we should explain to them what it really means.

Once we understand the real meaning and history of the term, it's a label we should be proud to wear.

The world may scoff, but you can call me a Fundamentalist any time.

May 5, 1992

What the Nightly News Ignores
Religion and the Campaign

"I pray virtually every day . . . and I read the Bible every week."

That was Bill Clinton in an interview with *U.S. News & World Report* during the recent presidential campaign. He went on to say, "I really believe in . . . the constancy of sin, the possibility of forgiveness, the reality of redemption."

Not to be outdone, President George Bush announced that his party was "proud to celebrate our country's Judeo-Christian heritage, unrivaled in the world." He boasted that his party's platform is the only one that contains direct references to God.

What is going on here?

Both parties are appealing to religion to a degree unprecedented in recent years. Their political handlers obviously feel that a religious appeal will work with today's voters.

And they're right.

Polls reveal that Americans are turning to religion in droves. Last year *Newsweek* ran a cover article on the return of the baby boomers to church. Some 80 percent of boomers consider themselves religious.

A GOP poll asked voters to describe their greatest objective in life. A full 56 percent said a closer relationship to God.

Even marketing researchers are recognizing the trend. In an article in *Fortune* magazine, tucked in among descriptions of new home products, is a prediction that interest in religion will continue to rise. Futurist Arnold Brown says, "people are searching for absolute values and a sure grasp of right and wrong."

He predicts "a return to the eternal verities," a "groundswell of longing for some permanent, transcendent set of values."

Those are strong words.

And if he's right, it's no wonder politicians are giving a higher profile to religion these days. The politician who claims to speak for the people has to show respect for the people's concerns. And religion is undeniably one of their major concerns.

But not just any religion. The most vibrant religious force in America today is Evangelicalism, says Dean Kelley of the National Council of Churches. In an age of sex and drugs, Kelley says, people see Evangelicalism as "the base center for the nation's morality."

Even people who are not Evangelicals (like Kelley himself) are attracted to it, he says, as a bulwark against further moral decline.

The only people who seem puzzled by all this positive attention to religion are those who work in the media. Media figures have jumped all over the candidates for using religious language in their campaign speeches. They see it as nothing but a cynical political ploy—or worse, as a play on religious prejudice.

But historian Garry Wills says that's because media folks have so little to do with religion in their own lives. A mere 4 percent of media leaders attend church. Yet, Wills points out, religion has always had and continues to have a pervasive influence on America's culture and politics.

The fact is that in all societies religion is inescapable, because we are made in the image of God. No one can completely suppress the religious dimension of life. No one is ever completely irreligious.

So despite what you may hear from the media, it's not necessarily either cynicism or demagoguery when politicians use religious language.

It's a recognition that religion truly is at the core of American life.

October 6, 1992

Who Conquered Paradise?
The Battle over Columbus

This year Americans commemorated five hundred years since Christopher Columbus made his famous voyage to the New World. But not everyone joined in the celebration.

In Minneapolis, the city council adopted a resolution condemning Columbus for opening a door to genocide and the enslavement of the American Indians.

In the Dominican Republic, where Columbus first came ashore, the commemoration was marked by violent protests denouncing Columbus as an invader. Protesters set up barricades of burning tires and threw gasoline bombs.

As far away as Japan, university students staged a mock trial that found Columbus guilty of murder, plunder, and destruction of the native culture.

These are pretty extreme reactions—and that ought to tell us something deeper is going on here.

These aren't merely debates over historical facts about Christopher Columbus as an individual. No, the anniversary has turned into a battle of symbols: with Columbus as a symbol for Western European culture and the natives representing non-Western culture.

The symbols are so oversimplified they have all the marks of a second-rate morality play. The natives are presented as goodness incarnate, living in an uncorrupted Garden of Eden. The Europeans are the serpent that invades the garden. One movie about Columbus is even titled *The Conquest of Paradise.*

As Christians, of course, we know paradise was lost long before that, in the time of Adam and Eve. Since that time, every culture has been marked by sin and corruption. Every culture, apart from the redeeming grace of God, falls into cruelty and injustice.

There's no question that the Europeans broke their treaties with the Indians and mistreated them miserably. But Indian culture had its barbarism, too. Some of the first natives Columbus encountered were cannibals. The word *cannibal* even derives from their tribal name.

So let's get away from the battle over symbols. No culture has a monopoly on evil and corruption. When we study history, the real question isn't who was the good guy or the bad guy. The real question is, How can *any* culture aspire to higher things?

What are the true and universal values that can serve as a guide for all cultures?

The irony is that the universal values most critics use to denounce European culture came from *Europe*—from the Christian faith that spread first across the European continent. Christianity teaches a universalist ethic that demands respect and love toward all people, not just toward the clan or tribe.

Europeans haven't always *followed* the Christian ethic, of course. But the reason we *recognize* their failings is that we've accepted the Christian values they brought to the world.

So when the politically correct thought police attack Western culture, go ahead and agree with them. We can all freely admit the weaknesses of European culture.

But don't stop there. Ask the critics how they *know* a culture is good or bad—by what standard do they judge?

The standard they use to condemn the sins of the Europeans was imported . . . from Europe.

And that's something we can all celebrate.

October 9, 1992

Just for the Record

Are Christians Hypocrites?

Ask a non-Christian neighbor why he doesn't go to church, and what's he most likely to say? Oh, they're just a bunch of hypocrites in there. Fakes. They act pious in church, but it isn't real.

And money—churches always hit people up for money. Greedy television evangelists defrauding little old ladies of their last dollar.

The charges make for colorful diatribes against the church. There's only one problem: They don't fit the facts.

Actually, Christians *do* put their money where their mouth is. A recent survey shows that believers give more money to help the poor than nonbelievers do.

The survey is reported in a book by Robert Wuthnow and Virginia Hodgkinson called *Faith and Philanthropy in America.*

On average, the survey found, local congregations spend nearly *half* their funds and time on services to human need. Unlike the funds the government takes out of your paycheck for welfare, *this* money is not devoured by some voracious bureaucracy.

And maybe that's why, for the past thirty years, half—that's half—of all charitable giving in the United States has come from people who gave in the name of religion. That's counting all forms of charity: both religious and secular. Most of the money given to secular charities—like the Red Cross and the United Way—comes from religious believers.

Here's another fact: The more religious a person is, the more likely he is to be generous. People who attend church frequently are three to four times more generous in their giving than are people who attend church infrequently or not at all.

And here's something unexpected: Poor Christians give a larger percentage of their income than do rich Christians.

Of course, charity is not just a matter of money. What about the gift of time and energy? Here, too, believers outdo their nonbelieving neighbors. The survey found that members of churches and synagogues are 50 percent more likely than nonmembers to volunteer their time to charitable activities and community service.

About 150 years ago, a Frenchman named Alexis de Tocqueville traveled through the United States and wrote down his observations of American culture. Compared to Europeans, Tocqueville wrote, Americans have a strong sense of individualism. But it is balanced by a uniquely American habit of joining together in voluntary associations to serve some common good.

The voluntary associations Tocqueville observed were mostly churches and Christian charities.

In our own day, many people seem reluctant to acknowledge the positive role Christians play in society. Secularists don't like to admit that religion is good for American culture.

But *Faith and Philanthropy* shows that religion does have a positive impact on society. It is an empirical fact: Charity in America has strong religious roots.

Secular leaders may not like that. They may argue that people don't *have* to be religious to be generous and kind. But the historical fact is that religious faith has always been the major spur to helping the poor. No secular moral tradition has been able to influence people in the same way.

So let's not hear any more about how the church is just a bunch of hypocrites. It may be a common excuse why people avoid church.

But it just isn't a fact.

June 5, 1992

Pluralism on the Field
Praying in Public

When you settle into your easy chair for that great annual American extravaganza—the Super Bowl—you'll probably see some great football. But one thing you *won't* see is athletes praying. And here's why.

Over the past several years, Christian athletes have grown increasingly outspoken about their faith. So many Christians play for the Washington Redskins that when they trounced the Detroit Lions, one newspaper announced, "The Lions were thrown to the Christians last night."

The report mentioned halfback Earnest Byner's conversion and his baptism in Darrell Green's Jacuzzi. Byner joins Art Monk, Charles Mann, and several other teammates in his open profession of faith.

But this new boldness is not always well received. Christian athletes sometimes get razzed by their teammates. Like the time Brett Butler spoke in the San Francisco Giants' clubhouse about his conversion to Christ—and someone turned on a laugh machine.

But the most hostile critics are in the media. After the 1991 Super Bowl, a scathing article appeared in *Sports Illustrated,* attacking athletes who pray publicly. Christians on various teams had been meeting on the field to pray. And during the Super Bowl, a small group of New York Giants knelt together on the sidelines.

The writer for *Sports Illustrated* was incensed by it all. Praying during a game, he argued, is coercive—the players are imposing their beliefs on a captive audience.

Millions of television viewers are being subjected, he said, "whether they like it or not," to the spectacle of grown men bowing their heads in prayer. Shocking. The writer urged the NFL to ban the prayers.

I don't know if the NFL officials read the article but they followed its recommendations to a *T.* League owners voted to ban prayer sessions on the field. Players may still pray in locker rooms or kneel in the end zone after a touchdown. But organized prayers are now *verboten.*

This raises serious questions about our understanding of pluralism and freedom. Just who is doing the coercing here? There's no coercion when a camera picks up a group of athletes praying. No one is forcing the television viewer to pray. Or even to watch. If they object, viewers can just switch the channel or turn the television off.

Isn't that what people always tell Christians?

When Christians turn on the television and find comedy acts or movies that mock religion, we're told we're free not to watch. We're told that's pluralism. The very suggestion that maybe actors should stop saying certain things in public raises accusations of censorship.

But the very same people demand that *athletes* stop saying certain things in public. Like prayers.

What happened to pluralism this time?

The pluralism argument goes both ways. If we allow freedom for religious criticism, we have to allow freedom for religious expression.

A little more religious expression might not be a bad thing for sports. Athletes have always had a reputation for hard drinking and skirt chasing.

Wouldn't it be a good antidote for young people to hear a little more about Reggie White's prayer meetings, which he leads after every game for the Philadelphia Eagles?

In my book, *that* would be a healthy dose of real pluralism.

January 22, 1992

Looking East
How the Church Survived Stalinism

Last year I visited Eastern Europe and was amazed at the depth of Christian faith I saw there. It was even a bit of a let-down coming back to the States.

What a contrast. Here we have so much—Bibles, churches, seminaries, and yes, even Christian radio programs—yet we do so little with it. Over there they have so little, yet they do so much with it.

It's easy to see why Aleksandr Solzhenitsyn predicted that if spiritual renewal comes to the world, it will come from the East.

Solzhenitsyn spent ten years in the Gulag, the Soviet prison system, where he converted to Christian faith—so he knows firsthand what he's talking about. He reports that the strongest Christian faith and character are found not in the West, with its comfortable churches, but in the persecuted churches of the East. Let me give you one example of how the church thrived under communism.

Fifty years ago, Josef Stalin decided to destroy the Lutheran church in Russia. The Lutherans were to be a case study in how all the Christian denominations might eventually be liquidated.

First, Stalin had the pastors killed or imprisoned. Then the church buildings were confiscated. Bibles, hymnbooks, and religious writings were destroyed.

Lutheran families were broken up. Men were forced into the army. Women and children were loaded into boxcars like cattle and scattered throughout the remote regions of the Soviet Union—some to the deserts of the Islamic republics, others to the arctic wastelands of Siberia.

In a shockingly brief time, the Lutheran church of the Soviet Union was wiped off the face of the earth.

Today, if you go to St. Petersburg, you can view the only remaining physical evidence of the once-flourishing denomination: a stately Lutheran church building. It's been turned into an indoor swimming pool.

But that's not the end of the story. Not by any means.

The Lutheran women worked stubbornly, painfully, to keep their church alive. They had no pastors, no church buildings, no Bibles or hymnbooks. But that didn't stop them.

They sought each other out across miles of desolate countryside. They met in one another's homes to pray and minister to each other. They wrote down all the religious instruction they had learned by heart: Bible verses, Luther's catechism, hymns, liturgies. They held religious services. And, at the risk of imprisonment, they passed on the faith to their children.

Over time, some of the husbands managed to rejoin their families. Some of the surrounding people converted. A community of believers was formed that appointed elders and deacons.

The Lutheran church was reborn.

It now meets in more than five hundred house churches. Western Christians have sent them Bibles. And they have recently established a seminary. Soon they will have trained pastors again.

The church has outlasted communism.

How many Western churches would survive a deliberate attempt to exterminate them? Could your own church live on without a pastor, a building, even a Bible?

Jesus promised that the gates of hell would not prevail against His church. We in the West believe that by faith; the church in Russia knows it by bitter experience.

Will we have to learn it the hard way, too? I pray not.

Western Christians need to realize that living in the midst of affluence exposes us to just as much temptation as living in hardship.

We who are relatively pampered need to get just as serious about our faith as those who are persecuted.

January 31, 1992

Trading on Christianity
A New Age Bestseller

Marianne Williamson was a typical 1960s burnout.

In her youth she had been a radical when such things were chic. But afterward, she never seemed to grow up. She switched jobs several times, had several affairs, abused drugs.

In her own words, she was a total mess.

That's when Williamson discovered an obscure New Age self-help program called *A Course in Miracles*. She began to follow the program and eventually to teach it. Finally she wrote a book about it, called *A Return to Love.*

Immediately it became a bestseller.

So Marianne Williamson has finally found her niche in life—as a prophetess of a New Age religion. She's been featured on the "Oprah Winfrey Show," profiled in *Newsweek,* and her book has been number one on the *New York Times* self-help bestseller list for weeks.

What's the book's message? Simply put, that sin is an illusion. Hatred, anger, jealousy—they aren't real. "Only love is real," Williamson tells her readers. "Everything else is an illusion."

So don't bother asking God for forgiveness. All the bad stuff you *think* you did is merely an illusion.

Obviously, this is a far cry from Christian teachings about God and sin. At least, it *should* be obvious. But Williamson uses a lot of biblical lingo that has misled even some Christians. As *Newsweek* says, *A Return to Love* "reads at times . . . like a Christian religious tract."

The trick is that Williamson takes Christian terms and redefines them. Listen to these mushy New Age definitions. Williamson describes Christ as a kind of pantheistic deity: "the common thread of divine love that is the core and essence of every human mind."

This isn't Christ as the second person of the Trinity; it's Christ as a "divine spark" in everyone.

The idea of crucifixion Williamson redefines as "the energy pattern of fear." Resurrection is "the energy pattern of love."

Nothing in those definitions about Jesus' historical death on the cross or His historical resurrection.

And when Williamson talks about serving God and doing His will, what she really means is getting in touch with a divine energy source inside yourself.

No, Williamson is no Christian. But she understands the power of the Christian message. So she has hijacked Christian terminology to communicate her New Age religion.

When a book like this hits the top of the bestseller list, it's a poignant reminder that we live in a spiritually hungry age. People are eating whatever they can find in the religious supermarket—without checking the label first.

As a result, many Americans are swallowing New Age beliefs and don't even realize it. A Gallup poll found that only a quarter of Americans have heard of the New Age movement, and only a tiny fraction say they believe in it. Yet vast numbers of Americans accept certain New Age beliefs and practices.

About half believe in extrasensory perception. More than a third believe in mental telepathy. A quarter of all Americans believe in astrology. A quarter believe in reincarnation. And a fifth say they've been in touch with the dead.

What a testimony to the sorry state of America's spiritual condition. People are starving spiritually, yet what they're picking up to eat is the spiritual equivalent of a Twinkie. They're filling up on spiritual junk food—when what they really need is the plain but nourishing bread of the gospel.

April 16, 1992

Faith and Facts
Historical Evidence for Jesus' Life

The young man was obviously excited to meet me. "Boy," he said, "when I argue with nonbelievers about Christianity, I sure wish I had *you* here to help me."

I knew the young man meant it as a compliment, but frankly, I was distressed by his attitude. He had fallen into the trap of thinking he couldn't defend his faith on his own.

But each of us is called to be prepared to give a defense of the hope that is in us. And I'd like to offer some ways to do it using historical evidence presented by Paul Johnson, an eminent British historian. In a speech entitled *A Historian Looks at Jesus,* published and distributed by Prison Fellowship, Johnson says that the more he studies the historical facts, the more his faith is strengthened.

Many modern historians consider the Bible to be a collection of ancient myths. But Johnson argues that by normal standards of historical analysis, the Bible is a highly dependable historical document.

For example, skeptics used to say that the New Testament wasn't written until hundreds of years after Jesus lived—after a jungle of myth and legend had grown up and distorted the original events. But we now know that the New Testament books were originally written a mere twenty to forty years after Christ's crucifixion.

That's within a single generation—less than the time separating us from the end of World War II. Far too brief a span for myths and legends to take hold.

In fact, if we compare the historical evidence for Jesus to the evidence for other figures who lived in ancient times, there's just no comparison. Consider: Though we don't have the original documents of the New Testament, we do have several thousand copies—some of them from only a hundred years after Jesus lived.

Compare that to the Roman writer Tacitus. He's considered a first-rate historical source. Yet we have only twenty copies of his work, and the earliest manuscript is dated a thousand years after he lived.

And no one doubts the authenticity of the Greek philosopher Aristotle. Yet the earliest manuscript of his work that we have is dated fourteen hundred years after he lived.

We all know about Caesar. Yet the earliest copy of his *Gallic Wars* is dated a thousand years after the original.

There can simply be no doubt any longer that the New Testament is an authentic document, Johnson says—that it describes real events. Jesus is better authenticated than any other figure from ancient times.

So if people ask how you know Jesus was a real person, respond with your own question: Was Caesar a real person? Was Aristotle? If they say yes, tell them the evidence for Jesus is much stronger.

Or you can turn the question around: If people doubt that Jesus was real, tell them they'll also have to throw out everyone else we know from ancient history—Tacitus, Aristotle, Caesar. The evidence for their lives is much weaker than the evidence for Jesus' life.

There's just no middle ground: Either you believe the New Testament account of Jesus is authentic—or you become a complete skeptic about all of ancient history.

So you don't need an expert at your elbow every time you talk to a non-Christian. Just give him a little history lesson.

The evidence is on our side.

March 30, 1992

Scrolls and Tablets
Historical Evidence for the Old Testament

The biggest news for biblical scholars these days is that they can finally study the complete Dead Sea Scrolls.

The scrolls were first discovered more than forty years ago in a rocky cave outside Jerusalem. But many of the scroll fragments were hidden away, accessible to only a tiny group of scholars. Finally, a few months ago, twenty metal boxes were hauled out of a secret vault in a California library and opened to the world.

It was the entire scroll collection on film.

Of course, the portion of the scrolls released earlier had already made dramatic contributions to biblical scholarship. For example, the earliest copy of the Old Testament used to be from the Middle Ages. Skeptics argued that we couldn't trust it—that it had been changed over the centuries by careless scribes and by editors who inserted their own religious teachings.

But among the Dead Sea Scrolls were portions from almost every book in the Old Testament, a thousand years older than previously existing copies. Amazingly, the two versions match nearly word for word.

Proof that the Old Testament was copied accurately through the ages.

Another example: Skeptics have always tried to get rid of anything in the Bible that smacks of the supernatural—things like prophecy. They argued that Psalm 22 could not have been written by King David because it gives details of Jesus' crucifixion—a form of punishment that had not even been invented in David's day. Critics concluded that the psalm was written much later, just before the time of Christ.

But copies of the Psalms were also found among the Dead Sea Scrolls. And if *copies* were already in existence at that time, clearly the originals were written even earlier.

That silenced the critics.

The Dead Sea Scrolls are only one of many archaeological finds confirming the reliability of the Old Testament. Consider a few others.

Critics have always jumped on the early chapters of Genesis, where we read about several puzzling customs—Sarah giving Abraham her handmaid as a surrogate wife; Abraham adopting a slave as his heir; Esau's sale of his birthright for a paltry bowl of porridge; and so on.

These customs are so alien to the modern reader that critics treated them as fairy tales, invented centuries later and projected into the past like so many Paul Bunyan stories.

But in recent decades, clay tablets have been dug out of the Near Eastern deserts describing exactly the same customs. Proof that the descriptions in Genesis fit the time they were written.

In fact, many of these customs are unique to the patriarchal period. There's no record of them at any later time. So it is impossible for Genesis to have been written by anyone living later. We would have to suppose that the writer just happened to *invent* customs true to the times, though by then long forgotten.

It's as though ancient Greece were forgotten, but we just happened to invent stories about a couple of philosophers named Plato and Aristotle.

So next time you hear people dismiss the Bible as a patchwork of ancient folk tales, tell them about the Dead Sea Scrolls. Tell them about the clay tablets. The historical evidence supports the Bible all the way back to the time of the patriarchs.

Historian Paul Johnson puts it well: "It is not now the men of faith, it is the skeptics, who have reason to fear the course of discovery."

March 31, 1992

Character Witness
The Restraints of Christianity

I was talking to a friend recently—a nonbeliever—and he said, "Chuck, everything you say about Christianity sounds good. But what bothers me is the historical record: The Crusades, the Inquisition—all the terrible things done in the name of Christ."

"True," I said. "But just remember, that's nothing compared to the things done in the name of secular faiths. Think of Hitler—6 million Jews murdered in the holocaust. And Stalin—some 50 million people slaughtered in the Gulag. The fruits of atheism are much, much worse than any abuse of Christianity."

My friend stopped short. "You're right," he said.

Christianity doesn't make people perfect. But it does make us better than we would have been without it. Remove the restraint of God's law, and the worst barbarism breaks forth.

In *A Historian Looks at Jesus,* Paul Johnson tells the story of novelist Evelyn Waugh, who had a gift for making sharp comments that wounded even his friends. A woman asked him,

"Mr. Waugh, how can you behave as you do and still call yourself a Christian?"

Waugh replied, "Madam, I may be as bad as you say. But believe me, were it not for my religion, I would scarcely be a human being."

The point is, Christianity does make us better people. But in some of us, God starts out with pretty difficult raw material.

Edith Schaeffer once said that the Fall affects each person differently. Physically, some people are strong and athletic; others are weak and sickly. In the same way, some people have a naturally good disposition; others are born with an abrasive personality.

Becoming a Christian doesn't erase these inherent differences. It just gives us tools to work on them.

C. S. Lewis put it this way. A crotchety old lady may be considered a poor witness for Christian faith. But who is to say how much *more* cantankerous she might be if she were not a Christian?

And a nonbeliever who is a gentle, pleasant fellow—who is to say how much *better* he might be if he *were* a Christian?

For myself, I'm sometimes accused of being a hard-driving man. But I know what I was like before I became a Christian. When I worked in the White House, it was said I would run over my own grandmother to get what I wanted.

So don't be intimidated when your friends bring up the tired old lines about the Crusades and the Inquisition. Just remind them how much worse people are when Christian restraints are removed.

After all, when a Hitler or a Stalin commits atrocities, he is acting out the ideology he believes in: He's revealing the logical consequences of his beliefs. But when a Christian is cruel, he's acting in *violation* of his beliefs.

And when Christians act in accord with their faith, even in small measure, the result is a goodness that the world knows nothing about. Around the world, Christians have built schools, universities, orphanages, and hospitals. They have supported law and public morality. They have rescued children thrown out to die. They have helped the poor and visited the prisoner.

The evidence from history is clear. Despite our human faults, Christianity has made the world and the people in it—not perfect—but far better than they would have been without it.

April 1, 1992

Africa Bleeding
The Necessity of Christianity

"Africa is bleeding," Bishop Desmond Tutu of South Africa wrote recently. The African nations have thrown off colonial rule only to fall prey to military dictatorships and one-party Marxist regimes.

"The awful truth," Bishop Tutu says sadly, "is that in Africa there was far greater freedom in the colonial days than there is now."

An amazing admission from a man who has *fought* colonial rule all his life.

The history of Africa demonstrates in concrete terms the powerful role Christianity plays in restraining evil. When Christianity departs, that restraint is gone, too.

Again, historian Paul Johnson is our guide on the subject. In a speech entitled "The Necessity of Christianity," Johnson acknowledges that the colonial days were not perfect by any means. Yet the colonial powers were largely Christian—in culture, if not in personal belief.

And wherever the colonial powers went around the globe, they brought with them basic principles derived from biblical faith: things like the rule of law, individual responsibility, political freedom, care for the weak, respect for learning.

When African nations threw off colonial status, many of them lost that Christianized heritage. Look at Angola and Mozambique, Johnson says. They once formed the jewels in the Portuguese Empire. But independence brought in Marxist states and civil war, poverty and starvation.

Farther north is the tragic case of Uganda. Under colonial rule, Uganda was Christianized by Anglican and Catholic missionaries. It was considered the most delightful country in all of Africa. Winston Churchill called it "a paradise upon earth."

When Uganda was given independence, it fell victim to the military regime of Idi Amin. Amin's mother was a pagan witch, and Amin himself seems to have practiced ritual cannibalism, keeping human organs in his refrigerator.

Under his rule the rivers were choked with the bodies of his victims. Today Uganda remains a ruined country, ravaged by civil war.

Most pathetic of all perhaps is Ethiopia, the only African country to retain its Christianity from ancient times. In 1974, a Christian emperor, Haile Selasse, was assassinated at the instigation of the Soviets. They installed a puppet Marxist regime in his place.

Since then, Ethiopia has been stricken by wars within and wars without. Its population has been decimated by famines, created in part by deliberate decisions on the part of its Marxist rulers—just as Lenin and Stalin once used famine to destroy dissidents within the Soviet Union.

All in all, Johnson says, if we survey the world today, we see that wherever Christianity has been forced to retreat, oppression and violence have rushed in to fill the vacuum. It is just as Bishop Tutu said: Africa was better off in the colonial days.

Not because colonialism itself was necessarily a good system but because the European colonists brought with them the political and social fruits of the gospel.

The good news is that the decline of communism throughout the rest of the world is now reaching Africa as well. The *Washington Times* reports that all across Africa, Marxist regimes are either being voted out or being forced to give up their autocratic powers and create free parliaments.

So the verdict of history is in. Secular ideologies give birth to blood and hunger. Christianity gives birth to the fruits of the Spirit.

Not only in individuals but also in nations.

April 2, 1992

The Persian Gulf War
The Untold Story

The Persian Gulf War—what images do those words bring to mind? SCUD missiles exploding? Iraqi soldiers surrendering? Welcome-home parades?

How about thousands of American soldiers kneeling in prayer?

That's one you missed? Small wonder. The story was almost completely passed over by television. It was pieced together from letters sent home by chaplains serving in the Persian Gulf.

Jeff Houston, a minister from Missouri, wrote that he was holding four worship services every day. Four a day! Each service averaged more than 160 in attendance. Daily there were new professions of faith.

"I have discovered that there really are 'springs in the desert,'" Jeff wrote home. "The men are so thirsty for the water of life. . . . This is more like a revival than a war."

Another chaplain wrote that many nights a soldier would lie awake talking with a buddy in the next cot about what would happen if he was shot. Is that the end? Is there an afterlife? Without fail, the next day five or six guys would drop by the chaplain's tent to ask him questions about life, death, and God.

Colonel Dave Peterson, chief of all the Persian Gulf chaplains, said, "In twenty-five years in the army I have never seen as much spirituality."

This is not to say that the ministers had an easy job of it. Saudi Arabia is an Islamic nation, and soldiers were forbidden to wear crosses in public. Chaplains were forbidden to carry out missionary activities as they did in Europe during World War II and in Vietnam.

In some places, chaplains were required to call themselves "morale counselors." Worship services were dubbed "morale meetings."

In spite of these restrictions, the Bible was the most widely circulated publication among the troops. Thousands of Bibles with desert camouflage covers were distributed.

Why was there such a great spiritual hunger among the soldiers?

C. S. Lewis suggests an answer in his popular book *The Screwtape Letters,* a fantasy based on a correspondence between two devils. In the story, war breaks out and the younger devil is delighted. He knows that war can bring out the worst in people—cruelty, cowardice, savagery.

But the older devil is wiser. He knows war can also bring out the best in people. Confronted with the threat of death, many people wonder for the first time about *life.*

They begin to ask what things are truly worth living for.

For many soldiers, the Persian Gulf War was just such a time. Living under stress and uncertainty, facing danger and death, soldiers sensed their need for God.

It's a pity it takes something like a war for this to happen. When things are going well in life, we pay a courtesy call on God once a week and then go our own way. It's only when the bombs are falling that we get serious about God.

Yet in reality each of us faces the possibility of death at any moment. Maybe we don't have SCUD missiles landing in our backyard, but more people die from car accidents every year than ever died in a war. More than twenty-four thousand people are murdered each year in America. And cancer is no respecter of age or status.

If we honestly consider how fragile life really is, each of us has reason enough to get serious about God—right now.

September 19, 1991